Flights to Hell

'I don't want to take any more planes. Please, Lord, help me' – a scribbled note found in the wreckage of Japan Air Lines Flight 123 which flew out of control for one hour before the Boeing 747 crashed on a mountainside killing 520 passengers and crew.

'What goes up must come down' – proven fact

Flights to Hell

Allan Edwards

THOMAS & LOCHAR

British Library Cataloguing-in-Publication Data

    Edwards, Allan
        Flights to Hell
        I. Title
        363.124

        ISBN 0 946537 81 X

© Allan Edwards 1993

Maps drawn by R.E.G. Davies

Typeset by XL Publishing Services, Nairn
and printed in Great Britain at
Redwood Books, Trowbridge
for Thomas & Lochar
PO Box 4, Nairn, Scotland IV12 4HU

Contents

Foreword

Many books have been written about airliner accidents. Most of these have dwelt on the death and destruction with a morbid fascination in the tragic dramas. Some have attempted to sensationalise the tales of crushed metal, disfigured bodies, and distressed survivors, with ghoulish determination. This book, though dealing with the same facts and figures, the same incidents and events, and the same disasters, is not such an aberration of responsible reporting.

Allan Edwards was a journalist, and as such, was in a position to observe and to narrate the often frightening detail of major airliner accidents and crashes, in most parts of the world other than the Soviet Union, where authentic information has not been available. But he did more than report the events. He analysed them, investigated them, and most important, studied the work of the accident investigators from official agencies, and reported on those too. He was no callous ambulance chaser. He examined the reports, compared them with his own conclusions, and in this book has tried to synthesise the results in language that is bereft of journalistic jargon and eschews the sometimes unintelligible language of official reports.

This is not to state that he glosses over the sheer horror – a word that, being short, is too often misused in the headlines – of accidents and crashes that have often incinerated the passengers, or crushed them to death, or asphyxiated them. He does not resort to euphemisms. Nevertheless, he concentrates on the responsible selection of the vital facts of each case, and shows how lessons could be, and were, learned from the often unavoidable tragedies.

The author sometimes expresses his own opinions, but few would disagree with his views. He is especially disgusted with the looters who are always quickly on the scene of accidents, some as fanatical souvenir-hunters, some blatantly seeking money and personal valuables from dead bodies. I am reminded of the picture of the 1931 crash in which the famous football coach Knute Rockne was killed. The group of spectators look as though they are at a party.

Allan Edwards writes in an easy style, mixing the facts, the opinions, and the conclusions, with some observations that at times are almost poetic. I liked his description of an English winter sky as of 'dishcloth clouds against a background of dirty washing up water' and his vivid appreciation of the procedure of projecting chickens (dead ones) into jet engine compressor intakes to test the effect of bird strikes. They emerged the other end, he claimed, 'plucked, gutted, and cooked.' Aside from these more colourful comments, his paragraphs often include sensitive impressions of the mood of airline passengers, past and present.

The readable text is supplemented by an excellent appendix listing every accident, major or minor, narrated and analysed in the book. And there is a thoughtful index which adds considerably to the quality of the finished work. It is thoughtful because the references are made through the mind's eye of the reader, and not as if by some mindless computer; and in this day and age, we are grateful that there is one at all.

Allan Edwards has expressed the hope that this book may become a standard work. I have a feeling that it may do just that.

R.E.G. Davies

Maps

The selection of maps which begins overleaf supplements the text (see page references for each map) and has been chosen to illustrate the more dramatic episodes in the chapters of accidents.

THE *HINDENBURG* DISASTER

7 May 1937
(pages 32-33)

Note turn of almost 180°

Scale – feet
0 2000 4000 6000

Hangar

Mast and Mooring Circle

10 mins. out
590 ft., 73 mph

5 mins. out
390 ft. 26 mph

2 mins. out
300 ft.

8 mins. out
490 ft., 33 mph

12 mins. out
650 ft., 73 mph

Airship had to arrive
at 6 a.m. or 6 p.m.
Ground party of
240 required

LAKEHURST
NAVAL AIR STATION
NEW JERSEY

LAST FLIGHT
OF THE
R101

5 October 1930
(page 29)

Bedford
19.36

Luton

LONDON

Dover

Calais

Boulogne

Hastings
22.35

E N G L I S H
C H A N N E L

Pte de →
St Quentin
23.36

R. Somme

Poix
01.00

Allonne Ridge
01.07

Beauvais

R. Seine

PARIS

SCALE

0   25   50   75   100 km.
0   20   40   60 Miles

REGD

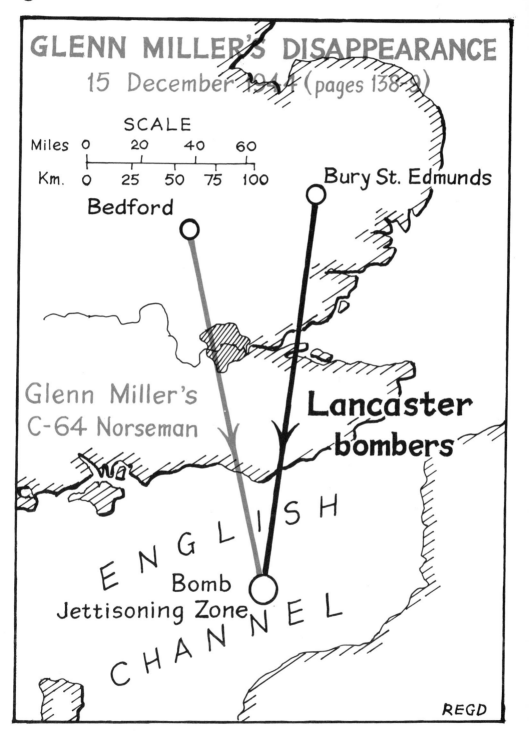

③

GLENN MILLER'S DISAPPEARANCE
15 December 1944 (pages 138-9)

SCALE

Miles 0   20   40   60

Km. 0   25   50   75   100

Bedford

Bury St. Edmunds

Glenn Miller's
C-64 Norseman

Lancaster
bombers

ENGLISH

Bomb
Jettisoning Zone

CHANNEL

REGD

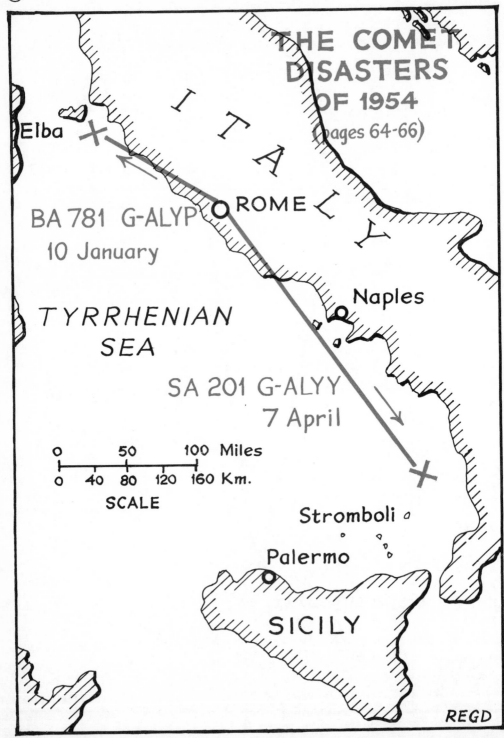

④

THE COMET DISASTERS OF 1954
(pages 64-66)

ITALY

Elba

BA 781 G-ALYP
10 January

ROME

TYRRHENIAN
SEA

Naples

SA 201 G-ALYY
7 April

0   50   100 Miles
0   40   80   120   160 Km.
SCALE

Stromboli

Palermo

SICILY

REGD

⑤

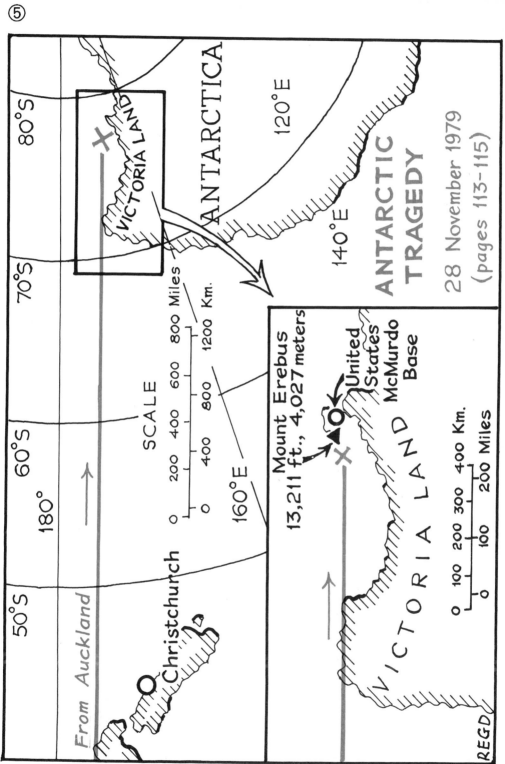

ANTARCTICA

120°E

140°E

ANTARCTIC TRAGEDY

28 November 1979

(pages 113–115)

VICTORIA LAND

80°S

70°S

60°S

50°S

180°

From Auckland

Christchurch

SCALE

0   200   400   600   800 Miles

0   400   800   1200 Km.

160°E

Mount Erebus
13,211 ft., 4,027 meters

United States McMurdo Base

VICTORIA LAND

0   100   200   300   400 Km.

0   100   200 Miles

REGD

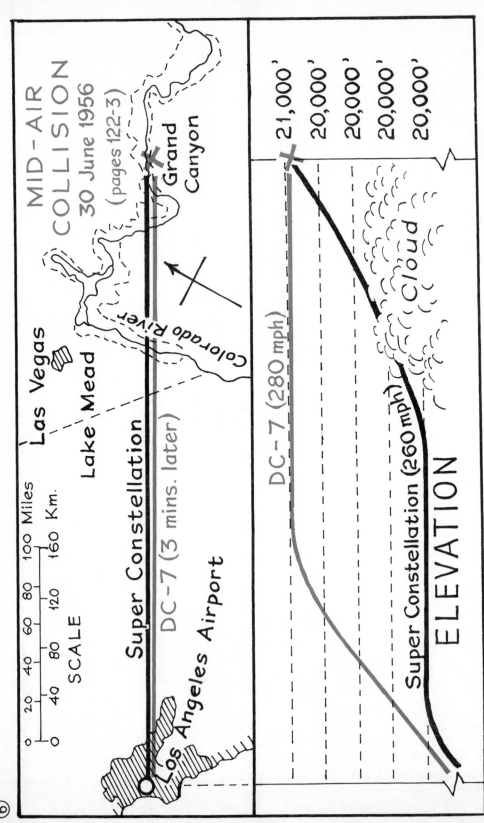

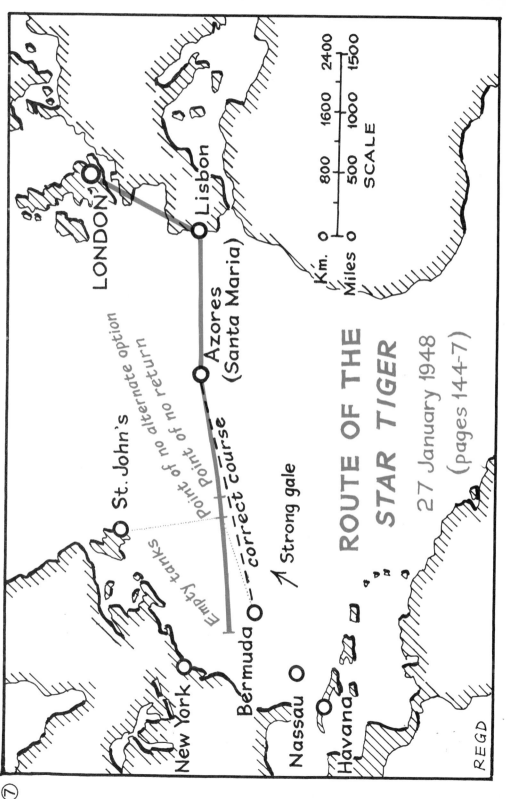

ROUTE OF THE
STAR TIGER

27 January 1948
(pages 144-7)

LONDON

Lisbon

Azores
(Santa Maria)

St. John's

point of no alternate option
point of no return

Empty tanks
correct course

Strong gale

Bermuda

New York

Nassau

Havana

SCALE

Km. 0   800   1600   2400
Miles 0   500   1000   1500

REGD

⑦

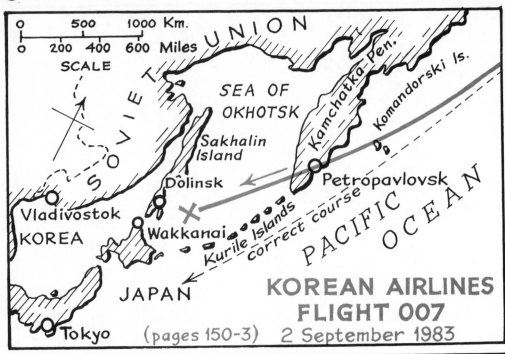

⑧

SCALE
500   1000 Km.
200 400 600 Miles

SOVIET UNION

SEA OF OKHOTSK

Kamchatka Pen.

Komandorski Is.

Sakhalin Island

Dolinsk

Petropavlovsk

Vladivostok

KOREA

Wakkanai

Kurile Islands

correct course

PACIFIC OCEAN

JAPAN

Tokyo

(pages 150-3)

KOREAN AIRLINES FLIGHT 007
2 September 1983

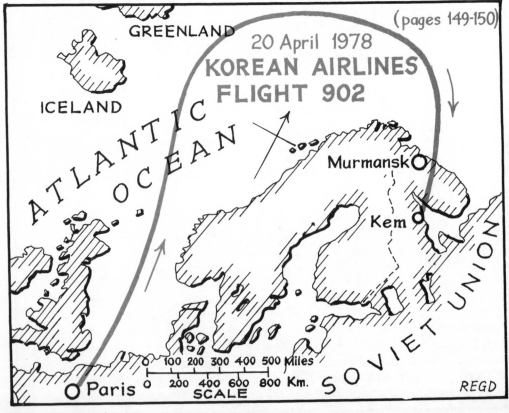

GREENLAND

(pages 149-150)

20 April 1978
KOREAN AIRLINES FLIGHT 902

ICELAND

ATLANTIC OCEAN

Murmansk

Kem

Paris

SOVIET UNION

100 200 300 400 500 Miles
200 400 600 800 Km.
SCALE

REGD

⑨

Introduction

'I have to look into all of the passengers' eyes as they check-in,' the airline ground stewardess told me. 'Any that seem even slightly suspicious get a mark against their name so that the boarding gate security staff pay special attention to them. We've got to watch out for the bombers and hijackers, you see.

'Of course, nearly all the passengers' eyes show one thing in common: they're nearly all afraid of flying.'

And so we are. We have conquered the air in a single lifetime, yet still we fear the flying. Mr Big Shot, the international entrepreneur who flies a hundred thousand miles a year, comes to the check-in with disdainful nonchalance. He's going to plot three takeovers and a corporate killing at forty thousand feet but nagging away at the back of his mind is the thought that the plane might meet disaster. The grandparents who have never flown before and are off to see their emigrant children and grand-children believe that over three hundred tonnes of 747 can never get off the runway; there's a professional golfer slipping down the world rankings because he spends entire flights looking out for the mid-air collision he's certain is going to happen; there's a macho-image rock-star who curls up like a baby and sucks his thumb at the slightest turbulence, convinced the wings are going to fall off.

Even some pilots are terrified of flying! There's a few white-knuckled merchants up there handling the inter-continentals.

'When I was cabin crew there was a senior pilot who needed the "snack bag" within two minutes of every take-off,' the stewardess told me. 'Any poor first officer flying with him had to handle the noise-abatement hassle, radio frequency changes, flap retraction and auto-pilot settings on his own. The pilots cover up for each other, you see. The old chap was on his third marriage – all those nights away I suppose – was paying a fortune in alimony and was terrified that if he failed his six-monthly medical or cockpit simulator check he wouldn't be able to meet his debts. Some pilots'll go on flying when they're not fit to through fear of unemploy-ment. After all, what other job are they trained for? I think he flew into a hill somewhere down South America way in the end.

'Some of the things I've seen are more like scenes out of that classic comedy film *Airplane* despite the safe and professional image the big lines try to project. There's more than one ex-fighter pilot likely to throw an airliner around thinking that he's back in Vietnam or the Falklands and is under attack.

'Of course I still fly when I go on holiday. It's nice to be waited on instead of handing round the snack bags and dealing with the gropers and besides, no one – me included – *really* believes that they're going to be killed in an air disaster.'

Indeed, as we look through holiday brochures to distant countries or plan pan-continental business trips, thoughts of aerial cataclysm come to the forefront of few people's minds. We can be propelled through space at the speed of a bullet in a machine that's a potential flying bomb but we have an in-built human defence mechanism: it won't happen to me – others will be the victims in those gruesome television pictures of crash scenes. And we resort to stock comforts: statistics say that any person can expect to fly safely for a thousand years before being involved in an air disaster – but that really means that the disaster can happen at any time during that thousand years, some have been killed on their first flight! We usually believe the saying that the drive to the airport is more dangerous than the flight but we are all so certain that we are the world's best driver – it is someone else piloting the plane!

One ponders if the Wright brothers dreamt of what they were starting!

Credit for the first powered 'flying machine' flight over the Kill Devil Hills, Kitty Hawk, North Carolina, in 1903 is always given to Orville and Wilbur. Poor Charles Taylor, the engineer who designed and built the essential lightweight petrol engine of *Flyer 1* in only six weeks and thus made the achievement possible, tends to be ignored. This flight was the fulfilment of a dream enshrined in human hearts. Mankind has always wanted to fly and his flights of fantasy are preserved in cave paintings and mythology.

The dream first began to be realised just over two centuries ago when the Montgolfier brothers' first paper balloon wobbled uncertainly into French air. The true airship still lay more than a century into the future, only just pre-dating the Wright aircraft.

The brothers' success was the culmination of centuries of experiment. The principles of heavier-than-air flight were reasonably well understood by the middle of the nineteenth century. The German Otto Lilienthal had made over a thousand flights in gliders whose simple principle was that a curved aerofoil section would reduce pressure over the top surface of a wing and thereby largely suck the machine into the sky – this is as true of a 'jumbo' jet as it was for the early crude gliders.

Only a decade was to separate the first tentative steps over North Carolina from the air battles over France. By 1918 the accelerated techno-logical progress allied to days of conflict saw engines of 420 horsepower able to lift stable machines above 6,000m (20,000ft). Flying was no longer a novelty, a daring escapade for rich experimenters or an impossible dream. No longer would the buzz of a 'flying machine' in peacetime skies seem such an alien sound that all heads would automatically crane upwards. The public had become air-minded. They, too, wanted to fly, and war-surplus aircraft such as the De Havilland DH4/9 and Avro 504 trainers were available to take them.

At county fairs and holiday resorts Joe and Josephine Public were 'taken up for a spin'. In 1919 scheduled commercial flights using converted DH4 and Handley Page 0/400 bombers began between Croydon and Paris.

Those early aerial exploits now seem like ancient history yet that age of 'stick and string' flying machines, of Zeppelins and of flying circuses, is less than a lifetime ago.

The first man to pilot an aircraft, Orville Wright, and the first man to walk on the Moon, Neil Armstrong, walked this earth at the same time.

It is possible for people born before the first powered flights to have flown faster than the speed of sound in the Anglo-French Concorde and the Russian Tupolev Tu-144 'Concordski' during its brief period of service in the 1970s.

Two hundred years ago, before the age of railways, people would commonly live and die without leaving the environs of their town or village. Seafarers and returning soldiers would tell of adventurous lands and strange peoples that lay several months' sailing time away across terrifying seas and around perilous shores. Now the 400 series Boeing 747 is entering service; this new version of the classic 'jumbo' (an affectionate name-tag that aircrew hate but which will be used occasionally in this account owing to the benefit of conjuring an instant image in the mind of the layperson) is able to half-circumnavigate the globe. Non-stop flights from England to the antipodes are a near-reality. There can be no sighted person on this small blue world who has not now seen an aircraft stitching a path through the heavens. Air travel is the norm. And it affects everyone, even those who never fly. Almost every home contains some item that has been carried in an aircraft. And to some countries air travel is vital: their economies depend on the tourists that aircraft bring.

Glossy brochures in travel agency windows have lured holidaymakers with pictures of golden beaches fringed with palm trees. The reality is that these scenic shores are now blighted by concrete hotels of drab uniformity. For many years now British package-tourists have squeezed themselves into seats set at a closer pitch than on a London Routemaster bus for a 'bargain' flight to the Mediterranean, a holiday as cheap as staying at home. On these flights the Boeings take los gamberros britanicos (the British 'lager lout' which aircraft have transported all over the world) to the Liberian resorts. Pity the poor aircrew who have to control these drunken and ignorant members of society. 'It used to be easy to stop trouble,' a senior pilot for a charter line told the author. 'The sight of the captain's epaulettes was enough to get the most troublesome back into their seats and quiet. The old-timers will say that flying's got too cheap, that we're carrying the rabble now.' It's certainly true that flight crews now face a real risk of being assaulted.

'If I get a rowdy bunch I take the auto-pilot out and fly through some "turbulence". They soon go quiet when their heads are over a "snack bag"!'

As long ago as 1957 more passengers crossed the North Atlantic by air than on board the blue riband liners. The great days of the ocean grey-hounds, of the British 'Queens' and of 'United States', were over, vessels rendered obsolete like the battleships before them by the frail but speedier craft of the air. Now it is not only the rich or jetsetting businessmen crossing the 'big pond', but package tourists of average incomes.

Of course, it's not a romantic trip any more; no more sleeper berths in the rumbling Boeing Stratocruiser, no longer does the captain leave his cockpit to stroll down the aisle with a friendly word. The contemporary airliner is a people-mover: its vastly expensive technology can only be prof-itable if airborne with small crews and large payloads for as long as possible. Money is lost for every moment it is grounded.

'It's only a little crack in the engine pylon. There's a full charter load here for Las Vegas. We'll fix it after that trip.' The pages of this history will show that such risks are sometimes taken. And Las Vegas would probably be a ghost town in the Nevada desert were it not for the coming of airliners.

Our age has also witnessed a new and potent armament in the instru-ments of war: aircraft are now the siege weapons. On the night of 13–14 February 1945, 735 Avro Lancasters of the Royal Air Force swam through the interlunary night sky to Dresden deep in the heart of Nazi Germany. These frail bombers whipped up a maelstrom of destruction that obliter-ated the heart of the most beautiful rococo city in Europe and killed at least 50,000 people, mostly non-combatants: women, children and refugees from the advancing Russian armies. It can be seen as perhaps the greatest air disaster of all in terms of the loss of life, and arguably an unnecessary funeral pyre when the defeat of the Third Reich was already a certainty.

Within months the flames of Dresden would be over-shadowed by radioactive mushrooms blooming over Japanese cities. Less than half a century after the first heavier-than-air flights the Boeing B-29 Superfortresses *Enola Gay* and *Bock's Car*, each carrying a single bomb, ushered in the nuclear age. Many of us have grown up beneath the shadow of the nuclear bombers' wings.

One such type is the General Dynamics F-111. It was an accident to one of these two-seat fighter-bombers that introduced the author to the subject of air accidents when he was a trainee journalist. One of these green and tan machines from the U.S.A.F. base at Upper Heyford in Oxfordshire began to have engine problems as it overflew North Buckinghamshire. Soon the heavy machine was out of control and it was time for the crew to 'take to the silk' (parachute) or use the ejector seats – except that the F-111 is fitted with neither. It has a jettisonable cockpit and forward fuselage that floats to earth on three parachutes. The crew acti-vated the charges that blew the machine into three: nose radome, 'survival cell' and main body. It was the autumn of 1972, the time of the Apollo moon shots and the residents of the village of North Crawley who saw the cockpit section floating down thought that it was a returning spaceship. As the cockpit 'capsule' thumped to the ground just off the end of a line of terraced cottages and in a chicken coop (with detrimental effects to the poultry) the wings and main bulk of the F-111 erupted in a fireball close to a farmhouse a mile away.

The story filled four pages of the local newspaper. The author must confess that while writing the copy he tried to mention that the wreckage just missed a school, this being almost a cliché in the aftermath of British air crashes. In fact, in such an overcrowded island it is almost impossible not to crash close to one (later pages will reveal the disaster of a bomber crashing on a school).

This comparatively minor incident demonstrates the newsworthiness of air disasters. Even a minor 'prang' to a private light aircraft can be head-line news in the immediate area.

However, sensationalism is not the intention of this book. This is a history of air safety. The less reputable and sensationalist members of the media breed have been offered many sacrifices for ritual slaughter in recent years: Air India and Pan American 'jumbos' have been ripped apart in mid-air by terrorist bombs, DC-10s have broken-up over France and ploughed into volcanoes in the Antarctic, the most popular airliner type of all – the Boeing 737 – have had engines exploding on take-off, lost massive sections of cabin roofing over the sea and even had engines falling off while climbing. As the public's demand to fly outstrips the capacity of manufacturers to produce the machines, we have entered an era that less-informed journalists have branded as that of the 'geriatric jets' as machines over twenty years old shed parts of their structure in flight.

'How Safe Is It To Fly?' banner headlines ask. Very safe, is the realistic answer. However, it could always be safer, and the greatest tragedy of all is not to learn from a disaster how to avoid it happening again. The lesson is not always learnt. While completing this work the author was often asked such questions as: which is the safest airline? Should airlines be seen as culpable when a manufacturing fault might have caused disaster? And should an airline safety index be built up based upon the number of take-offs and landings their fleets have completed, for these are the most dangerous times and would always put short-hop charter operators low down a graph of safety.

It is notable however that a second-hand aircraft offered for sale from the fleet of one of the major operators such as British Airways or Lufthansa will command a premium price on the basis that it is more likely to have been rigorously maintained without the engineers having taken 'short-cuts'.

At the time of writing the giant Eastern Air Lines of America is in receivership following the deregulation of Ronald Reagan's presidency which allowed any operator with an elderly DC-9 or early-production Boeing 737 to compete with the household names on that nation's routes.

Eastern found their ability to match these new operators crippled by the costs of running the massive maintenance bases that they had established in the 1970s. Travellers usually consider the price first when purchasing their tickets; they do not realise that the cheaper flight might only be possible because the aircraft is older and perhaps rather tired, its rivets suffering from that engineering cancer termed metal fatigue, the engines burning a little too much oil, the pilot desperately in need of rest but under management pressure to keep the planes flying.

In Europe the greatest threat at present is the sheer volume of traffic in overcrowded skies. The navigation system here was established in 1946 to ferry refugees home, and basically the same system is in use today. The computers of the twenty-two nations' air traffic control systems are not compatible. A conference landline circuit links London, Paris, Brussels, Madrid and Frankfurt, but otherwise controllers have to telephone each other. In the United States a giant computer screen in the basement of the Federal Aviation Administration building in Washington, DC, can show every commercial flight airborne at any moment over the country. Despite the formation of the European Economic Community no agreement has been reached about establishing a single air traffic control authority for these skies. In 1988 Lufthansa estimated that its airliners spent ten thousand hours on the ground waiting for clearance to take-off and another ten thousand hours flying in fuel-wasting holding patterns waiting to land.

'Flow control' exists throughout Europe now: no aircraft can take-off until there is space for it within the air traffic control system of its destination. It is the passenger who finally pays the extra operating costs that such congestion causes.

With deregulation a possibility in Europe too, what will the operators do to relieve this congestion? Probably, they will invest in larger aircraft because such machines will give them priority at airports. New routes will be developed even when not justified just to strengthen their case for more 'slots', and they will fill up the order books of manufacturers just to stop new operators muscling in. It is estimated that by the turn of the century there will be two *billion* air passengers per year. Can the existing infrastructure take the strain? Is safety becoming a gamble?

Flying an aircraft is actually quite boring. Computers and gyroscopes control it, and can even land it at some airports. Seated in plush chairs, lulled by the hum of air-conditioning and almost imperceptibly rocked as the machine rides the air-currents, body-clocks thrown awry by travelling through the time zones and irregular hours, is it any wonder that crews fall asleep on the flight deck? On intercontinental flights most airlines expect a stewardess to visit the cockpit approximately every twenty minutes just to ensure that the pilots are still awake. Manufacturers are considering fitting alarm bells that will ring if no control is touched for, say, five minutes. A stewardess cannot be on the flight deck as the pilots make the landing approach however. Crews have been known to fall asleep during this function, or to attempt a landing on a motorway, or even at the wrong airport!

This book does not have a chapter titled 'Pilot Error'. It is more important to look at the background to why the pilot made an error, where appropriate. Was too much expected of him or her?

Who decides what went wrong in the wake of a disaster? Great Britain has led the field in the independent investigation of air accidents. As early as 1919 the Accidents Investigation Branch was formed – in their own words – 'as a result of public concern about the numbers of aircraft accidents at that time'. Since November 1987 this team of detectives have had the suffix 'Air' added to their name. The Chief Inspector of Accidents at the time of writing is Donald Cooper, AFC. Like most of the team he is a pilot. Full details of the AAIB are given in an appendix to this book, but one major facet must be stressed here: this body works to discover the cause(s) of accidents. It is not its function to attribute blame.

Nowadays aircraft accidents are big business once the litigation lawyers move in. Victims of air disasters, or their relatives, can become multi-millionaires if blame can be attributed to a person or organisation. Inevitably, so long as aircraft fly a few will meet disaster. Are the vast sums now being awarded in compensation truly justified? The victim could have been killed by a lightning strike at the golf course the next day. Such lawsuits can take many years to resolve: for example, the compensation claims for the relatives of those killed in the 1973 DC-10 disaster near Paris were only being finalised as this book was being researched. Lawyers are looking to attribute negligence on the part of a human being – God carries no third-party insurance.

America's once thriving light aircraft manufacturers have now pruned many of the smaller designs from their catalogues out of fear of compensation claims which could bankrupt them. Although this may open up a market once dominated by native companies to foreign competition, there is also the possibility that the average age of the light aircraft may simply become older, and therefore more dangerous.

Flying in a light aircraft is, on average, fourteen times more dangerous than a large airliner. Should an American aircraft come to grief the cause(s) will be investigated by that nation's equivalent of the AAIB: the National Transportation Safety Board (N.T.S.B.).

This body was only established many years after Britain's lead and in the wake of a notable crash. On 5 May 1935 a Douglas DC-2 of Transcontinental & Western Air (T.W.A.) took off from Albuquerque, New Mexico, on the second leg of a flight from Los Angeles to Newark, New Jersey. In just hours and a single lifetime later it would backtrack above the coast-to-coast trails of the wagon trains that had taken months to rumble their perilous way west. On board were nine passengers, including Senator Bronson Cutting, a politician revered (at least by his party compatriots) in Congress. As Captain Harvey Bolton set course across the Rockies he flew into a storm and the twin-engined airliner (from which the classic DC-3 which did more than any other craft to establish the airways of the world was evolved) was buffeted by hail and wind. Bolton discovered that his transceiver was not transmitting. He could still receive signals however and hoped to pick up transmissions from an emergency landing field.

The unpressurised DC-2 was unable to climb above the storm. Flying at treetop height, Bolton took her into a ravine. It was a dead end with solid rock looking up out of the murk. Bolton could not heave the aircraft round. He and his co-pilot were killed along with three passengers, one of them Cutting. Six passengers survived.

This incident was the catalyst for the 1938 endorsement of the United States Civil Aeronautics Act that created a pair of government bodies responsible for air safety: the Civil Aeronautics Administration and the Civil Aeronautics Board for Accident Investigation. These are now respectively the Federal Aviation Administration and the National Transportation Safety Board (also responsible for other transport modes).

If one is truly determined not to die in an air disaster one should never fly. There is of course always even then the chance of being struck by a falling plane but the odds of this are even less than the chances of being struck by lightning! The one hundred per cent safe form of transport will never exist, and it follows therefore that there is always a degree of compromise. What price are the voyagers willing to pay for their journeys and is this sufficient to cover their expectations of safety standards (always higher than the price they are willing to pay) while still leaving an operating profit?

Passengers can also be their own worst enemies; some never listen to the safety lecture before the airliner leaves the ramp nor watch the choreographed mime of the stewardess indicating the emergency exits. Some do not fasten their safety belts and some smoke in the lavatories despite the 'do not' signs.

The very nature of an 'accident' is that it is an event believed to be inconceivable. For example, for the sake of a small light bulb worth a few cents, the first wide-bodied jet disaster occurred. An Eastern Air Lines Lockheed L-1011 TriStar was approaching Miami shortly before midnight on 29 December 1972. This then-new jumbo-generation machine, powered by three turbofans, had only rolled off the production line five months previously but it had already accumulated nearly one thousand hours in the air and five hundred landings; enough service to burn out the filament of the green bulb that should glow when the nosewheel was down and locked. As the giant gently descended towards the runway the co-pilot pulled the green lever on the centre console that lowered the undercarriage. There was the familiar rumble and shudder of the gear dropping down. 'Hey, we've only got two greens,' he said as the cycle ended. The two lights representing the mainwheels 'down and locked' beamed brightly but that for the nosegear was unlit.

This was a minor problem. But they would have to fly another circuit now to check the position of the landing gear.

Even if the nosewheel had remained stubbornly in its well there were still back-up systems that could get it down: pumping it by hand, or if that failed disconnecting the hydraulic supply to let it simply fall into place by gravity. As the pilot radioed the control tower to declare that he was over-shooting on this approach, both pilots and the flight engineer were certain that all three landing oleos were in fact down and locked and that it was just a blown bulb.

Air traffic control directed the flight into a holding pattern at 600m (2,000ft) to the west of Miami International. Below lay the dark mass of the Everglades. Perhaps in pre-historic times when this world was still cooling much of it appeared as the Everglades remains: a humid marsh-land neither land nor sea, a soggy carpet threaded by swaying fronds of sawgrass stretching several feet high. Water gurgled slowly over the mud down clear leads while the night was filled with the eerie sound of the calls of frogs and toads. Only the distant glow of the lights of Miami and the occasional roar of jetliners overhead signposted modern times, otherwise it could have been a landscape of pre-history.

The TriStar flew a rectangular orbit above that tract of wilderness as the crew struggled with the obstinate bulb. The airliner was flying on auto-pilot as they hunched over the centre console. It was awkward to get access to the bulb, which would not come free of its mounting. As the pilots cursed it, the 163 passengers and cabin crew were beginning to wonder what the delay was. Most of the passengers were returning from vacation. It had been below freezing in New York. They expected soon to step out into the balmy 75°C of Florida. Some were visiting friends and relatives to share the arrival of a new year, new hopes and dreams. In another conti-nent the B-52 bombers of that nation's air force were pounding Hanoi and Haiphong as President Nixon tried to force an end to the Vietnam war.

The crew cursed that bulb. It would be so easy to change it on the ground. It had jammed in its housing. The flight engineer had been leaning over between the pilots' seats to see if he could twist it out. Now they decided that he should drop down through a trapdoor into the nose compartment that housed the computers from where a visual check could be made of the gear's position. At about that time a soft chime sounded from the flight engineer's panel. It was the altitude warning: the TriStar had dipped below 500m (1,700ft). Distracted by the recalcitrant bulb, no one on that flight deck heard the chime. They were confident that the electronic wizardry of the auto-pilot was still in control. But it had been disconnected!

The electronic brain could be disconnected by pressing on a button on each pilot's control column, throwing a lever on the centre console, or – and this was to enable the airliner to be hurled across the sky instantly if mid-air collision or some other crisis loomed – by a force of 6–8kg (15–20lb) pressure on either of the control antlers. As the pilot leant over to his right to struggle with the bulb his knee must have nudged the

column; an insignificant nudge, but enough to activate the disconnect. He
did not notice that the auto-pilot height setting indication on his instrument panel had blanked out. That for the co-pilot remained on, still
showing 600m (2,000ft) even as the airliner nosed down slightly, whis-
pered through the darkness and gathered speed a little. The brooding
mass of the Everglades offered no visual horizon for the pilots to orientate
themselves to, to sense this descent.

In the final moments the co-pilot suspected that something was wrong.
But it was too late to avert disaster. There was not even a ground-proximity
warning *whoop-whoop* from the siren that sounds if a crew tries to land with
the wheels up, for all three undercarriage gears were indeed down and
locked. Travelling at 6km (4 miles) per minute the aircraft ploughed into
the Everglades and broke up, flinging passengers out into the swampland.
The sawgrass ripped and tore at their bodies. A fire lashed through the
wreckage, though fortunately it did not take hold. The frogs fell silent.
Pieces of airliner splashed into the mud, water gurgled and steamed
where the three giant turbofans lay, their red-hot combustion chambers
cracking at the sudden slaking. There was a brief time of almost silence
and then the injured began to cry out, for there were survivors in that
wreckage, shocked and frightened, lost and helpless. Other airliners
searing through that midnight sky saw the flare of the fire-flash and
reported it to air traffic control where the operators were just realising
that a 'heavy' (wide-bodied airliner) that had been flying a holding
pattern had disappeared off the scopes.

Of the total of 176 people who had been aboard, 77 survived, pulled
from that swampland; dirty, cut, bleeding, some half-naked, some with
compound fractures, soaked in kerosene, traumatised. Helicopters flew
them to Miami. Two died later in hospital. The entire flight deck crew
perished.

The air industry soon took steps to prevent a repetition of the incident.
The National Transportation Safety Board recommended that a flashing
light on both pilots' instrument panels should be activated if either
disconnected the auto-pilot owing to a nudge on the control column.
Following the distribution of the report to the Federal Aviation
Administration, an Airworthiness Directive was issued by that body
obliging such a modification to all machines of the type. The disaster also
instigated the fitting of terrain warning avoidance radar that should
prevent aircraft ploughing either into the ground in circumstances similar
to the Everglades incident or into high land; though such equipment is
now commonplace we shall discover in the wastes of the Antarctic that it is
not foolproof (see p. 113).

Not all of the stories recounted in this history end in death and destruction. They were selected not on the basis of the death toll, but to best show
the development of air transport and improvements in air safety. It has
been estimated that civilian airline operations will be responsible for the
deaths of some one thousand passengers per year up to the end of this

century. It is for the reader to decide if this statistic is acceptable.

It is not the intention of this work to scaremonger. In Great Britain there are over five thousand deaths on the roads every year: that's eleven full 'jumbo' loads. When the figures are published at each year end they provide a one-paragraph report in most newspapers. Throughout Europe over fifty thousand people are killed in road traffic accidents per year. This figure far out-numbers the *total* number of passengers killed in civilian airline accidents since air transport began 80 years ago.

The drive to the airport is the most dangerous part of the journey.

1
Lighter Than Air

It is sometimes hard to believe that man's desire for flight was only realised just over two centuries ago. Success came not from imitating the birds, by attempting flight in machines with flapping wings, but by employing the simple scientific truth that heat causes air to expand so that it becomes lighter and lifts. Man learnt to make machines that could become lighter-than-air: balloons.

The principal aerial pioneers were Joseph and Etienne Montgolfier, the sons of a French paper manufacturer. After experiments with models they constructed an almost cylindrical envelope 14m (46 ft) in diameter and 21m (70ft) high with a capacity of 1,700 cu m (60,000 cu ft). Strung below this was an iron grid on which straw could be burnt. The heat rising through the open neck of the envelope warmed the air enclosed there to lift the contraption, including the basket built around the iron grid and any brave soul willing to risk his life in it.

After successful tethered flights with animals on board, King Louis XVI suggested that two condemned convicts should ride the balloon for its first free flight. However, incensed that credit for such a momentous occasion should be credited to 'common criminals', one Pîlatre de Rozier volunteered to make the first attempt. The Marquis d'Arlandes also pleaded to take part in history. Accordingly these two men soared up and over Paris on 21 October 1783 to land somewhat bumpily in a field 9km (6 miles) distant. The conquest of the air had begun.

Two years later, however, Pîlatre de Rozier, trying to emulate Jean Pierre Blanchard and an American Dr John Jefferies, died in an attempt at floating across the English Channel. This balloon had its upper half filled with hydrogen (which is lighter than air and can provide lift) and the lower section inflated by a fire burning beneath the envelope, Montgolfier-style.

Miraculously, this potentially explosive contraption managed to take off from the French coast and rose to about 450m (1,500ft) before the inevitable happened: there was a blinding flash as the hydrogen ignited. Burning debris plummeted to the sea. The first authenticated pilot was dead.

While the free-flying balloon has the ability to lift into the air, it is at the mercy of the wind once it is airborne. Inventors repeatedly tried to find methods of propelling balloons: teams of rowers, and sails, were just two methods experimented with, the perpetrators of the latter idea not realising that an airborne balloon drifts with the wind so sails would only hang limp.

Balloons, however, did go to war. In 1870 France was invaded by Germany and Paris was besieged. Trapped in the city were some of the greatest pioneer balloonists. On 23 September 1870 Jules Durouf soared out of the city over the Germans' heads carrying a package of despatches. Three hours later and 100km (60 miles) away he landed safely at Evreux. Over the next week three more flights were successfully made, but the problem was that this route to the outside world could only convey one-way traffic and over half of the balloon experts were now away from the city with no way of returning. The answer was to set up a balloon production line and find others willing to fly them on the understanding that each ascent was both a test and operational flight of a new balloon and would also be the first solo for the crew. Acrobats from the Paris Hippodrome were recruited, but these gentlemen had a tendency to shin down the mooring ropes to the ground at the least threat, at which moment the now considerably lightened balloon would soar away with the precious despatches usually still on board.

Why exactly there seemed to be an almost inexhaustible supply of Navy men in Paris during the siege has not been recorded, but these formed the crews for most of the later missions, flights that did not go without incident. More than one balloon came down on German-occupied territory and on 12 November the *Daquerre* was shot down, the first victim of anti-aircraft fire! Just as Royal Air Force (RAF) bombers were forced to do years later, the balloonists resorted to flying by night. The most tragic victim of these flights was a sailor named Prince who declared before ascending from Paris just before midnight one December: 'I am going to make an immense voyage that will be talked about for years to come.' His balloon drifted over England's Lizard Point the next day where he dropped his despatches. However, instead of venting the hydrogen from his balloon to descend he drifted on. There was only the Atlantic beyond, and he was never seen again.

The next advance in flight had to be a machine that could return to its starting point, and this was finally achieved on 9 August 1884 when the *La France* airship of Charles Renard and A.C. Krebs took off from Chalais Meudon to cover several kilometres (miles) before returning. Her envelope was almost 50m (170ft) in length, a horizontal cylinder, the true infant of the giants that would soon come. *La France* was powered by electricity, a nine horsepower Gramme motor that needed 95kg (210lb) of battery for each one. But the power-to-weight ratio desperately needed to be improved.

The 'horseless carriage' engines being developed by Carl Benz and Gottlieb Daimler seemed to offer promise. A Dr Wölfert fitted such a petroleum engine to an airship in the 1890s. However, the combination of exhaust sparks and hydrogen gas was akin to lighting a fuse to dynamite. In June 1897 the detonation came, killing Wölfert and a passenger; the first members of a terrible roll call of death that would only end with the destruction of the *Hindenburg* in 1937.

The name that is linked forever with the airship is that of Count Ferdinand von Zeppelin. Born on 8 July 1838, he was commissioned as an army lieutenant in 1857. This career ended during the Franco-Prussian War when he was rumoured to have deserted the patrol which he was in command of when fighting broke out. He was the only survivor. Although perhaps privately seeing the Count as reprehensible, his peers did not allow allegations of public disgrace; at least not until 1887 when he seems to have made the mistake of criticising the Kaiser. He retired from the army and it was expected that his name would fade into obscurity.

But he began to pursue the quest of flight. Ask a mountaineer why he climbs and he will almost inevitably say: 'Because it's there.' Why does an aviator chase the clouds? 'Because I want to fly,' he must surely say, yet the Count does not seem to ever have made such a statement. Nevertheless, he invested almost all of his wealth in constructing his first airship, the LZ1, in a floating hangar on Lake Konstanz. She was 126m (420ft) long and 12m (40ft) in diameter, with a capacity of 11,300 cu m (400,000 cu ft). A true rigid airship unlike the dirigibles (akin to the modern 'blimp' whose shape is retained through the cut of the envelope and the pressure within) that had come before, she was powered by two Daimler marine engines of just sixteen horsepower. But she flew with the Count and four others on board. Directional control was almost non-existent and her fore-and-aft pitch could only be adjusted by sliding a 250kg (550lb) weight along a rail. She was airborne for over an hour however before settling gently and undamaged on the lake, on 2 July 1900.

LZ1 was not brought out again until 17 October 1900. The first flight had made as little impression on the newspapers as the Wright brothers were shortly, strangely, to experience.

The *Frankfurter Zeitung* asked a freelance journalist, Hugo Eckener, who happened to be nearby, to cover the story and write about it if anything seemed worthwhile, beginning Eckener's long association with the air.

LZ1's second flight was barely more successful than the first. Bankruptcy loomed for Zeppelin, but he had aroused the interest of an aluminium manufacturer in Ludenscheid, and the State of Württemberg granted him permission to raise funds by lottery. The construction of LZ2 became possible. This second ship was similar in most ways to her predecessor except in the power units, which were 85 horsepower Daimlers.

Her first flight almost brought disaster: the forward engine stopped as she was being towed from the hanger. The tail dropped to the water, damaging the rudders, but then she recovered and, powerless, drifted towards the high ground on the Swiss side of Lake Konstanz. A motor launch took her in tow just in time.

The second flight of LZ2 on 17 January 1906 seemed at first to be a triumph; she soared to 450m (1,500ft) and reached an airspeed of over 48kph (30mph). However, the engines failed and she drifted away, to be dashed to pieces in trees on the north shore of the lake.

Zeppelin, assisted now by Eckener who was acting in the role of public relations advisor, would not be defeated. With funds from friends and another lottery, LZ3 was completed. With 85 horsepower she successfully flew 96km (60 miles) in two hours on 9 October 1906, repeating the feat the following day. The German government at last took interest, placing an order for two airships. The LZ4 flew successfully along the River Rhine until the forward engine failed in 1907. Zeppelin managed to fly her to the Daimler plant at Stuttgart on the remaining one, but while she was there a wind sprang up and the sailors clinging to the guy ropes could not hold her. She smashed to the ground and caught fire. There were no injuries, but it was a portent of what was to come.

Still undeterred, Zeppelin formed an airline, Deutsche Luftschiffarts AG. The first passenger ship, *Deutschland*, was wrecked by her ex-army captain, but without injury. Others were built and the flights were certainly not without incident: *Swallow* broke up and caught fire at Düsseldorf, yet when the operations of the world's first passenger airline were curtailed by the outbreak of war the service had carried 35,000 passengers safely.

When war came Zeppelin handed his airships over to the German government for military use: after all, that was what he had first designed them for. He was not the only producer of such machines: in Danzig a Dr Schütte and Heinrich Lanz, the chairman of an engineering concern, had developed a wood-framed rigid airship that pioneered the true cigar shapes of the British R100 and R101 in later years. These Shütte-Lanz ships bore the brunt of the war in the air, though they were erroneously described as Zeppelins by their would-be victims.

It is hard to believe now with our knowledge of the vulnerability of the airships just how much fear they instilled into the civilian populations of cities such as Paris and London; fear that had been captured and accentuated by such fiction as H.G. Wells' *The War in the Air*. In a pre-emptive strike, Winston Churchill, then First Lord of the Admiralty, ordered attacks to be made on the airship lairs. On 8 October 1914 two Royal Naval Air Service Avro 504s took off from Antwerp carrying puny 9kg (20lb) bombs. Flight Lieutenant Marix dropped his accurately on the airship shed at Düsseldorf. Zeppelin Z9 erupted.

The full story of the airship is beyond the scope of this book but a brief resumé of their defeat and destruction is relevant in this history. Throughout World War I the airships only appeared above their main target of London twelve times, but the effect on morale was far greater than any bombing damage that they could achieve. They brought warfare to civilians.

So impregnable and unreachable did these giants seem floating silently and menacingly above upturned, fear paled faces. Drifting 6,000m (20,000ft) high, rimed in ice, their crews trembled with cold, gasping for oxygen, knowing that one spark, one shot from a seemingly so harmless in comparison aeroplane, could instantly turn their ship of the sky into a funeral pyre. Any extra weight diminishes the performance of an airship, so the crews had no parachutes.

On 31 May 1915 Londoners first heard the drone of Maybach engines high in the night sky. Five people were killed as bombs rained down on the north-east of the city. Searchlights illuminated the airship, but the retaliatory shellfire fell short.

The beginning of the end for the military airship was presaged on 7 June 1915 when Flight Lieutenant R. Warneford, flying a Royal Naval Air Service monoplane to attack the airship sheds at Berden St Agathe, sighted L37 in flight over Belgium. From 1,800m (6,000ft) he overflew it and dropped six Hales bombs on to her envelope. Warneford's light butterfly-like aircraft was nearly destroyed by the eruption of the airship. He was awarded the Victoria Cross – Great Britain's supreme award for gallantry in action – but was killed just ten days later in a flying accident near Paris.

One was brought down on English soil on 2 September 1916 by Lieutenant W. Leefe Robinson of the Royal Flying Corps. To the cheers of those on the ground it fell in flames at Cuffley, Hertfordshire, north of London. Night flying and incendiary bullets were developed to meet the threat of the airship.

Soon afterwards the L33 under the command of Captain Boeker was brought down by artillery fire almost intact at Little Wigborough in Essex. This time it was possible for engineers and scientists to inspect it. The post-war designs of Great Britain would initially be strongly based on it.

Germany now relied on Gotha bombers for almost all their aerial attacks on England. The total death toll from both airships and aircraft bombing was 1,413, a prelude to the true blitz that would commence in 1940.

Just as the destructive power of nuclear fission was harnessed for peaceful power after World War II, so the airship, despite its propensity for self-immolation, would be seen as the long-range travel of the future. It could be made safe but for the millionth chance, its champions declared. Of course, the same had been said for the 'R.M.S. Titanic'!

The German airships had been grounded, some destroyed in their hangars by their crews who simply vented the hydrogen and then cut the cables by which they were strung from the roof girders. The United States and the United Kingdom would initially be the chief proponents of lighter-than-air travel; soon, however, to be rivalled again by resurgent Germany.

Based on their study of L33 the British Admiralty contracted Armstrong Whitworth's to build the airship R33 after the war (the fact that the number was the same was mere coincidence, the British sequence included the non-rigid blimps, the new craft simply taking the first available number), while Beardmore and Company produced the R34. This latter airship was 192m (643ft) long with a hydrogen gas capacity of 55,200 cu m (1,950,000 cu ft). Powered by five Sunbeam Maori petrol engines of 250 hp, she left East Fortune, Scotland, on 2 July 1919 under the command of Major G.H. Scott. With 32 crewmen (one of them a stowaway discovered after take-off) and taking the great circle route via Newfoundland – which unwittingly through the basic meteorological knowledge of the time gave maximum headwinds – the 22,050 litres (4,900 gallons) of fuel just took her to Mineola, Long Island, New York State in five days. A brave venture indeed; but a portent of the future was that Alcock and Brown had conquered the North Atlantic the previous month in a converted Vickers Vimy bomber.

Leaving on 9 July the R34 returned in seventy-five hours. Now, if only airships could be made big enough, a trans-Atlantic or even global service for passengers was possible. After all, the aeroplane was really too small and fragile, perhaps just capable of carrying a few passengers across the English Channel, no more than that, surely? The R34 lasted for a further eighteen months until she flew into a Yorkshire hill. She limped home to East Fortune before collapsing beyond repair.

Meanwhile in Germany Eckener revived the Delag pre-war airline with LZ120 *Bodensee*, a small ship of 11,050 cu m (390,000 cu ft) capacity. She was placed into service between Friedrichshafen and Berlin, flying the distance in just six hours. She safely carried 2,300 passengers, and a sister ship, *Nordstern* was constructed before the controlling Allied powers intervened, and took them over as war reparations.

The United States wanted to take command of some of the wartime German airships but after their wrecking, cash instead was demanded in compensation. Eckener offered to construct a new airship instead. The LZ126, alias *Los Angeles*, was delivered via the Atlantic in 1924. Almost alone in the tragic history of airships she survived to be scrapped in 1939, even lasting through once being blown vertical at her mooring mast.

Inspired by the R34 Atlantic crossing, the Americans also ordered a new airship from Great Britain. R38 made her first flight trials in June 1921. An American crew crossed the ocean from Lakehurst, New Jersey, to train with and ultimately operate her. The gas cells within her latticework structure were filled with hydrogen as on 23 August she performed a full-speed test over the River Humber; helium, the uninflammable inert gas, was only available in America if she crossed the Atlantic. Four days before she had buckled amidships when Commander L.H. Maxfield of the US Navy had pushed her to maximum revolutions. Now, at 100kph (60mph), he strained her again with violent rudder swings. Horrified watchers suddenly saw her split in two. The heat of the engines ignited the escaping gas as both sections fell into the water. Of the 49 men on board there were only 5 survivors, 4 of these being British. Many were burned to death in blazing pools of petrol on the water. After this, America decided to build its own airship.

ZR1, to be christened *Shenandoah – Daughter of the Stars*, was completed at Lakehurst on 13 August 1923. But even the fact that she was to be inflated with helium (which provides 92 per cent of the lift of hydrogen) did not save her from disaster. She had flown for 750 hours and covered

44,800km (28,000 miles) as a US Navy airship, before her end came on 3 September 1925.

Against the judgement of her captain, Lieutenant-Commander Zachary Lansdowne, she was ordered to cross the country from Lakehurst, New York, to perform manoeuvres with the fleet off California. Thunderstorms were rolling across the Mid-West states. Lansdowne's fears were realised over Ohio shortly after midnight. A seemingly solid bank of ominous black storm cloud was ahead, sweeping towards the massive airship. Lightning streaked through the clouds, which held strong up and down draughts, capable of destroying even contemporary airliners. The incredible length of *Shenandoah* meant that she could be subjected to opposing air currents at bow and stern simultaneously. With such tremendous twisting forces upon her structure, it is remarkable that she survived so long. For almost four hours the crew fought to save her, making almost no headway. Early risers in the town of Caldwell saw her in the slate grey dawn. She was caught in the mighty, invisible hands of that storm, suddenly whipped higher with her tail up and nose down. As she went higher, to 1,500m 1,600m (5,000ft, 6,000ft), there was the added danger of her gas cells splitting. This was no wartime Zeppelin 'height-climber' designed to operate at over 6,000m (20,000ft). As she rose, her helium expanded in the lower atmospheric pressure. Zachary ordered venting of the precious gas. Slowly, her 2m (6ft) second climb was checked, but instead she lurched down into an even faster dive. Water ballast was released as she plummeted. At 900m (3,000ft) she began to slow, at 660m (2,200ft) she was almost level, but then either conflicting air currents caught her nose and tail, or the lattice framework could take no more: she split into two ahead of the forward engine pods. At the same moment the underslung control cabin sheared off, plunging to earth, killing Lansdowne and all inside instantly. The aft section also quickly fell to earth, but the forward half of the airship free-ballooned for almost an hour.

By venting the gas cells Lieutenant-Commander Rosendahl brought off a semi-controlled descent that saved the lives of 29 of her remaining 43-man crew.

As the injured lay helpless on the ground, in danger of dying from exposure, the ghouls of disaster came: the looters, sensation seekers. On buck-boards and in Model Ts they came to rip and tear at the wreckage for macabre souvenirs; carrion-feeders who before nightfall would strip bare the wreckage of *Shenandoah*. Their despicable like would appear again at later disasters: inside the wreckage of a Trident near Heathrow before the emergency services had even arrived at the wreck, and on the wind-swept moors around a once little-known town called Lockerbie.

The destruction of *Shenandoah* was not to be the end of the United States' involvement with airships, however: in October 1928 contracts were signed with the Goodyear Tire Company of Akron, Ohio, for two further ships, each of 184,000 cu m (6,500,000 cu ft) capacity. The tragedies that befell these, *USS Akron* and *USS Macon*, will be told shortly. Meanwhile, it is time to look again at progress being made in Europe.

France, the original pioneer, turned its back on lighter-than-air transport following the loss of its Navy's *Dixmude* off Sicily on 21 December 1923. All fifty aboard her perished when it was struck by lightning and fell in flames to the sea. The airship was the ex-Zeppelin LZ114, taken by France as a war reparation.

For a time after constructing the *Los Angeles* Eckener's Delag company had been reduced to making saucepans but by the mid-twenties, with the memories of the great conflict beginning to fade, he was able to raise the money and start construction of a new passenger airship without Allied objections. The *Graf Zeppelin* was christened in her hangar on 8 July 1928, 111,800 cu m (3,950,000 cu ft) ship of 232m (775ft) length. Her five Maybach engines could propel her for 9,600km (6,000 miles) with twenty passengers and twelve tonnes (tons) of freight. On her first trans-Atlantic flight in autumn 1928 she suffered a severe tear of the fabric on her elevators, but members of her crew managed to repair this while she hovered over the ocean. This first flight through adversity to New York was seen as evidence that the airship could be safer than the aircraft. In 1929 the *Graf Zeppelin* circled the globe. Meanwhile, in England, the Imperial airships R100 and R101 were almost complete.

4 October 1930 was an overcast day of scudding clouds streaming east. Early that afternoon a blue Daimler left the Air Ministry in London for Bedford, 80km (50 miles) to the north. It was trailed by a Trojan van. At the top of Hammer Hill, overlooking the flood plain of the River Great Ouse, the two vehicles drew to a halt. A strikingly tall, well-dressed gentleman stepped from the limousine and gazed down on Cardington, a small village on the south-east of the county town. Floating there at her mooring mast, gleaming silver in the setting sun, was the largest vessel in the world: R101. That night, with him on board, R101 would leave for India, the fulfilment of Christopher Birdwood Thomson's dream.

The story of the R101 is a romantic one, concerning Thomson's vision of an airship service that could link together the British Empire, and his love of a woman who shared and supported his beliefs but could not become his wife: Princess Marthe Bibesco. She was Roumanian by birth, French by upbringing; he was a forty-year-old British Colonel. They had first met at a soirée given by King Ferdinand and Queen Marie at the Cotroceni Palace in Bucharest 1915. The attraction between this distinguished soldier and the twenty-nine year old society beauty endured to their deaths; it was a tragic love because she had married the Catholic Prince Georges-Valentin Bibesco in 1902 and had a daughter by him. He must have known of the enduring affair between Thomson and his wife, but he did not divorce her. While her husband lived a life centred around motor racing and 'flying machines', separate from his wife and daughter, the beautiful Princess and the gaunt British Air Minister had to keep furtive trysts in the capitals of Europe.

Before leaving London Thomson had sent a telegram to his lover:

THE PRINCESS BIBESCO, POSADA, PAR COMARMIC PRAHOVA, ROUMANIA – OFF TO INDIA AT LAST IN R101 STOP MY THOUGHTS AS EVER WITH YOU STOP OUR TALISMAN FLIES TOO STOP ALL MY LOVE AND BLESSINGS

KIT

Their talisman was a carpet that had travelled the world from Sulaimaniya in Kurdistan. The Trojan van had picked it up from Thomson's home, and it now followed his Daimler down Hammer Hill towards Cardington. The Air Minister believed that it would grace the banquets to be held celebrating the flight of R101, at Ismailia and Karachi.

Thomson's first interest in air transport came at the turn of the century when serving with the balloon section at Kimberley during the South African war. This sparked a belief in air power within him that endured through his military career, although he had no further contact with this form of transport until many years later. In 1919 he resigned his commission to stand as a Labour candidate for parliament in the Bristol Central constituency. This attempt at entering government failed, but it did bring Thomson close to the future first Labour Prime Minister, Ramsay MacDonald. In 1923 Thomson had a seat on the committee that was examining the prospects for an Imperial airship service under the chairmanship of Air Vice-Marshal Sir Geoffrey Salmond.

Labour came to power in 1924, Thomson being appointed Air Minister with a seat in the House of Lords as Lord Thomson of Cardington, and a place in the Cabinet. He presented his colleagues with a formal proposal for two 141,500 cu m (5,000,000 cu ft) airships to take one hundred persons and sixteen tonnes (tons) of freight over 5,600km (3,500 miles) at 100kph (60mph). These were to be prototypes for a future fleet linking the Empire. The approved expenditure was £1,400,000 spread over three years, with the design and construction to be divided between the Air Ministry, who would take over the premises of Short Brothers at Cardington, and the Vickers-owned Airship Guarantee Company Limited based at Howden. Their airship would be the R100, the two planned craft being of independent designs with the intention that the future Imperial fleet ships could incorporate the best aspects of the differing approaches.

The first Labour government fell in November 1924, but work continued on the R100 and R101. In 1929, two years after the target completion date, the two ships came together at Cardington, a year that also saw the return of Labour to power and Thomson to the Air Ministry.

R101 was the more graceful craft, a cigar shape that offered lower drag than the traditional parallel-sided ship. The primary difference between the two giants, however, was in power plant: Rolls Royce Condor petrol engines for R100, but five Beardmore Tornado diesels originally designed for Canadian railcar use fitted in gondolas slung beneath R101.

R101's first flight was on 14 October 1929, a five-hour trip to London and back. Thomson had his first journey on 18 October, a six-hour circuit encompassing Birmingham. But all was not well: the engines proved to be both unreliable and overweight, and problems were also experienced with the fourteen gas bags – these were torn and punctured as a result of rubbing against the framework. In seven flights R101 flew for 73 hours in 1929, but although the airship programme was nearly £½ million over-budget by that time, the India and trans-Atlantic flights would have to wait until the next year.

The summer of 1930 was to be that of airships. Even Eckener and his *Graf Zeppelin* came to Cardington that year, his ship pausing there to pick up its master who had dined with Thomson after arriving by sea from America where he had been trying unsuccessfully to secure helium. On 29 July R100 left for her only long-distance flight: to Canada and back under the command of Captain R.S. Booth but, in a confusing chain-of-command, with Major Scott (of R34 fame) as Officer of Flying Operations. Scott insisted on flying through storms, an unnecessary and foolhardy 'push on' attitude. The trip was successful, however, R100 locking back on Cardington's tower on 16 August.

Meanwhile, R101 had been causing considerable problems. She went to the Hendon air display, that curious between-wars carnival of a toothless RAF whose doped silver wings of Hawker biplanes and Vickers bombers glinted in the sun, but limped home after losing hydrogen as a result of the gas bags being chafed against the framework. She was certainly not fit to undertake any long distance flight. India was out of the question unless more lift could be found to counteract the ten tonnes (tons) that would effectively be lost in the lighter air of the tropics. It was decided to cut R101 in two and insert an extra bay containing two more gas bags, a 'stretching' process commonplace in the development of modern airliners.

By September the modified R101, now suffixed C, was floating at her mast, dominating the skyline of Bedford. She was an incredible 233m (777ft) long. The new 13m (45ft) long bay had been inserted, and also most of the fabric of the outer cover, much of which had rotted, had been replaced with new cotton and linen doped into place. However, that at the nose of the ship and stretching back for 25m (86ft) was not touched, the compound curves there having forced such a method of fitting in the first place whereas the fabric on the centre of the hull had been pre-doped. If only that forward fabric had been replaced disaster might yet have been averted.

The wind was freshening, a vanguard of a deepening trough of low pressure, as twilight came on 4 October 1930. The electric lift yo-yoed up and down the mooring tower as the passengers boarded and their luggage was stowed. Everything taken on board the ship was weighed, since every item needed many times its own volume in hydrogen to be lifted. The weight manifest later revealed that the four officers, thirty-eight crew and eleven of the passengers took on board 4.5–9kg (10–20lb) of personal luggage each. However, no such restriction applied to Lord Thomson: porters loaded two green cabin trunks, four suitcases, two cases of champagne that were intended to toast the triumph of the flight at a state dinner at Ismailia, a dress sword and, as the very last item, the ten foot roll of carpet. 'My precious carpet from Sulimaniya,' Lord Thomson declared. 'We'll have it down for the dinners at Ismailia and Karachi to do the thing in style.' It was placed in the forward gangway. We do not know how much it weighed, perhaps the equivalent of a person or two standing right at the prow of the ship.

With the Tornado diesels in the forward two gondolas turning in reverse, R101 was slipped from the mooring tower at 19.36. An amethyst spray of water ballast sparkled in the twilight at Captain Carmichael ('Bird') Irwin balanced the ship. Perhaps the water ballast ejected from the nose was to counterbalance the weight of that carpet. Despite the strengthening wind, R101 did not immediately set course: first she was to make an anti-clockwise circuit of salute six hundred feet above her hometown. This circle took her north of the riverside town as far as a farm on the outskirts: Twin Woods Farm. Who could envisage then that in just a decade Europe would once again be embroiled in war and that the flat plateau of farmland would be departure point for one of the great mysteries of the air – but Glenn Miller was a struggling musician who had not yet had his first big break with Ray Noble as the airship overflew his future departure point to destiny.

It was 20.19 before R101 bade her farewell above Clophill Crossroads, pointed her nose towards London. Her planned route would take her across France and down the Mediterranean to Ismailia (a distance of 3,580km/2,235 miles) and then a second leg via Baghdad and the Persian Gulf to Karachi (a further 3,400km/2,125 miles). However, even as she pointed her snout south/south-east she was struggling. The number five, aft, engine had been stopped as the airship circled across the River Great Ouse. Engineers Bell and Binks were struggling in the confines of the gondola to change what they believed was a faulty oil pressure gauge.

Unfortunately, it was not decided to return to the tower. The next day would dawn with clearing weather and the crew, most of whom had been on duty for over twenty-four hours, could have rested before setting out on a route that no airship had trailblazed before. It is not known who made the decision to push on, the cautious Irwin or 'press on regardless' Scott who was 'Officer in charge of Flying Operations', an ambiguous title that makes the historian question who was in charge of the airship that night. Before departure 'Bird' Irwin had made it quite clear to journalists thronged around the base of the mooring tower that he was the captain; however, the very presence on board of the R34 hero must have undermined his authority to a degree.

The ship was making some forty knots as she overflew the Midland Railway line towards Luton. With all five Tornados operating she should have been able to achieve seventy knots, but this had never been tested! Engine failure had plagued the test flight of Wednesday 1 October when with four officers, thirty-eight crew and fifteen passengers she had left Bedford in the afternoon, passing over London and Southend before riding out the night over the North Sea. It was not known whether the fabric of her envelope could withstand the strain of driving at full speed into weather that had now developed into a true gale.

How history could have been altered had disaster struck during that proving flight for one of the passengers then was Air Vice-Marshall Hugh Dowding, architect of Fighter Command's victory in the battle of Britain a decade later!

Soon, R101 came over the home of Richard Clarkson at Hoo End near Luton. Clarkson was then an apprentice for De Havilland. In later years he would be the chief aerodynamicist of the Comet and Trident airliners, types whose tragedies will be recounted later. As the airship rumbled over Clarkson estimated its height at six hundred feet. He saw two persons silhouetted against the port lounge windows. She was making 37mph against a headwind of 22mph as she bore towards the capital.

Binks and Bell restarted the number five engine at 20.56 over Brookmans Park to the north of London. The airspeed rose to 100kph (63mph) as she crossed east London, bearing for the landmark of Greenwich Observatory. The rear engine had again been shut down, and was not coaxed back into life until midway across the Channel.

It was 22.35 when the airship passed over the sea 6km (4 miles) east of Hastings, still flying at less than 300m (1,000ft). Figures were seen gazing down for a final glimpse of England. A cold buffet had been served. The sound of dance music drifted into the wind. The BBC were broadcasting Ambrose and his orchestra playing 'My Baby Just Cares For Me' as the R101 rumbled out above a sea whipped into whitecaps.

The storm was pushing the airship port of its intended track, a fact confirmed by calcium flares dropped from the control car. Landfall on the French coast was made over Pointe de St Quentin at 23.36 GMT (00.36 BST). On five engines again, R101 was making 54 knots.

As the log was filled in by Irwin at 01.00 they were 1.6km (1 mile) north of Poix. Now instead of passing 16km (10 miles) west of Beauvais she would have to pass east of that town and over the 220m (730ft) high ridge at Allonne. **See Map 1.**

Sefton Brancker, the Director of Civil Aviation at the Air Ministry, was almost certainly asleep by then. Had he known his location he would certainly have recalled the Allonne ridge from an incident two years before: he had been a passenger on an Imperial Airways Armstrong Whitworth Argosy en route from Le Bourget to Croydon when it had suddenly plummeted 60m (200ft) in the lee of the ridge, slightly injuring two passengers. Brancker wrote to the Air Ministry Meteorological Service about the incident. In reply Captain Entwhistle explained that in the prevailing conditions downdraughts would have occurred. Imperial

Airways pilots now knew to avoid overflying that ridge, but R101 was bearing straight for it as the watch was changed.

Second Officer Maurice Steff took command as Irwin retired to his bed. C.H. Mason now took control of the elevators and P.A. Foster the rudder wheel. It would take them some minutes to get the 'feel' of the ship; until then some yawing of both altitude and direction was to be expected. Up above, Squadron Leader Michael Rope was inspecting the gas bags from the narrow walkway that ran from fore to aft within the envelope.

Crewman Harry Leach was having a final cigarette in the smoking room (like that to be built into Germany's *Hindenburg*, entered through an air lock and shielded from the gas bags around it by metal sheeting) beneath the wireless cabin when at 01.07 he felt the ship nose down into a dive, throwing him to the floor. As R101 levelled off he had time to pick up some glasses and a soda syphon that were rolling around the floor before the second fatal dive came. Up above, Rigger Church, to die later in hospital, was given an order – almost certainly by Rope – to release half a tonne (ton) of emergency forward water ballast. The crash came before Church reached the prow of the ship.

In the aft engine gondola Binks and Bell felt the first plunge as the telegraph clanged and its pointer indicated that the engine revolutions should be reduced from 825 to 450. They had time to obey the instruction before the impact came.

The Chief Electrician, Arthur Disley, was dozing in the switch room. Immediately after the first dip the Chief Coxswain, George Hunt, came in yelling, 'We're down, lads!' Then the impact came – only a minor jolt, as the prow of the ship ploughed into the woodland, with most of R101 landing on the open hillside, but strong enough to push the forward engine gondolas up into the envelope and the gas bags with predictable results. With a mighty roar the largest machine in the world became a funeral pyre visible for eighty kilometres (fifty miles).

The ceiling collapsed on to Harry Leech. He heard screaming from the passenger cabins above as fire erupted all around him. A hole appeared in the side of the ship and he scrambled to safety, falling to the wet grass. Binks and Bell prayed for salvation as fire surrounded their gondola, expecting to be burnt alive and that the petrol tank of the Tornado's starting motor would explode at any instant. Then a water ballast tank in the hull above burst, drenching them and driving back the flames long enough for them to escape.

Five others clawed their way out of the holocaust, not really knowing how they escaped, just driven by the primitive instincts of survival. Two died later in hospital. Everyone else on board that ship of dreams perished in the flames – flames that were a beacon to disaster that brought help running. But no one could do anything to stem the blaze of over 119,000 cu m (5,000,000 cu ft) of hydrogen which lasted for many hours, the latticework structure slowly collapsing, glowing white-hot. The next day, when the last of the hydrogen had burnt away, only the ensign at the tip of her tail remained unburnt, gently flapping in the calm winds of the new day.

They brought the bodies back to England on board HMS *Tempest* on 7 October. Forty-eight coffins lay in Westminster Hall, London for last respects to be paid; but only twenty-six of the forty-eight coffins bore names, the other remains being incinerated ash, unrecognisable, including the remains of Thomson and Brancker. They were buried together in the little churchyard at Cardington, within sight of the shed where R101 had been born and where R100 was cut up without ever again seeing daylight, destroyed by the disaster on the Allonne Ridge just as surely as her sister ship. Today, the ensign in the church and the monument above their communal grave are reminders of the tragic events. The giant sheds, still stand, used until 1991 by Airship Industries to construct small helium-inflated blimps that buzz above sporting events with little ducted-fan engines, puny shadows of their predecessors.

Plans for an airship service linking the British Empire died with the crew and passengers of Airship R101. What exactly had gone wrong during those final minutes? Hunt's cry of 'We're down, lads,' apparently shouted just before the impact, shows that those in the control car knew that there had been some catastrophic failure and that disaster was inevitable. Did Michael Rope find the forward gas bags deflated because the fabric of the envelope – which had not been renewed around the bow, the point where the greatest pressures and strains were – had split so that the pressure of the incoming air had squeezed out the hydrogen, even ripped the gas bags loose? Rope might then have thrown himself down the ladder to the control car to warn Steff, shouting to Church to lighten the prow by dumping ballast as he passed him. Leech must then have run back down the gangway to try to warn the crew.

Perhaps the fatal error was Steff's: instead of reducing engine revolutions, he should have ordered up elevator and full power which with water ballast ejected and dynamic lift on the envelope might have enabled her to gain height. Possibly the accident was caused by a downdraught that tore her from the control of the crew. If so, would they have had a narrow escape if it were not for the weight of that carpet stowed in the bow?

Princess Marthe Bibesco came to that hillside to pay her respects before the girders were carted away for scrap. Now only the Germans and the United States were in the airship business, the latter it seemed with the likelihood of safety – after all, their airships would be inflated with helium which could not explode.

Mrs Herbert Hoover, wife of the US President, christened USS *Akron* for the Navy on 8 August 1931, a 194,000 cu m (6,850,000 cu ft) capacity ship with eight engines mounted within the envelope for better streamlining. She was built by the Goodyear Company and named after her town of birth. For eighteen months she was an airborne aircraft carrier, launching Curtis F9 biplane fighters and bringing them back into her internal hanger by catching them on a trapeze arrangement slung beneath. On 4 April 1933 USS *Akron* flew into a storm off the New Jersey coast. She was twisted apart just as *Shenandoah* had been. Only three members of the seventy-six man crew survived. But the US Navy did not learn.

Just days after the *Akron* disaster, on 21 April 1933, her sister ship USS *Macon* first flew. En route to the West Indies in late 1934 she too flew into a storm, this time without fatal consequences, although she was seriously damaged, her girders twisted and broken. The damage was repaired piecemeal when time allowed, so that on 11 February 1935 as she flew out to take part in manoeuvres over the Pacific, the upper elevator spars had not been renewed, merely patched. As she encountered turbulence the elevator was torn off, holing three gas bags, so she slowly drifted down to the sea. This time the death toll was just two crewmen out of eighty-three on board.

Now only Eckener in what was now Nazi Germany was flying the flag for airships. On 6 May 1937 ferry boats on the River Hudson blew their whistles as the *Hindenburg* came in over the harbour after her first North Atlantic crossing of the year. She passed over the Empire State Building at 15.30. New Yorkers gazed up as her 240m (800ft) long shadow darkened the canyons of the city's streets. Giant swastikas were emblazoned on her tail. At Lakehurst a landing party of 248 waited to moor her. At 16.00 Captain Max Pruss approached the field, but rain squalls and glowering clouds that threatened thunder made him sheer away. For three hours she circled.

With her four 1,100 hp Daimler Benz diesels grumbling at low revolutions, Pruss brought her back just after 19.00. Passengers lined the gallery windows in her hull, waving to their friends and relatives below. Herbert Morrison of radio station WLS Chicago was giving a running commentary.

The first mooring rope came down on to the wet sand of the mooring circle. Customs officers strolled out to greet the travellers, the diesels growling at idle as she hovered 20m (75ft) from the ground. 'Passengers are looking out of the windows waving, the motors are just holding it,' Herb Morrison said. Then came the sight that shocked the world. 'It's flashing! Flashing!' Herb screamed. 'It's bursting into flames! This is one of the worst catastrophes in the world. Oh, the humanity and all the passengers!'

A jet of flame had shot from the top of the airship, racing across the top of the hull. Ballast water spurted from the rear tanks as Pruss tried to keep his vessel level, not realising at first just what had happened. She came down stern-first as passengers smashed the perspex observation windows and leapt out, away from the flames. The motor engineers jumped from their gondolas. The fabric of her envelope blazing from stem to stern, *Hindenburg* crunched on to the sand, the bow rearing up again momentarily as it bounced on the inflated bumper beneath the control cabin. The fabric skin of her envelope burnt away like paper.

Sixty-one of those on board lived, though many were seriously burnt or suffered broken limbs from their desperate leap to earth. Pruss died of injuries received helping to pull passengers clear of the white-hot girders in which they were trapped. Eckener survived. **See Map 2.**

On 11 May, as ten thousand mourners watched the coffins of European victims being loaded on to the SS *Hamburg* in New York harbour, Germany voiced bitterness at the Americans for not having sold them helium. The cause of this final airship disaster remains a mystery. Many different theories have been put forward, including sabotage, a gunfight on board, and a whip-lashing internal cable. The airship tried to moor in an atmosphere charged with the static of a storm. When the first mooring line went down did it strike a spark as the ship was electrically earthed?

The only certainty is that the whole future of the airship died in those crackling flames. Even when lifted by helium, airships would always be subject and victim to the vagaries of weather. Today's blimps – dirigibles that are not true airships – are but minnows compared to those whales of the past. Those who witnessed them will never forget their awesome spectacle, those of us too young to have seen one must strain our imaginations to envisage how they filled the skies.

It is believed that the *Graf Zeppelin II*, the last of the giants, but never to see passenger service, prowled off the east coast of England during the early days of World War II, eavesdropping on radio transmissions. But, along with the grounded *Graf Zeppelin I*, she was broken up by 1940, the metal of her structure reprocessed to make warplanes.

The future belonged to heavier-than-air craft.

2
Take-Off Accidents

The take-off is often the most terrifying stage of any air journey. Most passengers feel some quickening of the heartbeat as the engines roar to a crescendo and the ground begins to rush by faster and faster. Some people then begin to imagine that there is something wrong, that the aircraft is going to crash at the end of the runway.

Seated overlooking the expanse of the wings it is easy to start to disbelieve the laws of flight. The more initiated know that the drooping leading edge slats are diverting air across the top of the wings so that it flows faster there than that passing below, lowering the pressure on the curved top surfaces to produce lift. The flaps push down against the airflow beneath the wings to provide a cushion of air on which the aircraft can ride.

Every airliner is the result of thousands of hours of testing; before it even flew for the first time models of it were tested in wind tunnels, computers predicted every characteristic of its performance; test pilots flew the prototypes harder, treated them rougher than everyday airline pilots ever should.

We know that this machine can fly, we have seen it with our own eyes; but strapped in the cabin, no longer masters of our own destiny, we disbelieve it. This hurtling mass of humanity, metals, plastics and volatile fuel is just too heavy; it is not possible.

And then the aircraft is airborne and the rumbling of the wheels stops as the ground fades away far below.

Only rarely, tragically, do people's fears prove to be justified; only rarely do aircraft fail to become airborne, instead careering through runway thresholds, or staggering briefly into the air damaged or overladen so that the laws of gravity reassert themselves, bringing this symbol of Man's ingenuity over the elements down to destruction.

Nowadays the performance of an aircraft can be accurately predicted before it even leaves the design office. The take-off distance needed for different loadings, runway altitudes, temperature, even the scenario of an engine failing as it hurtles down the runway too fast to stop before the end, committed to flight – all these are known before construction of the first prototype commences. The task of the contemporary test-pilot is largely to confirm the computer predictions and then to accumulate kilometres (miles) and time in the air to prove the durability of the type and its long-term freedom from fatigue failure.

The creators of the early aircraft had no practical experience to draw upon. The Wright brothers, for instance, used wing-warping instead of the far less complicated and efficient principle of the aileron. Gradually the advances made established a fund of knowledge on which to draw.

By the late 1920s and early 1930s the basic principles were firmly established, but there was still an element of trial-and-error in aircraft design. There is a saying that 'what looks right is right'. This is not always so, but proved to be the case in the early 1930s when the Douglas DC-2 rolled off the production line. Piloted by Dirk Parmentier (who will feature again later in this history) a KLM (Royal Dutch Airlines) example of this type, flying to airline schedules, came second in the 1934 England–Australia air race, finishing only a few hours behind the purpose-designed and constructed de Havilland Comet (not to be confused with the later jet airliner) piloted by C. Scott and Tom Campbell-Black.

By adopting a more circular fuselage, Douglas quickly evolved this good DC-2 design into the classic DC-3 (known as the C-47 when fitted with a strengthened floor and large rear doors for cargo purposes). No aircraft, except possibly Boeing's 707 series, has contributed more to safe, reliable air transport. It established same-day coast-to-coast travel across North America, usurping the passenger train there; it was the Allies' transport lifeline throughout World War II; and afterwards, many of the type being military-surplus machines, was the basis on which airlines worldwide were established. Almost 18,000 were built, and even today some of them still serve. Their pugnacious nose and smoothly streamlined shape, graceful wings and square, strong tail fin are the very essence of harmonious design and aesthetic balance. The design is truly a work of art, relatively undated even now.

As the type trailblazed the post-war routes, the DC-3 was an aircraft whose performance, through sheer experience, was almost totally predictable. Except, that is, in ice. Add a layer of ice to the wings of an aircraft and its aerodynamic properties are no longer certain. Ice is an insidious enemy of air safety. In the pioneer days of air travel it blocked carburettors so that engines stuttered and were starved of fuel, it blocked air intakes to cause overheating, and made already heavy manual controls seize solid.

By the late 1930s the danger of ice cloud was universally recognised, but many aircraft were already capable of climbing above it into clear air. Nowadays airliner wings and engines are protected by de-icing equipment, while of course the pilot and his controls are no longer exposed and vulnerable.

However, these safeguards do not protect an aircraft standing on the ground, and it is essential that power plants and wings are cleared of ice (if it has formed) before take-off, afterwards relying on the de-icing gear to keep them clear during flight. The history of air safety is littered with tales of aircraft which struggled but briefly into the air with a glazing of ice on them.

The most remarkable escape from this situation was for the five people aboard DC-3 G-AGZA of Scottish Airways just before Christmas 1946.

The north-west suburbs of post-war London were dusted by light snow on 19 December. This whitened the normally silver Dakota as it stood on the concrete hardstanding of Northolt airfield with a scheduled flight to Glasgow. Incredibly, it began its take-off run without even being brushed clean. Perhaps the pilot thought that the snow would be swept away by the slipstream as it accelerated down the runway. To onlookers it seemed that the take-off run was longer than usual and that when it did struggle into the grey sky it was in a tail-down attitude. The DC-3 was airborne only briefly. As it cleared the perimeter fence the tail wheel struck the ice-reamed hawser of a telegraph wire, streaming it behind as it grazed the roofs of a line of terraced houses. It came down on a detached house, sweeping the rafters and tiling to the ground, but with the chimney stack surviving and its pot level with the Dakota co-pilot's windscreen. The machine balanced there, supported by the bricks of the walls. There was no fire. The two passengers and three crew walked down firemen's ladders to the ground, unhurt.

In the early 1950s Manchester United was England's premier football club. Under the management of Matt Busby these young footballers, 'Busby's babes', swept most opposition aside. On 5 February 1958 they drew 3–3 against a Yugoslav team, the Red Devils, in the European Cup in Belgrade. It was enough to see them through to the final in Milan. The flight back from Yugoslavia was the next day. British European Airways had supplied a 47-seat Airspeed Ambassador (known as an Elizabethan) for the charter, under the command of Captains Thain and Rayment. It was snowing as the twin-engined, high-winged aircraft took off. There was a cordial atmosphere in the cabin, most of the passengers having flown together before. Besides the football players there were leading sports writers from the British press, and football league officials. Talk was inevitably of the prospects for 'Busby's babes' in the final. Five seats were occupied by other passengers, including the wife and baby daughter of the Yugoslav Air Attaché in London, making a total of 38 passengers.

The Elizabethan's wheels threw up whorls of slush as she set down for a refuelling halt at Munich in Germany. With the task completed, the two captains walked around their airliner. It had stopped snowing now, though the low clouds threatened more to come. The Elizabethan had been standing in the open for an hour. As a precaution, de-icing fluid could have been sprayed on to the upper surfaces of the wings, and the snow brushed off. Thain and Rayment saw water dripping from the trailing edge of the wings and decided that these actions were not necessary. They did not climb up ladders to inspect the all-important top surfaces of the wings and tailplanes. On most aircraft the pilots can look out of the cabin windows to see the wing surfaces, but this was impossible on this high-winged type. Pilots of other aircraft who had taken off from Munich that day had requested de-icing sprays. The captains may have felt that the water dripping from the wing showed that any ice there was melting, but the chill factor induced just by taxiing at freezing point could cause freezing on a wing.

An hour after landing at Munich the passengers were called out from the terminal. At 14.15 the Elizabethan began to taxi. James Thain had flown the aircraft to Belgrade and now Ken Rayment was taking it back. The aircrew rostering had been manipulated by these two men to put them together on this duty. They were good friends who shared an interest in poultry farming when not flying. It is a curiosity that many pilots have an outside interest in this work; strange that men whose work is flying should have an interest in birds that cannot!

Although junior to his friend, James Thain was officially in command of the flight, and would have to take responsibility for any decisions. Company regulations stipulated that the pilot in command must occupy the left hand seat (as is universal practice), but Air Ministry rules did not actually forbid pilots exchanging seats. Ken Rayment, although acting as co-pilot for this flight, was more used to occupying the left hand seat and therefore having his right hand on an aircraft's centre-console mounted throttle with his left hand on the control column. The pilots agreed between themselves that they would exchange seats so that Thain, although officially in command, that afternoon occupied what should have been the co-pilot's seat on the right as they taxied towards the runway.

Runway 25 on which they aligned the aircraft was felted by some two centimetres (one inch) of slush etched with the tyre tracks of other aircraft which had taken off and landed safely through it. Ken Rayment pushed the throttles forward and the run began. One of the traits of the Airspeed Elizabethan was for its Bristol Centaurus piston engines to suffer boost surging if an even slightly over-rich fuel mixture was fed to them. Now, as the Elizabethan gathered speed, the engines' harmony suddenly became discordant and the boost pressure gauges fluctuated. 'Abandon take-off,' Rayment called.

The Elizabethan slowed to a halt. Radio officer Bill Rodgers called the control tower to ask permission to backtrack along the runway for a second attempt. This was given. As the aircraft slowly returned, the two pilots discussed the problem. A slower opening of the throttles generally made the engines of the type behave better and this was the policy adopted as the second attempt at take-off was made, Thain holding the aircraft on the brakes as power built up before letting her run down the grooves pressed into the slush.

But again the power began to fluctuate and the attempt was abandoned. The pilots decided that they would like to have the port engine examined before trying again, so the Elizabethan returned to the ramp and the passengers trudged back to the departure lounge.

No obvious faults had been found with the port engine; meanwhile a car had driven out to inspect Runway 25, returning to report that there was a minimum of one centimetre (half an inch) of tyre-cut slush on the main section, but that for the last third of its length it was lying undisturbed. Other pilots who had taken off from Munich that day said at the subsequent enquiry that they thought the slush was deeper than this.

The Elizabethan lined up on the runway again just before 15.00. To those in the passenger cabin, many of them very used to flying as they promoted football around the world, the acceleration seemed slower this time. In the cockpit Thain was opening the throttles gently and calling out the speeds: 60 knots, 70 knots, 80 knots – the port engine began to surge slightly but acceleration continued. Rayment stopped steering by means of the nosewheel now that there was a fast enough airflow acting on the triple fins. Thain juggled with the fuel mixtures to overcome the power surging. 'Third time lucky,' many of the passengers thought as speed continued to build up. They must surely soar into the sky this time.

'Speed 105,' Thain called. '110, 115!'

Rayment pulled back on the control column to raise the nose by 4°. At 117 knots Thain called, 'Vee one!' Now the decision had to be made whether or not to take-off or abort. The surging seemed to be under control; speed was still rising. In moments Thain should call 'Vee two,' flying speed.

But now the Elizabethan was hurtling into the untrodden slush carpeting the final third of the runway. Speed began to fall, 115, 110, 105! Thain forced the throttles against their stops. Perhaps Rayment then pressed on the brakes, hoping to stop. Whether he did or not is one of the mysteries of this disaster. If he did, he changed his mind almost immediately and tried to heave the airliner off the ground. Her nose went up, but the mainwheels still tramped through the slush. He called for the undercarriage to be raised; she just might have enough speed to fly and with its retraction drag would be reduced.

For a moment she actually did seem to fly. Back in the passenger cabin a few were staring out; surely they should be airborne by now? How long is this runway? Are we near the end of it? Was the speed falling off again? Suddenly the boundary fence loomed up ahead. The Elizabethan ripped through it, careering towards a house and a tree directly in its path.

The impact with the house tore off the left wing outboard of the troublesome engine, and part of the tail. The frantically revving engine buried itself inside the empty house, setting it alight. The trunk of the tree slammed into the left side of the cockpit, smashing the thin panelling near Rayment. Now the disintegrating airliner spun round, demolishing a wooden garage and setting light to a truck inside. What was left of the tailplane was torn off by this impact. The forward section of the aircraft bounced and jarred over the frozen ground for another sixty metres (seventy yards) before coming to rest. By then many on board were dead, some were unconscious. For a few seconds there was a shocked silence and then people began to cry out.

Thain was unhurt, but Rayment was severely injured. For a few seconds nobody moved. Psychologists call it 'negative panic' – half of the brain knows that something must be done, while the other half is trying to comprehend just what has happened. Fires blossoming outside were the spur to action. The unhurt Rodgers pulled the electrical master circuit breakers to stop any arcing that might cause an explosion. He then tried to get through the door to the passenger cabin, but it was blocked by luggage that had piled up against it. Thain tried to help Rayment, but the latter cried that he should help Rodgers with the passengers first.

The pilot and radio operator managed to crawl out of the galley window and drop to the ground. Along with two stewardesses they began to pull the injured clear. Of the 44 on board (38 passengers, 6 crew), 20 were already dead. The flames were quickly brought under control, thanks to hand-held extinguishers from the aircraft and the emergency services which soon arrived. Rayment remained trapped in the smashed cockpit as snow began to fall heavily, slipping into unconsciousness before he was finally released. Meanwhile the news was being flashed around the world: the golden team of football had met disaster.

Captain Hans Reichel of the Luftfahrt Bundesamt Accident Investigation Team arrived on the scene six hours after the crash, examining the wreckage in the glow of arc lights. The conclusion he reached, later given as the cause at the German enquiry, has remained controversial to this day. He said that there was an 8cm (3in) thick layer of snow covering the wings, presumably having accumulated after the crash, but beneath this and bonded to the metal was a centimetre (half an inch) of ice. Reichel concluded that this ice had been present throughout the Elizabethan's take-off attempts, and that it had both added weight to and destroyed the aerodynamic shape of the wings. This conclusion dismissed the possibility of the aircraft having been slowed by the slush on the runway. Sixteen other aircraft had taken off safely from Munich that day, but they had all been de-iced first so ice on the wing did, at least initially, seem to be the culprit in this case. This made Thain and Rayment culpable because they had not ensured that their aircraft was treated.

On 20 February another footballer died bringing the death toll to 22. Ken Rayment died on 15 March in the Rechtader Isur hospital. Thain was suspended by British European Airways, and his licence was revoked by the British Air Ministry pending the enquiry. It was re-instated on 12 October 1960, following the enquiry's conclusion. He was dismissed by British European Airways the day after his licence was re-instated.

After an accident where pilot error is suspected it is normal to suspend the pilot's licence until after the enquiry. Even if the suspicion is found proved it is normal to renew the licence afterwards provided the accident was not the result of deliberate negligence.

The German enquiry's conclusions were never totally accepted in Great Britain, and in 1963 the effects that slush on a runway could have on an aircraft's take-off acceleration, including the now obsolescent Elizabethan/Ambassador type, were investigated in England. It was concluded that just half a centimetre (quarter of an inch) of slush would apply such a braking effect to this type that fifty per cent more runway would be needed than necessary in dry conditions. This perhaps proved that at Munich, on that day, the Elizabethan would have needed a take-off run of 2,250m (7,500ft); yet Runway 25 that had been used had only been 2,000m (6,600ft) long.

The Germans reopened the enquiry into the disaster on 18 January 1965, but although listening to the evidence of the British slush tests still regarded the apparent icing on the wing as the cause. The British Ministry of Aviation now officially disagreed with the German findings and in April 1966 issued its own deductions. The Germans were unmoved even through a reopened British hearing on 10 July 1968. By then the disaster was ten year old history, a crash that would probably have been forgotten except by those involved if it were not for the sensationalist element added to the incident because of the football team's involvement.

The deaths caused by that crash on a freezing day in 1958 were not totally in vain if they have made pilots think about the possibility of ice on their wings or slush on the runway before take-off.

James Thain concentrated on his poultry breeding business until his death at the early age of fifty-four in 1975. Barely a day must have gone by without his thinking that he should have been seated in Rayment's place on that fateful day. Perhaps Thain was the twenty-third and last victim of the Munich air disaster, but he was officially exonerated.

13 January 1982 was the worst day of winter in Washington, DC, as snow swept in from the Mid-west of America. By mid-afternoon the streets were clogged with traffic as offices closed early and workers set out for home. Traffic had jammed solid on the 14th Street Bridge across the River Potomac River by 16.00. Drivers waited impatiently. Here, aircraft taking off from Washington National Airport would often be sighted. For ninety minutes the air above the clogged traffic had been silent while the runways were cleared. Now there came the roar of a jet approaching. But the sound changed to an ear-splitting scream. Suddenly the aircraft became visible, looming up out of the swirling snow, tail-down and aiming for the bridge.

The Air Florida Boeing 737 was forty-five minutes late as the seventy-eight passengers boarded. It had been de-iced, but had since been standing outside for almost an hour in the snow flurries. This dusting of snow had streamed from her wings as she roared along the runway, before Captain Larry Wheaton hauled her off the ground and into the icy sky.

A few on the bridge saw her coming, her nose pointing at the sky, but she was descending. The wheels had been retracted, the engines were pushing her, but she was not truly airborne; instead she was just waffling along, tail-down and aiming straight for the 14th Street bridge. Perhaps she might just clear the bridge, gain power and yet thrust herself above these clouds and into the light.

But no. The blade of the tail skid, designed to support the tail should the nose rise too high on take-off or landing, slammed into the parapet of the bridge and a car, slicing through it like a knife. The rear of the fuselage and the sweep of the tailplanes destroyed other cars as if they were mere children's toys. The impact was too much for the Boeing's fuselage, and the nose was forced down, the entire tail section from forward of the rear pressure bulkhead snapped off. It rolled across the road, sweeping other vehicles aside, smashed through the parapet on the other side of the bridge and tumbled off the edge.

The fuselage and wings of the aircraft seared on beyond the bridge and, with engines still screaming, plunged through the ice into the freezing river. Some people died instantly from the shattering impact; while others drowned in that freezing water that bubbled now with kerosene from split fuel tanks. Not far away the water boiled and frothed as the heat of the engines was quenched.

There were some survivors. The rear of the fuselage half-floated and, gasping for air, at first not comprehending what had happened or where they were, just driven by the reflexes of survival, a stewardess and five passengers bobbed to the surface amidst the ice floes. Some car drivers slithered down the banks of the river to help those struggling in the water. One of the heads bobbing there disappeared, not to rise again. A police helicopter hovered over the tail section with the survivors trying and failing with frozen hands to grip its skids. The helicopter co-pilot climbed down on the skid of his machine, hauled them on to it and held them tight as the pilot flew over to the bank, leaving each one there and returning for the others before they slipped beneath those icy waters not to surface again.

The National Transportation Safety Board headquarters are in Washington. Even as the drama in the river was taking place, the 'Go' team were trying to get through the stationary traffic to the scene.

Four motorists and seventy-four on board the Boeing died that day, because in the haste to leave the airport the killer ice had been allowed to re-form on the aircraft's wings and engine probes.

The rostering of aircrew is a complex operation that has to take into consideration such factors as permissible hours of duty, agreed rest time between flights, leave and type-training. These circumstances mean that two members of cockpit crew may be rostered to fly together for three consecutive days; or they may not share the same cockpit for months.

Captains, co-pilots and engineers may be friendly or might verge on the hostile. Promotion through airline ranks can be a slow process. It was especially so back in the 1970s when there was an element of 'dead men's shoes' about the career as would-be successors waited for a captain to retire, die young, or be taken off flying duties through ill-health. There can be few aircrew who do not worry about the six-monthly medical check, their careers relying on that clean bill of health from the doctor. As a pilot grows older these fears increase; and all the time he is working with younger men who covet his left-hand seat. Little wonder then that some senior captains can become autocratic.

British European Airways' Captain Stanley Key was not universally popular with his colleagues; in fact in 1972 some rather obscene graffiti about him had appeared on the engineer's consoles of their Trident airliners. In the BEA crewroom at London's Heathrow airport on 18 June 1972 Key was canvassing against a threatened international strike of aircrews. He lambasted a first officer who had spoken out in favour of the strike, in what was later described as the worst outburst of temper ever known in that place. This was witnessed by Second Officer Jeremy Keighley, a young man only recently passed out from the joint British European Airways and British Overseas Airways Corporation training school, and must have unnerved this raw member of flight crew.

Stanley Key almost immediately and publicly apologised to the second officer who had been on the receiving end of his outburst, but the damage that was to indirectly result in the destruction of a Trident airliner and all on board that afternoon had been done.

Key was a short, stocky man of fifty-one. For many years he had been suffering from arteriosclerosis. This disease had progressively worsened so that now his heart arteries had narrowed by as much as seventy per cent; yet the annual electrocardiogram did not reveal this. During his outburst in the crew room his blood pressure would certainly have risen. This pressure must then have ruptured the blood vessel in his left coronary artery. Now blood pressure on the arterial wall would force a separation of the arterial lining. Key was a doomed man, yet the chest pains he must have felt could have been dismissed by him as mere indigestion.

Shortly afterwards Key, Keighley and twenty-four year-old Second Officer Simon Ticehurst who were on stand-by duty that afternoon were called to take command of Flight BE548 to Brussels, owing to a delay in the arrival of its rostered crew, in triple-engined Trident 1 jet G-ARPI. Key had 15,000 flying hours to his credit, 4,000 of them in control of this type of aircraft; possibly time enough to learn bad habits.

The Trident, along with such machines as the Boeing 727, Vickers VC10 and French Caravelle, had tailplanes mounted high above the fin, the normal attachment point being occupied by the engines. The drawback of this arrangement was that if the aircraft stalled, and this stall became really steep, it was possible that the elevators (that to recover would be depressed down to lower the nose of the aircraft into a dive to gain speed and recover) could be removed from the airflow altogether. This is known as a deep stall and recovery from it is impossible.

One Trident had already fallen victim to this during airworthiness certification tests on 3 June 1966. With four crew on board Trident G-ARPY had entered a deep stall at 3,000m (10,000ft) and crashed at Felthorpe, Norfolk, killing all.

By the time the Trident had been designed it had become convention to fit a 'stick shaker' to the control columns of airliners. This system literally shakes the control column as a warning to the pilot(s) that the aircraft is on the verge of stalling. As a further precaution against Tridents entering deep stalls, they were now additionally fitted with 'stick pushers' that would force the control column forward and the elevators down before the airliner could pitch nose-up to the degree that a deep stall condition was entered.

Unfortunately, British European Airways' pilots had found the stick-push system to be unreliable, often operating when they said it should not have done. An unreliable warning system will be treated with contempt, although like the boy who cried 'wolf' once too often, it may one day be telling the truth.

Some would say that the weather on 18 June 1972 was a typical British summer's Sunday afternoon, with weeping clouds at just 300m (1,000ft).

At the last minute a BEA Vickers Vanguard freighter crew also boarded the Trident flight. One man was accommodated on a seat vacated by a babe in arms, another took a crew seat while Captain John Collins, himself a qualified Trident pilot, took the jump seat behind Key in the cockpit. The take-off weight would now be 50,000kg (110,229lb), just 2,000kg (4,409lb) short of the maximum permissible.

G-ARPI was pushed from the departure gate at 16.08. Ticehurst, at the engineer's console, must have seen there the obscene graffiti relating to Key. One can imagine an icy, tense atmosphere in that cockpit as they taxied towards the runway; Key probably rubbing his chest to alleviate what he thought was indigestion as the final pre-flight checks were completed, Keighley and Ticehurst responding nervously, fearful of the far-senior pilot with the mercurial temper.

Today, airliners are of course equipped with both area and individual microphones at each crew position, but even so the recordings are not always clear after an incident, the 'black box' is not totally indestructible and conversations can be masked by the blare of warning sirens, bells and pre-recorded voice-alerts.

As the Trident reached the runway threshold it reported a 'slight problem' to the control tower. The crew did not elaborate on this, and investigation after the accident did not discover its nature. It may have been the amber lamp for low pressure on the stick-push system. What was discovered later was that there was a locking wire missing on this system's three-way valve. A jolt could have caused the warning light just forward of the leading edge slat lever on the pilots' centre console to illuminate. The system would still function – but would the crew now believe that a stick-push was a genuine warning?

The aircraft had three minutes of clearance to either take-off or taxi clear of the runway. Whatever the problem was, it was either resolved or the faulty mechanism isolated within just over a minute, for at 16.08 she was rolling, screaming down the runway, the nose soon lifting, pointing towards the dirty dishcloth clouds that floated in a washing-up water sky. Just nineteen seconds after take-off, 106m (355ft) high and at 170 knots, the auto-pilot was engaged. She should have been flying at 177 knots, but Key had mis-set the auto-pilot control.

At 16.09:44 the Trident reached 210m (700ft), already into the first tendrils of cloud. A left turn towards the town of Epsom was made using the auto-pilot control knob. Back in the crowded passenger cabin sighs of relief must have been being exhaled. The snub-nosed airliner began buffeting a little as it speared into the thick cloud at 300m (1,000ft). She had now been airborne for just ninety seconds. Keighley called this out. It was time for the power to be reduced. Heathrow is one of those airports surrounded by housing. Complaints of the noise made by aircraft taking off and landing have risen in proportion to the number of flights and reached a peak with the regular introduction of jet airliners in the early 1960s. Certainly, coming after the drone of piston engines and the whistle of turboprops the scream of the early jet engines was an ear-shattering intrusion. The argument was safety versus the public's declared right to normal conversation beneath the flight paths! Compromise usually won with many governments enforcing restrictions which mean reducing an aircraft's power soon after take-off, a move often vehemently resisted by pilots. In an emergency when flying low there is not always enough time to 'spool up' the engines for more power.

In recent years the problem has eased somewhat with the introduction of the quieter fan-jet engines but it was objections to noise, as well as to the sonic boom and unacceptable economics, that largely destroyed the sales potential of the Anglo-French Concorde; airlines were just not sure that they would be allowed to fly it into many airports.

Had Trident G-ARPI been allowed to continue climbing out at almost full power that day it just might not have crashed.

Just ninety-three seconds after take-off the flap-lever was moved to bring them in flush with the wings from their 20° droop. Even with their drag removed speed was falling and was down to 157 knots in the turn. As the aircraft was turning the first stall warning must have operated, shaking the control columns. The Trident desperately needed more power.

What actually happened now is conjecture. The only remaining evidence is from the flight recorder in the tail of the aircraft, digesting every control movement and twitch of the aircraft through the sky. Did the confused Key call, 'Droops,' thinking that the stall warning was because Keighley had retracted the leading edge slats; or did he himself retract them? Another possibility is that he said something like, 'Put it in,' meaning Keighley to enter the new height clearance given by air traffic control into the auto-pilot, this instruction being construed by Keighley as meaning to retract the droops. The only thing that is certain is that the Trident had to be at 900m (3,000ft) and flying at 220 knots before those droops could be safely retracted. At 16.10:24 climbing through 530m (1,770ft) at 157 knots somebody moved the lever, and the droops began to retract.

Just one second later the stick-shaker vibrated again followed instantly by the stick-push, the control column being pulled forward in an attempt to put the Trident into a dive so that it could gain airspeed. Perhaps Key was dying in that very moment, gripping the control column tight in confused terror. Perhaps Keighley, Ticehurst, or Collins noticed that something was wrong with the captain as the clang-clang of the auto-pilot disconnect warning rang in their headsets. More likely, Key still had a few seconds to live.

It took just six seconds for the droops to fully retract. At 16.10:32 they were fully in, altering the trim so that the Trident was tail heavy, already descending as the wings lost the extra lift that they had been giving. The 'stall recover operate' light again flashed and the stick-push tried to pull the column forward, but once more Key, or possibly Keighley, held the aircraft level. No one had yet isolated the auto-pilot disconnect warning. When the stick-push again operated just moments later someone ordered that the pneumatic pressure supplying its power should be vented to isolate it, which Ticehurst did. The very warning system that could have saved their lives had now been destroyed because too many times in the past it had lied.

Either Key or Keighley pulled the control column back, putting the aircraft into a climb; but this could not possibly be achieved now. At 16.10:43, less than twenty seconds after the stick-push had tried to alert them for the first time, the Trident went into a deep stall. Perhaps Key was still alive then, his last action being to almost unknowingly pull back on the control column, but they were all doomed from that moment when at 360m (1,200ft) the nose tilted up by 31°. The elevators were out of the airflow, and nothing could save them.

As the Trident entered the deep stall she lost airspeed from 190 knots to 54 knots, coming down at a 60° angle at 1,350m (4,500ft) per minute. What happened on that flight deck in the last few moments we will never know. Was Stanley Key already dead as the arterial lining of his left coronary separated to cause a massive haemorrhage? Almost certainly he was senseless or unconscious when the impact came, fortunate in that respect at least.

The aircraft burst through the clouds just above the dual-carriageway A30. Drivers barely had time to glimpse her and brake before she impacted, just missing the road and power cables to smash into a paddock, one of the few clear spaces in that area. The tail section broke away just forward of the pressure bulkhead on impact. The engines stopped and there she lay, suddenly silent. Heat haze shimmered above the seized engines that only moments before had been trying to force her aloft. There was no fire for the moment, but as fuel leaked from smashed tanks and feed lines, trickling down the hot engines, it threatened to break out.

Death came instantly to most on board, their spines broken and their internal organs ruptured by the fearful impact. A few bleeding to death. One person was found barely alive by rescuers, but died within minutes. Motorists abandoned their vehicles and ran into the paddock, some standing incredulous at the sight before their eyes, others risking their own lives by running into the wreckage to see if they could help. There was some looting. Some people actually snatched away pieces of the wreckage as black mementoes before the emergency services reached the scene, their progress hampered by the jam of halted vehicles blocking the main road.

Fire broke out fifteen minutes after the impact, but was quickly extinguished by the first fire tenders on the scene. As black tarpaulins shielded the crash site from the morbidly inquisitive and a police cordon prevented any further looting, the black box was taken away for analysis.

Investigators at Farnborough quickly discovered the reason for her helpless stall; the impact came just thirty-six seconds after the Kruger droop lever was moved by either Key or Keighley. Which of these was responsible and why will never be known.

As the Air Accident Investigation Branch were absorbing the facts of the take-off irregularities, the post mortem report on Stanley Key was delivered to them. The six-monthly medical test had failed to warn that Key was a doomed man before he even stepped on the flight deck that day.

No medical check can be totally foolproof. Stanley Key was far from being the first captain to die suddenly on his flight deck. On 24 May 1961 a piston-engined DC-4 freighter was in touch with Brisbane Air Traffic Control and seemingly making a perfectly normal approach on its flight from Melbourne. The pilot was cleared to make a visual approach in the dawn but at 04.40 when it should have been landing the aircraft was nowhere to be seen and did not respond to radio calls.

The wreckage was eventually found on a mudflat by Bulwer Island just off the mainland coast. The pilot and co-pilot were dead in the mangled remains of their cockpit. It was very odd that the throttles were recovered from the pieces in the closed position and that the co-pilot was strapped in his seat, although this had been torn from the floor on impact, but the pilot had, unusually, not been wearing his seat belt during the approach. A post mortem revealed that the pilot may have died from a heart attack just before the crash. It is possible that as he felt unwell he may have tried to leave his seat only to slump unconscious across the centre console, slamming the throttles shut. At low level and slow speed the co-pilot would have had no time to heave the body of the unfortunate pilot off the controls. Remember that all cockpits are cramped and trying to heave at a heavy corpse while strapped into a seat is almost impossible.

Captain Reed Pigman was the founder of American Flyers. By 1966 he suffered from both diabetes and a heart condition. He knew of this but still wanted to fly – so he simply falsified his medical record in the airline's files. On 22 April 1966 he was bringing his military charter flight in towards a landing at Oklahoma when he died. The Lockheed Electra turboprop smashed to earth killing all seven crew and seventy-seven of the ninety-two passengers.

In any year the deaths of up to six pilots while airborne should be expected. However, a competent co-pilot is there to assume control and make a safe landing – usually.

The 1972 Trident crash near Heathrow will always be known to the layperson as the accident caused by the pilot having a heart attack, but this is not really true. There are always at least two pilots on any airliner, often three, for a flight engineer, if carried, is also a qualified pilot. If the pilot at the controls is taken ill his colleague, or colleagues, should instantly be able to take over. Keighley was not able to take control of that aircraft and during its very brief flight it was flown in a cavalier fashion from the moment it took off too slowly.

Airline pilots are regularly tested on flight simulators. These are cockpits wired to a computer. They can accurately reproduce every facet of a type's performance, while views projected on to the windshield can represent the terrain around airports. Using this simulation a pilot can make many approaches to a major airport before he flies an aircraft into it. The other uses of a simulator are to check a pilot's performance and reveal bad habits, and to represent emergencies. So sophisticated are today's flight simulators that they even vibrate and produce the sound effects of the genuine aircraft. A 747 pilot can be making a normal approach to an airport when the simulator controller (seated outside the cockpit of the simulator) programmes the controls to represent all four engines failing. Pilots can then practise crashing without causing damage or deaths.

From the moment the Boeing 747 ushered in the 'jumbo' age cynics wondered when and where the first disaster would strike these new giants of the air. When it did come, a Lockheed TriStar was the victim (see p. 14). A few months after the Everglades crash a catastrophic structural failure of a Douglas DC-10 near Paris witnessed 346 deaths in a single-aircraft crash (see p. 72). The Boeing design flew for a year after that incident before disaster came to it in circumstances that were remarkably similar to Trident G-ARPI. On 19 November 1974 a Lufthansa 747 staggered into the air from Nairobi Airport with the leading edge slats retracted, stalled and slid along the savannah on fire. Fifty-nine perished.

On that warm November day the glossy white and silver 747 stood on the ramp being loaded with a consignment of newspapers. The flight had begun at Frankfurt and would terminate at Johannesburg. In the clear air of the African morning the relief crew for *Hessen* climbed aboard; 140 passengers were booked for this leg of the service.

United Nations Environment Program Liaison Officer Earl Moorhouse was seated just forward of the wings with his wife and two young sons. Soon after the disaster he wrote a dramatic account of the first major Boeing 747 tragedy (*Wake up, It's a Crash*, David & Charles, 1980). As the new crew prepared the galleys he glanced out at the wing to where the fat hoses pumped in fuel. It occurred to him that this aircraft was a gigantic flying bomb.

In the cockpit, so high from the ground that looking down was like seeing out from the third floor of a building, Captain Christian Krack began the pre-flight checks. Like all seventeen crew he was well rested. For three days they had stayed at the Intercontinental Hotel. At fifty-three years old he was one of Lufthansa's most experienced pilots with a total of 10,464 hours in his log book, 1,619 of them in the Boeing 747 type.

The aircraft weighed approximately 227,000kg (500,000lb), well below the maximum permissible take-off weight and allowing reduced engine power to be used on this occasion. At 07.42 the engines were started. Pneumatic power generated by engine compression needed to be bled off the mighty engines to push out the leading edge slats, but as the jets were started the valves were closed. As the engines spooled up to power Flight Engineer Rudi Hahn, a fifty-year old man with 2,650 hours flying experience with 747s, should have opened these valves as part of the pre-take off control setting. *Hessen* was fitted with both an area microphone in the roof of the cockpit and others linked to the intercom. The crew were not using the intercoms as they did the pre-flight checks, but on the cockpit voice recording tape above the roar of the engines co-pilot Hans-Joachim Schacke can be heard calling out: 'Bleed valves.' There was a pause and then Hahn replied, 'Open.' It had been agreed that Schacke would handle the take off. Now, when he moved the trailing edge flap lever to the open position as the Boeing trundled out to the runway, the leading edge slats should also be moved out by pneumatic pressure bled off the engines.

At 07.50 *Hessen* taxied out to the single main runway. Captain Krack elected to take-off in an almost northerly direction in the still air of that morning so that the flight could quickly turn on to its Johannesburg track. First they had to backtrack the length of the runway. During this time the trailing edge flaps were lowered by 10°. The leading edge slats should automatically then have also lowered.

There was no pause at the runway threshold. *Hessen* completed her 180° turn, spooled up power and began her roll, already cleared by air traffic control to soar up to 10,500m (35,000ft).

Everything seemed normal. At 145 knots Schacke pulled the control column back towards his stomach. For a few seconds the aircraft continued with her nosewheel seemingly pawing at the air and the four main undercarriage units tramping along the asphalt, then she lifted.

Possibly the first person to notice something wrong was US passenger and experienced pilot Tom Scott. He later declared that he felt the Boeing bounce at the moment of take-off, the kind of sharp bounce that often happens on landing.

The Boeing did not want to fly – that became clear in seconds. There seemed to be a lack of thrust and power from the engines. Instead of soaring into the sky it was staggering along at less than 30m (100ft). Tom Scott, seated between the wings, saw the wing shaking in pre-stall flutter. The whole airframe started to tremble; overhead lockers burst open and showered the passengers with their contents.

Schacke could not mistake the apparent lack of power. He was forced to lower the nose to prevent air speed falling below 140 knots. 'Engines OK so far,' engineer Hahn called out. The undercarriage retract lever had already been thrown, the retraction cycle was already in progress, massive doors opening beneath the belly of the machine to allow the four main undercarriage units to tuck themselves away. These doors were increasing the drag on the aircraft at a critical time. The stall warning stick-shaker vibrated the control columns.

Nairobi Airport's fire officer was watching the 747 take-off. His hand was reaching for the emergency alarm button before the Boeing even struck the ground. It was clearly shuddering into a stall, and an embankment carrying a road was directly in its path. Some of the passengers also saw this looming ahead. They knew that a crash was inevitable.

The still partially lowered undercarriage struck the embankment. The savage impact tore off wheels and oleo legs, momentarily bouncing the aircraft back into the air. She struck the roadway. Sparks arced back from the port wing as it scraped across the asphalt. Both port engines and their pylons sheared off. Fuel gushing from ruptured feed lines ignited. Still travelling at over 100 knots she struck again. New she began to break up. The fuselage split aft of the wings and again just forward of the pressure bulkhead. The port wing snapped off just outboard of the inner engine position.

The forward section of the Boeing seared across the scrub, flames leaping from the now ruptured fuel tanks in the remaining stub of the port wing. It began to swivel through almost 180°, jarring, crashing and smashing across the flat bush. Passengers had time to pray for this hell ride to stop. Finally she came to rest, the port wing stub a mass of flame licking at the fuselage. Many sat dazed, incapable of logical thought in those first moments of stillness. Some were injured, struck by jagged plastic ceiling panels or crushed beneath seat rows that had been torn from the floor. The first survivors to act decisively were the uninjured stewards and stewardesses, whose training took over. Steward Karl Kahn leapt from his seat and had to fight his way through the wreckage of one of the galleys to get to a port side escape door. Then he saw the flames leaping and licking at the fuselage on that side. There was no escape route there. He dashed across to the starboard side where stewardess Evelyn Rehm and a passenger were struggling to get a door open. The fuselage had buckled, jamming the doors. Finally, the strength of desperation got the door open. The first passenger leapt out before the rubber escape chute had even fully inflated.

Dazed, staggering and many of them badly injured, the survivors came sliding down the forward chute or that now inflated from the emergency escape door above the centre section of the wing and ran or limped away from *Hessen* as she was wracked by explosions. The first Nairobi Airport fire tenders reached the crash site within five minutes. Even before the first foam could be sprayed by these teams their chief was shouting into his radio for assistance. Smoke curled from the shattered airliner.

Sightseers and looters soon arrived. Some of those who had been pulled, or who had staggered injured from the Boeing, lay helpless on the veldt and saw thieves picking through scattered luggage and running away with bags and cameras, ignoring the hurt, the dying and the dead.

The flight deck crew survived. Hahn and Krack forced their way through the jammed door into the cocktail lounge behind the cockpit and then leapt down to the first class compartment. Flight Engineer Hahn badly injured his right shoulder as he landed on the broken floor. He stumbled out of a hole that had been torn in the fuselage and was led away in a numbing agony of pain by two strangers. Krack leapt out to the other side, but almost immediately climbed up the steep forward escape chute between passengers sliding down to help those in the economy cabin.

Co-pilot Schacke escaped through the hatch in the cockpit roof, lowering himself to the kerosene-soaked ground on the steel cord of the emergency escape reel, between fires. Hearing calls for help he also entered the shattered remnants of the economy class cabin. Between them the two pilots managed to stumble away with a severely injured woman, taking her clear of the fires to where a knot of survivors had gathered. As they turned to go back the wreckage shuddered to two explosions. Flames enveloped the forward section now, burning those still trapped in there. Some were conscious as the flames reached them.

Krack stood watching as the fire devoured his airliner. He shook his head in incomprehension. How could it have happened? Long after the last flickers of flame had been doused he was still standing there, watching as they brought out the dead.

Even before the next dusk came to the African bush, examination of the wreckage revealed why the aircraft had stalled – the leading edge slats had been retracted. The official report painted the cause in black and white: after the engines had been started the flight engineer had omitted to open the pneumatic system bleed valves. Although the lever to open the slats was in the correct position, there was no power to push them out. Even then disaster might just have been averted had the stall warning system been programmed to include the slat position. The stick shaker operated too late – a few seconds earlier and the pilots might have been able to push the levers forward for more power, might just have climbed away as it is now believed other Boeing 747 crews had done before.

All airline accidents investigated are recorded in the International Civil Aviation Operator's digest, which gives a brief resumé of the incidents. It does not record the circumstances of near-disasters. Like all businesses airlines are prone, rightly or wrongly, to conceal errors on the part of their staff that could have been dangerous. *Hessen* was not the first 'jumbo' jet to take-off with the leading edge slats retracted. Others had done so before, but the crews had clearly managed to increase power and climb away just in time. Nairobi Airport is at 1,500m (5,000ft). Perhaps the slightly thinner air at that height was the difference; the near-disasters before had possibly been at lower heights above sea level where there was just enough air to stream over the wings and hold the Boeings aloft while the power was increased. If only the crew of *Hessen* had known of these early mistakes by their contemporaries they might have checked the bleed valves more carefully before each take-off.

The mistake Flight Engineer Hahn made was as basic as forgetting to turn off the dipped headlights of one's car after driving in fog. Even as the survivors of the Nairobi crash lay in hospital recovering, the American Federal Aviation Administration was acting on the advice of the East African Chief Inspector of Accidents to take steps to prevent it happening again. As an interim measure all Boeing 747 operators were advised to ensure that a qualified observer should check that the slats were extended before aircraft were cleared to taxi. By early December a formal Notice of Proposed Rule Making was issued stating that an Airworthiness Directive requiring modifications to the Boeing 747 type's leading edge slat system was in the offing. After discussions with Boeing an Airworthiness Directive was issued requiring all aircraft of the type to be modified so that the stall warning system would consider the position of the slats, and a warning light on the pilot's instrument panel would show if any leading edge slat was not fully extended whenever the trailing edge flaps were at take-off setting. These modifications had to be made within five months.

The accidental authors of the first Boeing 747 disaster paid with their jobs. Captain Krack was suspended from flying shortly afterwards on medical grounds. The less culpable Schacke was reduced in rank. The memories will haunt them for the rest of their days.

Scientifically it is known what caused Lufthansa's *Hessen* to crash, but what passed through Hahn's mind in the moments when he should have opened those bleed valves is a mystery. It is the kind of question that few official accident reports can answer. The mistakes that aircrews make can often be pinpointed, but not always the true cause.

The events that took place on the runways of Los Rodeas airport on the island of Tenerife on 27 March 1977, when two Boeing 747s collided in the worst air disaster to occur to date, are known, although blame for this should perhaps be aimed not at the crews concerned but at a group calling themselves The Movement for the Independence and Autonomy of the Canaries Archipelago. Early that morning a bomb they had planted at Las Palmas airport, Canary Island, exploded, injuring several people at the check-in area. All flights destined for Las Palmas were now diverted to Los Rodeas.

The Boeing 747 of KLM Flight 4805 was one hour out of Las Palmas when it was told to divert to Los Rodeas. At 13.38 it came swooping down on to the single runway through wispy cloud that intermittently reduced visibility to 400m (1,300ft). Still airborne was another 'jumbo' jet, of Pan American. Its pilot asked permission to remain airborne in a holding pattern until Las Palmas was declared open again, this seeming to be imminent. However, he was ordered to land. The giant eighteen wheel undercarriage of the 747 came down on to the runway thirty minutes after the KLM machine had landed and taxied to the holding area. At this time the passengers of the Dutch aircraft were just disembarking, many muttering at the delay, unsure why they had been diverted to this unscheduled destination.

Captain Grubbs of Pan American was reluctant to disembark his passengers, believing that it would shortly be possible to take-off again for the short hop to Las Palmas. Meanwhile two company employees joined the flight for a lift to the other airport, giving a total complement of 396 persons. The Dutch flight carried a total of 248.

Las Palmas was declared open again at 14.30. Now the aircraft choking Los Rodeas could begin to be cleared. The runway and taxiway were constructed in the form of a tight loop. The departure ramp had become so congested with diverted airliners that it was not possible to use the main taxiway to travel down to the runway threshold. To leave, each aircraft was entering the main runway and backtracking at least part of its length, before taking one of the cut-offs back to the main taxiway to come out behind the waiting machines, then cruising the remaining distance parallel to the runway and looping around to join it.

Captain van Zanten of the KLM 747 had had to contact his operations office at Amsterdam to ask if he still had flight-time to take the service the remaining short distance. Such decisions were once at the pilot's discretion, but in more contemporary times, with growing concern at flight crews becoming over-tired and even falling asleep on the flight deck, flying time is regulated by the civil aviation authorities of most countries in agreement with the crews' trades unions. Captain van Zanten was told that he would not exceed his permissible time provided he departed before 19.00. With that matter resolved the Dutchman now decided to take fuel.

Behind the KLM 'jumbo' in the queue the Pan American crew seethed. They had not wanted this unscheduled landing and were ready to depart, but could not do so until the KLM jet moved. It was 16.51 before van Zanten asked permission to start his engines. The Pan American crew had now been on duty for eleven hours. They were more than a little annoyed at the additional and unnecessary delay that the Dutch captain had caused them.

There were two ground controllers on duty at Los Rodeas that afternoon, both harassed as they tried to clear the small airport of the extra traffic. They were using a frequency of 118.7 MHz for ground instructions and the approach frequency of 119.7 MHz for take-off instructions. The KLM 747 was cleared to taxi at 16.56 and to contact approach control. The first officer re-tuned the dials to 119.7 MHz and requested permission to backtrack the length of the runway. This was at first refused, the operator instructing the flight to proceed only as far as the third exit and to turn left there on to a cut-off that would take the aircraft to the main taxiway running parallel to the runway. The KLM first officer misunderstood this instruction and read back, 'First exit?'

'No, sir,' the controller said. 'Third.' Just moments later, however, the controller changed his mind, granting the request of the aircrew to travel the length of the runway and turn through 180° at the end ready for take-off. The KLM pilots seemed to be totally confused and again asked if they should leave at the first exit. The controller had to repeat his instruction to travel the full length of the runway and turn at the end.

Captain Grubbs had his engines running and was expecting to wait by the departure ramp until the KLM 747 had taken off. Now he was given instructions on the ground control frequency to follow the KLM aircraft on to the runway, but to leave by the third exit. Like the Dutch crew the Americans had great difficulty in understanding the Spanish accent of the controllers. English is the international airline language and all communications with the two fated airliners were conducted in this. It was the natural language of only one of the three nationalities involved, the Pan American crew.

At 17.02 the approach controller, handling the take-off instructions, called the KLM aircraft, 'KLM 4805, how many taxiways you pass?' These are the exact words and reveal the poor English of the controller.

'KLM 4805, I think we just passed Charlie 4 now.' The jumbo was still lumbering down the length of the runway. Meanwhile the Pan American 747 was just entering it and speaking to the other controller on a different frequency. The Pan American crew now asked for confirmation that they should turn off the runway at the third exit.

'Third one, sir. One, two, three, third, third one,' the controller told them. The Pan American jet began to rumble down that single runway, its windscreen wipers slapping as mist began to spread along the tarmac, the pilot and co-pilot hunched forward in their seats as they searched for the exit. Visibility at the time was approximately 900m (3,000ft), but as the KLM 747 turned through 180° at the end of the runway a cloud was sweeping along it.

At 17.06 the KLM crew were given air traffic clearance, the altitude and course they were to take once airborne; they were not given permission to take-off. In those moments the Pan American 747 was approaching the third exit and it too contacted the approach control. The controller was saying to the Dutch crew: 'Stand by for take-off. I will call you.'

'No, uh... We are still taxiing down the runway, the Clipper 1736,' the Pan American crew called.

Pan American first purloined the nautical term of clipper for their Boeing flying boats of the 1930s. Even today they include it in the names of the aircraft in their intercontinental fleet. The harassed controller now mis-named it Papa Alpha instead of Papa Clipper as he called it. 'Roger, Papa Alpha 1736, report runway clear.'

The American crew overlooked the controller's error, simply replying: 'OK, we'll report when we're clear.'

Meanwhile, veiled behind the thicker bank of cloud that was advancing down the runway, the KLM 747 was spooling up its engines, starting to advance, accelerating ever faster. Its flight engineer had forebodings. 'Is he not clear then?' he asked aloud.

'What did you say?' van Zanten queried over the roar of the engines.

'Is he not clear, that Pan American?'

'Oh, yes,' replied van Zanten ambiguously.

On the identical flight deck of the Pan American Boeing there was some alarm now. It was unthinkable that the KLM aircraft should begin its take-off run, but... 'Let's get the hell out of here!' Captain Grubbs called.

His first officer agreed. 'Yeh, he's anxious, isn't he?'

'Yeh, after he's held us up for an hour and a half,' the flight engineer added. 'Now he's in a rush.'

At that moment the KLM 'jumbo' appeared out of the cloud, an indistinct image at first, softened by the mist but rapidly hardening into a solid shape as it bore down on its sister aircraft. Captain Grubbs cried out: 'There he is...! Look at him...! That... that... that son-of-a-bitch is coming!'

The eyes of the KLM first officer were fixed on the airspeed indicator at that moment. The Boeing was travelling at over 190kph (120mph). He called out: 'Vee one!' The captain now had to decide whether or not to proceed with the take-off. In those moments van Zanten must have seen the Clipper ahead of him. There was no hope of stopping. He pulled back on the control column in a desperate hope that the 747 could lift, at least 'hop' over the Pan American machine. He pulled back too hard on the control column, the tail skid rasped along the runway for over 30m (100ft), throwing up a shower of sparks and adding a slight braking effect.

Captain Grubbs on the Clipper desperately steered to port, not caring if his aircraft became bogged down in the soft ground off the runway, just wanting to be out of the path of that KLM 747 careering towards him, its nose pointing at the sky, its main wheels stubbornly still rolling along the runway.

The KLM 'jumbo' did get airborne at the very last moment, but too late. The massive still spinning wheels of its starboard undercarriage units smashed into the first class hump behind the cockpit of the Pan American machine which had managed a slight turn to the centreline of the runway before the impact came. The KLM Boeing's undercarriage was ripped off, the first class hump of the Pan American jet disintegrated and the tail section sheered off. As the forward section of this aircraft lurched to a halt it was already on fire.

The passengers on board the KLM airliner had just moments to realise that something was wrong, a jolt as the wheels of their aircraft struck the American machine, perhaps a brief glimpse of the white hull of the other 747 flashing beneath them, but not even time to comprehend what had happened, before, less than 150m (500ft) from the point of impact, the Dutch machine slammed back down on to the runway, instantly erupting into fire as it skidded along, slewing around through 90° before coming to a halt, its blazing engines having been torn off in that wild slide.

All 248 on board the KLM 747 died as fire enveloped it and the fuel tanks, filled on van Zanten's insistence and the cause of the delay that led to the two aircraft being on the runway together, exploded.

Of the 396 people on board the Pan American Clipper, 70 escaped from the flames; most of these from the rear section. The cockpit crew miraculously survived, escaping through the emergency hatches in the cockpit roof and sliding to the ground on the steel cords. Fire overwhelmed most passengers and flight crew in the centre of the aircraft as they tried to escape. The final death toll was 583. Nine of the survivors were later to die from their injuries. It was the disaster that airline operators had dreaded since the birth of the 'jumbo' jet seven years earlier.

The emergency services of the airport and of Tenerife were totally overwhelmed by the scale of the disaster. The KLM jet was enveloped by flame before the first foam could be sprayed. Only the forward port side of the Pan American Clipper had unburnt paint on it the following day when the last of the fires was finally extinguished.

Only the over-optimistic would say the Los Rodeas accident could not be repeated. The only true error was in the KLM 747 commencing its take-off roll without having received permission. Los Rodeas does handle 'jumbo' jets on a regular basis and is not the only airport with such a capability that has only one runway: England's Gatwick has a similar arrangement yet handles far more traffic than the island of Tenerife and indeed is currently seeing a vast increase in passenger numbers. To have two jumbo jets simultaneously taxiing the length of a runway is not unknown even today; it is often the only way that overstretched airports can keep the traffic flowing. The only true protection against a repetition of the Tenerife disaster is most international air crew's knowledge of the events, and a good command of the English language by those involved. Perhaps the simplest and best safety feature that could be introduced would be a red/green traffic light at the runway threshold, a suggestion that at first might seem jocular, but would have prevented the KLM pilot at Los Rodeas starting his fatal roll.

Of course, had the terrorists not planted a bomb at Las Palmas neither aircraft would even have been at Los Rodeas. If van Zanten had not decided to top up his fuel tanks, or had made the decision sooner, other aircraft would have taken off between the two 747s. Even the cloud that crept along the runway at the critical minute seemed to conspire with events. It was estimated that the Pan American crew saw the advancing KLM aircraft nine seconds before the impact; ten seconds longer and the Clipper might just have got clear. One last sobering thought should be voiced: neither of the aircraft involved was carrying a full passenger complement – two 747s can carry over one thousand people.

The modern airliner is a machine both of enormous strength and frightening fragility. It can withstand g-forces when airborne equivalent to many times its own weight, and endures tonnes (tons) of internal pressure. But impact can destroy it within seconds. An airliner's power comes from the harnessing and then controlled detonation of highly flammable fuel.

As aircraft have become stronger and the chances of survivors remaining alive in wreckage have increased, protection from the potential danger of exploding fuel for those trapped in wreckage or trying to escape has become more important. It is tragic if someone who survives the destructive forces of impact should then perish in a resulting fire. From disaster reports in recent years it might seem that aircraft fires have become more common. This is not so. More people are surviving crashes that in the formative years of civil aviation and in earlier aircraft designs would have killed them on impact.

In September 1982 an unfortunate driver passing along the Malaga to Torremolinos road in Spain was killed as a giant Douglas DC-10 carrying nearly 400 people failed to stop before the end of Malaga Airport runway after the captain had aborted the take-off attempt. But fire claimed more victims as the aircraft drew to a halt.

The Spantax airliner was taking a charter flight to New York and was almost at take-off speed when the captain felt a severe vibration shuddering through the aircraft. He made the fatal decision of trying to stop, but far too late. The DC-10 ripped through the perimeter fence, struck several vehicles as it tore across the main road, and finally came to rest against a railway embankment 150m (500ft) farther on.

During the nightmare slide along the ground the DC-10 began to break up, one wing shearing off and smashing back into the tail section which became enveloped in flames. Panic broke out among the passengers as the slide finally ended. The tail section was severely damaged, seats having been torn from the floor and blocking the aisles. People clawed at the debris and against each other to fight their way forward. In their blind panic all too many did not see a second almost clear aisle leading to the front. The two rear doors were jammed as is so often the case after an accident, warping of the fuselage shell sealing them tight in their openings. A total of fifty were to perish as fire devoured the rear of the giant airliner; a further 344 survived.

One of the greatest tragedies of the Malaga disaster is that the aircraft could have taken off safely, the only fault being that the right nosewheel tyre had thrown its recapped tread. Aircraft tyres are subjected to huge forces – for example, acceleration from nought to over 160kph (100mph) almost instantly as an aircraft lands – and they occasionally fail, usually due to laxness in the manufacturer's quality control. In this incident the vibration was more alarming than dangerous. The pilot had only a split second to decide whether or not to attempt a take-off; that he made the wrong decision should not reflect adversely on him. One of the quietly voiced fears of contemporary pilots is that many runways in use are too short to enable a fully-laden wide-bodied airliner to stop, should problems be encountered near take-off speed.

At Manchester Airport on 22 August 1985 the British Airtours Boeing 737 had been accelerating for forty-one seconds down Runway 24. The co-pilot was handling the take off, Captain Peter Terrington calling off the speeds and pushing the throttle levers forward. '125 knots!' In just seconds the Corfu-bound Flight KT328 would lift into the early morning sky with its 131 holidaymakers.

That was when combustion can number 9 in the port Pratt and Whitney JT8D-15 engine exploded. The ejected dome and a small section of fan casing struck the underwing fuel tank access panel, ripping open a 106cm (42in) hole. Had the shrapnel struck the surrounding wing panels all might yet have been well, as they were stronger. Fuel gushed out into the airflow to be ignited by the hot exhaust of the engine. In the cockpit the crew at first only felt the problem as a thud as if a bird had been ingested or a tyre had burst. Captain Terrington called, 'Abort take-off.' Nine seconds after the detonation and only as the brakes were biting did the fire warning clang. As the plane slowed the pilots swung her to starboard on to a taxiway. Horrified watchers in the control tower had seen the red flame as the explosion occurred and could now see fire licking at the fuselage. By radio they informed the crew of the danger and advised evacuation of the plane on the starboard side. A seven knot breeze blowing from the port side was to make this incident worse than it could have been – if only the crew had turned to the left where the flames could have been blown away from the fuselage... yet it was a totally pardonable mistake.

The fire tenders were already rolling. They would be at the scene in less than a minute. Already there was hysteria in the passenger cabin. A stewardess had opened the port rear door before the aircraft had stopped rolling. A tongue of flame greedily licked inside. Within twenty seconds of the Boeing stopping the fire had broken through the aluminium panelling of the under fuselage into the cargo hold. There it was fuelled by suitcases. Less than a minute later it had broken through the cabin floor. Billowing black smoke filled the cabin.

Fifty-five died in the flames of a fuselage that became a cylindrical gas retort. Twelve perished of their burns, but forty-three were killed by poisonous fumes from burning upholstery and plastic panelling. Even the overhead lockers were quickly ablaze. Ammonia, hydrogen cyanide and carbon monoxide filled the death chamber. The overhead lighting was useless in such conditions; only draughts of fresh air from outside guided the coughing, retching passengers to the doorways. Driven by the flames, many pushed forward. A crushing jam formed at the 58cm (23in) wide passageway by the forward galley. A stewardess pulled a passenger away to clear the blockage with strength she would not have normally had. On orders from Terrington the purser had tried to open the starboard front door, but the cover over the inflatable chute jammed between the door and the frame, preventing a full opening. The purser ran to the opposite door; this time he was successful. The flames on the outside of the aircraft had not yet reached there, and a stewardess took over while the purser tried again with the right door. With difficulty, this time he got it fully open and the chute deployed.

Within two minutes the fire was so intense that the tail of the aircraft sheared off and crashed to the concrete. Most of those who were to survive were away from the wreck by that time.

An aircraft should be evacuated in an emergency in ninety seconds, but at Manchester that morning it took longer. The stewardesses stationed at the over-wing escape hatches perished at their posts. Crushes had formed there too where people had to fight over seats to get clear. In less than three minutes this flight of light-hearted holidaymakers was transformed to an incinerator. Despite the thousands of litres (gallons) of foam the tenders were pumping out, the flames burned right through the fuselage top from just behind the cockpit to the stump where the tail had been.

It was March 1989 before the official report was published. That the report took so long is not owing to any laxity by the Air Accident Investigations Branch. This was the first major disaster to befall a British airliner since the Trident accident of 1972, and the opportunity was taken not just to investigate the incident, but also to look at what improvements could be made to safety in the future. The 259-page report made some 31 recommendations, one of which the Civil Aviation Authority disagreed with: that a pilot in an emergency should stop on the runway and review the situation before taking further action. Rather, the CAA felt, it would be better for the machine to be brought to a halt in such a position that wind could not blow flames on to the fuselage.

The years between the incident and the report's publication did not see any possible safety improvement recommendations held in abeyance. As facts began to emerge, the CAA had already taken action on the following:

1   Engine inspection and repair procedures altered. The primary cause of disaster was the explosive rupture of the combustion-chamber outer casing which ejected the forward portion of number nine combustion can. The Pratt and Whitney JT8D is the most widely-used jet engine in the world. This particular example had logged 7,482 hours and in November 1983 had shown fatigue cracking from thermal causes; ie the continued expansion and contraction of operation. It had been repaired by direct fusion welding and was fitted to the aircraft in February 1984, logging another 4,611 hours before the catastrophe. Pratt and Whitney had advised operators that direct fusion welding reduced the engine life before fatigue cracking would become a major problem. The day before the incident the aircraft's log had recorded 'low idle' on this engine, a symptom of serious cracking that Pratt and Whitney were aware of. British Airways maintenance staff however simply adjusted the idle trim. A parallel can be drawn with a car's carburettor that needs changing, but instead is just 'botched up'. Two flights were safely made before the disaster with no apparent problems. British Airways would no longer attempt such a repair.

2   Fuel tanks to be strengthened against impact damage.

3   Seats adjacent to over-wing emergency hatches to have their pitch

altered so that they would no more than half-overlap the hatch.

4 Smoke detectors to be fitted in lavatories.

5 Investigation to be instigated of possible smokehood provision for passengers and water sprinkler systems fitted in passenger cabins.

Ill-informed journalists claimed that smokehoods could have saved the lives of all on board Flight KT328. In fact, these might have lulled some into a false sense of security. Twelve people burnt alive at Manchester. Perhaps it is more important that passengers should escape quickly without crushes forming. The Civil Aviation Authority had not at the time of writing decided to enforce smokehood provision in the near future. They did however draw up a specification for distribution to potential manufacturers. One company already in this field commented that the CAA specification represented a quantum leap forward in such design that would take some time to develop. It is possible that British Airways may unilaterally provide smokehoods soon; others would then surely follow.

In 1988 tests were conducted at the Cranfield Institute of Technology Applied Psychology Unit where a mock-up fuselage was filled with smoke while volunteers (who were selected as not being regular aircraft passengers) acted as 'victims'; a £5 incitement to the first few to escape produced a scramble so close to panic that the realism was too harrowing for many.

The other prime recommendations for future safety improvements include under-floor lighting indicating the way to the exits to be fitted to new machines and retrospectively added to those that will remain in service at the end of the 1990s. Upholstery and fittings that are both fire-resistant and do not produce toxic fumes when the worst does happen are also a prime requisite. In recent years airlines have often advertised on the basis of more comfortable, more widely-pitched seats than their competitors, while accepting that these plush fittings were filled with foam that produced deadly fumes when ablaze.

In the nineteen years before the Manchester incident there were 74 accidents where fire contributed to the death toll. The worst happened at Riyadh Airport, Saudi Arabia in 1980. A Saudia Air Lockheed L-1011 TriStar had just taken off when fire broke out in one of the cargo holds. The wide-bodied jet returned for an emergency landing and stopped. There it remained, silent, aflame. All 301 on board died of toxic poisoning.

A power plant or fuel that will be non-flammable in the event of disaster is not in the realms of possibility in the near future. Fire is a danger in any aircraft accident – unless one is flying a glider!

3
Structural Failure

Nowadays a further worry concerning flying has come to prominence: whether the structure of the aircraft is safe, or whether it will disintegrate in mid-air like a badly-glued construction kit. Until recently, this possibility had been almost discounted, even by the most timorous passengers. Some people remembered the disasters that befell the pioneering British Comet jetliners, but they seemed part of history. Regrettably, now is an age that has been dubbed that of the 'geriatric jets' when twenty- and thirty-year-old aircraft have started to shed parts of their structures from the weakness of age in that defect so aptly termed metal fatigue.

In the early days of flight many was the pioneer heavier-than-air pilot killed when his contraption disintegrated around him. The first passenger to be killed in an accident was the unfortunate Lieutenant Thomas Selfridge of the US Army.

It had taken five years from their first powered flight for Wilbur and Orville Wright to convince the military that 'flying machines' had a role to play in warfare. In response the Army stipulated that an aeroplane must take off with an 'observer' – the true function of this brave individual being to act as an artillery spotter – and return to the same place.

On 17 September 1908, watched by high-ranking officers, Lieutenant Selfridge climbed into the passenger seat (actually just a wicker basket) of Orville Wright's aircraft; a development of the original *Flyer 1* with a similar canard (that is, horizontal stabiliser leading) arrangement and a pusher engine behind the occupants. With a take off run aided by a launching rail, the fragile machine lifted into the sky with apparent ease despite the weight of the Army Lieutenant, and circled at just over 30m (100ft). As Orville pulled back on the stick to gain more height he heard something snap in the lattice framework behind. The machine nosed up into a stall and then plummeted to earth.

Orville Wright suffered broken ribs, pelvis and a leg; Selfridge was crushed beneath the hot engine and died on the spot.

For the next forty years frail aircraft fell in pieces from the sky with monotonous regularity. At the same time reliable airliners such as the classic DC-3, Ford Tri-Motor, Junkers–Ju 52/3m and Handley Page H.P.42 were emerging and starting to cross the globe.

Doubtless, structural failure accounted for many of the aircraft lost during World War II, although such losses were often relayed to the public as being 'the result of enemy action'. After the war structural failure began to be headline news and truly alarmed the public.

The war years had seen a spur applied to aircraft development; strides forward that would have taken years in peacetime took months under the pressure of conflict. Both the British and Germans had put jet aircraft into the skies while the war was still going on. Initial post-war American development was based on copies of these countries' engines, but with such a massive industrial and economic base it did not take long for their designers to make up lost ground on the British, the Germans of course being disarmed.

One of the aircraft that was attempting to retain British pre-eminence in military aviation was the twin-jet, double tail-boomed de Havilland D.H.110, an aircraft that in later service use was dubbed the Sea Vixen.

On 6 September 1952 de Havilland test pilot John Derry thrilled a crowd of over one hundred thousand at the Farnborough Air Show as he brought the all-silver prototype in with a high speed dive that aimed sonic booms at his audience. The fighter flew the length of the runway and climbed away, banking to port in a wide radius turn to the north of the town of Farnborough at over 640kph (400mph).

The thrill of the crowd turned to horror as Derry swooped the D.H.110 in for its second fly-by. Just over the airfield boundary and travelling at the speed of sound the aircraft reared up, disintegrating. The wreckage scythed down on the onlookers. Derry and his observer, Tony Richards, were killed instantly. But also killed, principally by one of the engines searing through the throng, were twenty-eight members of the public. A further sixty were seriously injured.

Initial eyewitness reports, that later became newspaper headlines, said that disintegration started with one of the engines breaking away from the airframe, but the official investigation was to reveal a different sequence of events. As Derry had levelled out, raising the right aileron, a compressive buckling had taken place along the leading edge of the starboard wing. This, combined with upward-bending G-loading, had led to the metal rippling and then splitting just outboard of the fuel tank. Air then entering the interior hollow of the wing had simply blown it apart, followed instantly by a chain-reaction disintegration of the entire airframe.

The failure could have been prevented by wing fences. These are now a common sight, particularly on military aircraft, and are simply a thin upright that prevents the airflow spilling outwards along the wing.

A tragic irony of this disaster is that instead of the all-silver D.H.110, John Derry should have been flying its all-black sister, but that had been grounded by a mechanical fault. The all-black aircraft had wing fences in the correct position.

This first Farnborough Air Show disaster demonstrated that during such displays aircraft should not fly towards crowds. Such advice was soon forgotten: at a subsequent air display organised by the US Air Force at their Upper Heyford base in Oxfordshire an English Electric Lightning supersonic fighter overflew awed crowds.

For regular passenger operation, aircraft truly bridged the Atlantic just prior to World War II with the Boeing 314 Clippers operated by Pan American. These luxurious flying boats were the epitome of pre-war air travel (with the exception of the airships), large enough even for the four radial engines to be serviced in-flight.

However, during the war years it was land-based aircraft that had to be ferried across the ocean to supply the forces operating over Europe. And with large multi-engined machines such as B-17s, B-24s and B-307 transports flying via Newfoundland this is exactly what was achieved; war paving the way for the airlines and aircraft that would follow these routes in peacetime.

Great Britain did not intend to allow the American designers and manufacturers to monopolise this potential market. Even before the European war was over the giant Bristol Brabazon was on the drawing board. This lumbering giant, impressive but overweight, was incapable of crossing the Atlantic with an economic payload. It also had a propensity for popping its rivets. It was simply too dangerous to allow this ponderous monster to enter regular passenger service.

Meanwhile, a team at the de Havilland Aircraft Company led by R.E. Bishop and Richard Clarkson were thinking along more advanced lines than such a propeller-driven machine. Right at the end of the war they had gained jet experience with their Vampire fighter, and they now wanted to capitalise on this knowledge and make a sleek jet airliner that would be pressurised allowing it to fly high where its power plants would be most efficient.

The first stepping-stone to the Atlantic dream was a version that could link Great Britain to Europe and the Middle East. As early as April 1949 the first (then) DH106 prototype roared into the sky from the airstrip outside the Hatfield factory.

Here was a fillip for austerity Britain: a belief that the country was still 'Great' was etched in jet contrails across the sky. But how soon was this majesty to disintegrate.

The first production machine, now christened the Comet 1, flew in January 1951. This could carry from 36 to 44 passengers at 780kph (490mph) over 2,800km (1,750 miles). With a reduced payload and maximum fuel the range could be stretched to 6,170km (3,860 miles). So advanced for its time was this beautifully streamlined aircraft that its aluminium skin was secured to the framework with Redux plastic glue, a method of construction that saved weight yet seemed to be capable of withstanding a sizeable internal pressure in the rarefied atmosphere at 12,000m (40,000ft).

To glue an aircraft together was not something new for de Havillands: it was a method of construction that they had pioneered back in the thirties when building the England–Australia Air Race winning DH88 (also named the Comet). In the war years the company had developed the basically plywood Mosquito, an aircraft whose performance was almost beyond peer, but naturally in wartime many were lost 'on operations'. It is interesting to speculate whether any that were reported 'missing in action' actually literally came unstuck.

On 2 May 1952 the four Ghost engines of Comet 1 G-ALYP powered it aloft for the first public flight to Johannesburg. The Queen Mother and Princess Margaret were shortly to fly in this British achievement, and in September development of the trans-Atlantic Comet 3 was announced. Just a month later, presumably sensing that the American manufacturers were lagging far behind Great Britain in commercial jet aircraft, Pan American joined the queue in ordering Comet 3s. Just a few days later came the first incident that marred the success story.

On 26 October a northbound British Overseas Airways Corporation Comet 1 crashed on take off from its stopover at Rome's Ciampino airport. The airliner had shuddered strangely on the verge of becoming airborne, and the pilot decided to abandon the attempt – a decision that was too late, for the Comet crashed off the end of the runway. There was no fire and all on board were evacuated safely.

On 3 March the following year, however, the five crew and six technicians on board Comet 1 *Empress of Hawaii* were not so fortunate: they died in the blazing wreckage when it failed to lift off from Karachi, Pakistan. The airliner had been on a delivery flight to Sydney from where it was intended to operate a Pacific service with Canadian Pacific Airways.

These two accidents seemed to share a common cause: pilots' inexperience of the stall characteristics of these new slippery, particularly streamlined machines where the onset of stall could be abrupt. This change in flying characteristics was rather like that which pilots had to adapt to when metal monoplanes replaced fabric-covered biplanes: then pilots had had to become used to a long, fast and straight approach to land instead of side-slipping down to the airfield blipping the throttle. Also, a jet has no propeller backwash across the wings to aid lift on the final approach; the correct airspeed is critical.

It was felt that with the Comets the abrupt stall characteristics were compounded by the hydraulic power that operated the flight controls. Until the 1930s the flying controls of an aircraft – that is, the rudder, ailerons and elevators – were almost always fabric-covered, and control was quite literally in the strength of the hands of the pilot who moved them into the airflow to achieve his three-dimensional placement. As aircraft became heavier and faster the control surfaces were metal-skinned both to increase strength and reduce drag. These controls were partly counterbalanced to assist the pilot, yet even so the captain of, say, a Lancaster bomber needed considerable strength to move them.

With the Comet 1, hydraulics replaced the brute force, but the negative effect of this power assistance was a lack of 'feel' transmitted to the pilot's hands.

In the wake of the flames of *Empress of Hawaii* Canadian Pacific Airways cancelled an order for two more Comets.

Pilot inexperience was also partly the reason given to explain the loss of BOAC Comet a G-ALYU on a westbound Singapore to London flight on 2 May 1953. This airliner broke up in flight just six minutes after take off from Calcutta Dum Dum airport on the leg to Delhi. The airliner was passing through 3,000m (10,000ft) when it disintegrated in weather that was described as a tropical storm. All 43 on board were killed and the wreckage was strewn over 20 sq km (8 sq miles). No distress call was made from G-ALYU, and death must have come instantly to passengers and crew. The Indian enquiry deduced that the port elevator spar had failed followed by the wing at rib seven. The manufacturer's early testing had in fact revealed fatigue failure at this point, but only after considerably more simulated flying hours.

Metal fatigue should briefly be explained. A simple example is anyone's ability to break a steel fork or spoon handle at its base by tiny but repeated bending movements. What actually happens is that the metal internally cracks with each bending stress until eventually all the strength is eroded and there are insufficient molecules interlinked to prevent a fracture occurring.

At the time of the early Comets metal fatigue was considered to be a rare phenomenon. One of the first mentions of it in aeronautical terms was a paper given to the Royal Aeronautical Society by P.B. Walker MA on 31 March 1949. Here was a first indication that static strength – that is, the load that any construction can withstand constantly – was not enough; consideration should also be given to the effects of loads being repeatedly applied and withdrawn. Even then, there was no mention of the stresses that can be induced by vibration.

The throttles of G-ALYU were found half-closed. The Indian deduction was that the aircraft had gone into a dive and that the pilot – Captain M. Haddon – had overstrained the elevators in attempting to effect a recovery. Some, but not all, of the aircraft's wreckage was sent to Farnborough for investigation by British authorities, but the earlier suggestions of control difficulties – the hydraulics system's habit of pitching the Comets into dives – perhaps blinded the Air Registration Board officials from seeing the true significance of any fatigue failure, although they did recommend more strenuous *static-load* tests of the Comet design's airframe.

As a metallurgist now knows, static load is not the only critical physical law in a machine's strength. A metal bar may be able to support a given weight permanently, but a weight of, for example, seventy-five per cent of this load, if repeatedly applied and removed, may eventually result in fracture. All aircraft are constantly subjected to such variable loads; they must be constructed so that such stresses cannot reduce the overall strength below the critical point where fracture of a vital structural component can occur.

In fairness to De Havilland, at the time of G-ALYU's loss they were testing a section of fuselage to fatigue tests in excess of the ARB requirements. These tests culminated in a stress fracture at the corner of a passenger window, but only after stresses that it was not believed would be met by the design in normal service.

Was this first BOAC Comet disaster caused by a pilot whose inexperience with the type over-stressed an airframe caught in a storm, or was it really the first Comet accident caused by metal fatigue alone? It will never be known.

A crash that was certainly caused by pilot error (or perhaps it would be more accurate to say pilot inexperience) befell Comet 1 F-BGSC of the French carrier UAT at Dakar, Senegal on 25 June 1953. It overshot the runway and lost its undercarriage, careering across a 60cm (2ft) deep and 21m (70ft) wide culvert before sliding to a stop. As in the BOAC incident at Rome, there was no fire and all seventeen on board escaped.

There was no escape, however, for the twenty-nine passengers and six crew of the Comet 1 forming BOAC Flight BA781 from Singapore to London on 10 January 1954. Callsign George Yoke Peter broke up at about 8,100m (27,000ft) off the coast of the island of Elba soon after its 10.31 (Local Time) take off from Rome on the last leg to London. Fishermen out in their boats that fine day (though there was some high-air turbulence reported) did not see the aircraft, but heard three explosions from the sky.

At the same time the captain of a BOAC Argonaut which had taken off from Rome ten minutes before the Comet was in radio contact with the jet. The final words of Captain Alan Gibson were: 'George How Jig from George Yoke Peter, did you get my...' He was obviously going to say 'weather report', as the jet airliner had overtaken the Argonaut already, but his sentence was never completed. The Comet had exploded, and its fragments and the corpses of its occupants, were falling down to the Mediterranean. Death would have come before comprehension as bodies were sucked upwards and skulls fractured on the cabin ceiling.

Too many had now died in Comets. Although no specific accusations could yet be made about the type's airworthiness, on 11 January 1954 BOAC voluntarily suspended all Comet operations. Sabotage was considered a possibility in this latest disaster, but most of the evidence lay on the bed of the sea. The Royal Navy were sent to dredge for it. **See Map 4.**

Meanwhile, Italian pathologists examined corpses recovered from the water and reported that they had been burnt after death (much of the wreckage had ignited when fuel had detonated through the heat of the engines) and showed violent decompression injuries.

After one month the Royal Navy's wreckage recovery operation brought most of the rear fuselage and tail of George Yoke Peter to the surface. These sections were shipped to the Air Investigations Branch at Farnborough, while newspapers speculated; the sabotage theory would not go away until a certain cause was found. Naturally there were many interested parties hoping that sabotage was the cause rather than a design flaw.

One other plausible explanation put forward was that an engine failure had resulted in a turbine blade flying off and puncturing the pressurised shell of the fuselage. The Comet, almost uniquely in the case of commercial aircraft, had its four engines mounted in the wing roots alongside the fuselage, a position that made the wing 'cleaner' and therefore more efficient, and would result in less yaw sideways in the case of engine failure. In response to this theory, armour plate was fitted around the engine nacelles as a shield against such an occurrence.

BOAC was losing £50,000 per week while their Comet fleet was grounded. With no explanation coming forward, services with the type resumed on 23 March 1954. But for less than a month.

South African Airways chartered Comet 1 G-ALYY which as Flight SA201 left London for Rome on the first leg of a Johannesburg service on 7 April. Lift off from the Italian halt was at 18.32 GMT with fourteen passengers and seven crew into good but overcast skies. At 18.57 the captain radioed that he was abeam of Naples, and ten minutes later he was contacted on high frequency radio by Cairo. There was no further word from the aircraft. G-ALYY disintegrated at about 9,000m (30,000ft) between the south-west Italian mainland and the island of Stromboli. That evening the then British Air Minister, Lennox-Boyd, withdrew the Certificate of Airworthiness for the Comet design.

Airframe G-ALYY had completed 2,704 flying hours at the time of its disaster; George Yoke Peter's log had shown 3,681. Armour plating around the engines now looked as if it was only adding unnecessary weight. Until the definite cause of the problem could be found De Havilland stood to lose £40-million of orders. The pieces of Flight SA201 were lost in deep ocean and impossible to recover. It was now vital to British prestige, the manufacturers and the operators that more wreckage of George Yoke Peter be recovered for analysis.

Meanwhile at the Air Accidents Investigation Branch at Farnborough, the thirty-six year old Director, Arnold Hall FRS, took charge of these remnants, and also Comet 1 airframe G-ALYU which was donated by BOAC. He wanted to test them to destruction in a water-filled tank of 33 × 6 × 5m (112 × 20 × 16ft) which was constructed on the premises. The wings of the airliner projected from this construction and were subjected to the blows of pneumatic hammers while the sealed fuselage was repeatedly filled with and vented of compressed air. By these means it was hoped that the stresses of flights could be simulated.

This rig was kept in operation twenty-four hours a day. After six months the first signs of fatigue were detected in the wings and after end of the undercarriage locating lugs. The cracks on the right wing were serious enough to need repair and would have resulted in the destruction of the aircraft had it been in flight. However, they were the kind of cracks easily detectable in their early stages by ground crews; no half-responsible maintenance manager would have allowed a Comet to leave its hangar with such damage.

The reconstruction of George Yoke Peter's tail section revealed a blue paint smear along the outside of pieces of its left fuselage. Analysis of this showed that it came from the aircraft's passenger seat tubing and was proof that the wings of the airframe had been attached at the moment of destruction. Clearly now, the catalyst of disaster lay somewhere in the fuselage construction.

The scientists turned their attention to the bonding glue. Had that been strong enough? No fault could be found there. De Havilland had even developed their Mosquito 'wooden wonder' as a high-altitude photo-reconnaissance aircraft with a pressurised cockpit by the end of the war without apparent problems, so the company could hardly be seen as inexperienced in the process (though with almost half a century's more knowledge now perhaps we should question the type's safety).

At the end of June 1954, as the water-cocooned fuselage of G-ALYU was being routinely pressurised in its tank to simulate a climb, the pressure gauges dropped to zero: the fuselage had failed. A section of skin near the corner of a forward cabin window had broken away. However, the scientists were not convinced that this was the definite answer; too much was at stake – the very credibility of British design and construction. The fuselage was repaired and further simulated routine journeys were 'flown' in the tank to the equivalent of 9,000 flying hours. Then, as the pressure was again being raised, there was a sudden and massive break 2.4m (8ft) long and 90cm (3ft) high on the port side above the wing. The stresses around the cutouts for the cabin windows were clearly greater than De Havilland had predicted. Two further cutouts on the top of the fuselage, where the automatic direction finding units and aerials were located, were also examined. Here hairline cracks stretching from rivet holes were discovered – positive evidence of fatigue.

Now accurate wooden models were made and, filled with explosive charges, launched from buildings so that estimates of the spread of George Yoke Peter's wreckage on the seabed could be relayed to the Royal Navy to help in their search. The only flying Comet in those days was G-ANAV which, with some rather brave technicians on board, was flying high altitude tests – unpressurised.

Vital sections of George Yoke Peter were discovered on the seabed in late August, including the ADF window area and some forward cabin windows. Almost three-quarters of the airframe had now been exhumed from its watery grave. There were signs of fatigue around George Yoke Peter's ADF window cutouts. Also, rivets towards the rear of this section of fuselage had been inserted too closely spaced so that a service engineer had had to, quite rightly, drill stress relieving holes to prevent the spread of cracks that were present there.

The Court of Enquiry into the disasters finally opened under Lord Cohen on 19 October 1954. The conclusion was that there was no just cause to adversely criticise de Havilland. This can probably be seen as a fair decision considering the contemporary facts: the company had entered virtually uncharted areas of technology and had taken as much care in testing as could be considered prudent. They paid a heavy price for being the pioneers. But 111 passengers and crew had paid the ultimate price.

To be historically accurate, however, Lord Cohen's conclusions should be re-examined. The Comet crashes happened after fewer actual flying hours than the test-rig failures had simulated. A possible explanation for the series of disasters is that the auto-pilots had malfunctioned. Comet pilots reported that the auto-pilots sometimes abruptly pushed the aircraft into dives. Perhaps then the pilots of the destroyed machines had over-stressed their airframes as they hauled back on the control columns to recover. The abrupt loss of radio contact with George Yoke Peter does rather seem to rule this out, though; Captain Alan Gibson would probably have managed to shout out what was happening to the listening Argonaut before destruction.

Another consideration not fully examined at the time of the enquiry was the possibility of fatigue cracking being at least partly induced by engine vibration. Early jet engines did not have the smoothness of later developments. It has subsequently been discovered that vibration resonance can cause cracks and breakages.

Over the years since the Comet disasters the general public – aided by Neville Shute's novel *No Highway* which was extensively based on these catastrophes, and the photographs of the airframe failing in the Farnborough test tank – have tended to believe the story accepted by the Court of Enquiry. Its findings were not conclusively satisfactory. The possibility of sabotage cannot be positively ruled out, though it has to be said that the weight of evidence is against this.

What is clear are the effects on the British aviation industry. The Comet 1s were withdrawn forever. The Royal Air Force Transport Command took delivery of a few Comet 2s with strengthened fuselages. The Comet 3 was purely a test-bed for the Rolls Royce Avon engines. The public did not fly in a Comet again until the advent of the Mark 4. On 4 October 1958 BOAC flew the Atlantic via Gander with one of these. However, it was only twenty-two days before a Pan American Boeing 707-120 series airliner achieved the same feat, and versions of this military-based (and therefore effectively part US Government subsidised – the 707's ancestry was really as the KC135 flying tanker to refuel the Strategic Air Command's B-bomber fleet in those cold war years) design and its Douglas DC-8 counterpart would soon be truly intercontinental, flying the Atlantic and Pacific non-stop.

Air travel for all, and large airbuses, were on the near-horizon. The American manufacturers would take the lion's share of this market. Great Britain's lead had been lost and has never been regained. The hopes and dreams were truly destroyed along with the Comet 1s, and also partly with the Avro Tudors (see pp. 143–148).

Great Britain did try to fight back: the Vickers VC10 is still considered by many who flew in it to be the most comfortable aircraft ever built. It did not compete with the 707 in operating costs per seat-mile but made up for this by generating higher revenues and higher load factors. The British Trident was aimed at the same market as the 727, and actually flew ahead of it; but design changes forced upon de Havilland (which should have resisted B.E.A.'s pressure) led to the production version being too small, with seat-mile cost penalties.

The Anglo-French Concorde offered a possible leap forward, similar to that achieved by the Comet. The supersonic transport was handicapped partly by the fuel crisis of the early 1970s, which pushed the price up and partly by objections to its high noise level on take-off and landing; but its marketability was severely curtailed by the restriction on supersonic flight over land, caused by the problem of the sonic boom; and by the impossibly high operating costs.

American manufacturers enticed the operators towards the subsonic 'jumbo' jets. French and British taxpayers paid a high price, although the Concordes flying now, at fares only affordable to the very rich, do clear the actual operating costs, which do not include any purchasing costs. No nation now is going to risk spending tax-payers' money – a politically sensitive factor – on building another supersonic aircraft. Boeing has no intention of doing so.

Great Britain's hopes of recapturing a share of intercontinental traffic types has to be as part of the European Economic Community. The A300, which began as a short-haul twin aimed at short-haul markets, has developed into a family of civil airliners, one of which, the A340, recently made a demonstration flight by encircling the globe from and to Paris, with only one stop, at Auckland, New Zealand.

On 16 April 1954 a then almost new Vickers Viscount four-engined turboprop of Air France took off from Bromma Airport, Stockholm. At 08.10, just seventeen minutes into the air, as the stewardesses were beginning to serve drinks and breakfasts, there was a violent explosion from beneath the aircraft.

Pandemonium broke out on board as the pressure plummeted, the passengers' ears popping painfully. The crew desperately tried to comprehend what had happened to their aircraft: engine number four, the starboard outer, was severely damaged and had to be shut down lest fire broke out. As they swung the crippled aircraft back toward Bromma and dived from 4,800 to 1,800m (16,000 to 6,000ft), number three engine began to vibrate terribly necessitating a reduction in its revolutions to 10,500 rpm.

Half an hour later, with the pilot and co-pilot desperately pressing against the rudder bar to counteract the asymetric power, a safe landing was achieved. Six passengers needed hospital treatment for shock.

Here was an accident easily explained: during cargo loading a ground mechanic had forced the lower horizontal locking bolt of the forward cargo hold door. Under the pressure in the air the door had sheared off, striking the engines as it flew away in the slipstream. Two decades later, the failure of a locking bolt on a cargo door would have much more serious consequences.

Douglas almost certainly contributed more to the development of safe, reliable, mass air transport than any other manufacturer when in the 1930s they developed the DC-2 into the classic DC-3. Post-war the DC-4, DC-6 and DC7 – the latter the last and perhaps most beautiful of the piston-engined airliners – capitalised on their predecessors' success, though its DC-8 inter-continental and short-haul DC-9 were largely eclipsed by their Boeing counterparts.

Following the introduction of the Boeing 747 by Pan American in 1970, to launch the wide-bodied, or 'jumbo-jet' era, the Seattle manufacturer's competitors were not far behind. Douglas's medium-haul transcontinental DC-10-10 went into service in 1971, and its tri-jet rival, the Locheed L.1011, came along a year later, with the European twin-jet short-haul A300 yet another year later, albeit in different markets. Douglas developed the basic type into longer-ranged aircraft, culminating in the McDonnell-Douglas MD-11, while the European Airbus Industrie brought out several versions of the twin, and a four-engined, long-range A340.

However, it seemed that this time the grace and almost perfect propor-tions were deceiving, for the DC-10 was to be the airliner involved in the worst crash to date. Other incidents led to its nickname 'dumbo', and many passengers were actually scared away from flying it. The saddest part of the type's catalogue of disasters is that they were avoidable. Because the lessons of an accident to American Airlines Flight 96 were not acted upon, 346 people were to die over France two years later, in 1973.

All manufacturers have to modify components of systems and controls (but seldom, happily, of structure) early in the service lives of their prod-ucts, as only actual day-in, day-out operations in all conditions can reveal any defects or shortcomings. However, it was not engineering incompe-tence that led to the downfall of the DC-10, but human failings that were at best disgraceful; at worst verging on the criminal.

At 19.20 (Local Time) on the cool evening of 11 June 1972, American Airlines Flight 96 took off from Detroit Metropolitan Airport into hazy, still air for the leg to Buffalo on a service that had originated in Los Angeles and was scheduled to terminate at New York's La Guardia. She was one hour late. There had been an eighteen minute delay at Los Angeles princi-pally caused by trouble in closing the rear cargo door, and a further five minutes were lost because of this at Detroit. Here, the ramp service agent had to use his knee to force down the locking handle before the 'door open' lamp on the flight deck would go out to indicate all secure.

Now all seemed well as the DC-10 speared through 3,000m (10,000ft) at 250 knots and the auto-pilot's vertical speed control was programmed for a climb of 300m (1,000ft) per minute up to the assigned height of flight level 23 (6,900m/23,000ft). Then, at between 3,450 and 3,600m (11,500 and 12,000ft) there was a muffled thud from towards the tail of the machine and the rudder pedals jerked to full port. The throttles snapped back to their 'flight idle' position while the fire warning bell clanged for number two (the tail) engine. With discordant harmony the cabin altitude warning horn blared – the giant fuselage was ruptured. The aircraft banked to the right while the red failure flag appeared for the airspeed indicator.

Towards the rear of the cabin Stewardess Sandra McConnell was thrown against the drinks bar there and landed by a gaping hole that had been torn in the floor. Her colleague Beatrice Copeland found herself staring into the cargo compartment.

In the cockpit Captain McCormick was fighting to bring the airliner level and pushing it into a dive towards denser air. He also had to deal with the warnings for the tail engine; mercifully there was no fire in it. At 2,400m (8,000ft) he tried to bring the DC-10 out of its dive, but now another horror faced the crew: all elevator control had gone. The throttles were thrust forward to bring her nose up. The tail engine remained stubbornly at 'flight idle', but mercifully the wing engines responded. Now there was time to take stock of the damage and to contact air traffic control for an emergency landing. The cabin staff's professionalism overcame their own fears as they calmed the fifty-six passengers.

With a gaping hole in the rear floor and aft port side, juddering frighteningly as the airflow tore at the damaged tail and with jagged metal being torn off, the DC-10 flew back towards Detroit, McCormick letting her descend at a gentle 60m (200ft) per minute, masterfully controlling height and direction by manipulating the throttles of the two good engines.

She made a fast final approach out of the fading evening light above the runway threshold. With no airspeed indication she touched down at a fast 160 knots (estimated). For a moment all seemed well as McCormick let the nosewheels sink on to the runway, but then she veered starboard, bumping over the lights and on to the soft infield. With the rudder inoperative only engine power could steer her; maximum power on number one (the port) and minimum on number three (the starboard) engines pulled her back to the runway where the brakes began to bite. As she rolled to a halt, the banshee wail of emergency vehicles trundling towards here, an emergency evacuation was carried out, the passengers sliding down the deployed chutes to land in crumpled heaps on the tarmac.

The reason for the decompression and damage to the flying controls and tail engine was quite clear: the rear cargo door had been ripped out. But why?

The American National Transportation Safety Board, the Federal Aviation Administration and Douglas looked into alleged locking difficulties with Convair, a division of General Dynamics and the actual manufacturer of the rear cargo door. Douglas was not in fact particularly helpful, only after some time and pressure telling the Federal Aviation Administration of over a hundred reports of difficulty in locking the rear cargo doors of the type.

What was not revealed at the time was a report by Dan Applegate, an engineer with Convair, who expressed deep concern with the safety of this particular door. Also, Douglas had not honoured the (admittedly unofficial) arrangement whereby records of reported difficulties or problems from the airline operators were passed on to the Federal Aviation Administration who might then have been able to notice a trend.

What the manufacturers had been privately doing to overcome the problems was to increase the power of the locking bolt actuators with a heavier gauge wire to drive home the locking bolt. This particular DC-10 had not been fitted with this modification. With such unmodified aircraft frequent use of a stand-by hand-crank was necessary to drive home the locking pin. Also, in the case of Flight 96, the use of a knee for extra leverage had actually distorted the locking pin rods.

Douglas saw the solution as a small peephole that would allow an outside observer to see that the locking bolts were fully home after closing the door. This was the kind of modification that could be enforced by a Federal Aviation Administration Airworthiness Directive. Indeed, early on the morning of 16 June the head of the FAA Western Regional office, Arvin Basnight, telexed Washington centre for approval to issue just such a document.

However, unknown to Basright, the previous evening Jackson McGowan, the President of Douglas, had been in telephone conversation with Jack Shaffer, the Federal Aviation Administration's chief in Washington. These two had come to a 'gentleman's agreement' along with Continental, United, and National Airlines (main operators of the DC-10) whereby instead of any modification to their fleets they would instruct their crews that no more than 23kg (50lb) of pressure was to be exerted when closing the rear cargo doors. Here was a suggestion both preposterous and ultimately calamitous. It would be virtually impossible for anyone to gauge how much pressure they were using.

On 6 July 1972 the National Transportation Safety Board formally recommended the Federal Aviation Administration that DC-10 aircraft should have peepholes fitted to enable a visual check to be made on the locking bolts after closure, that modifications to the latching system should be made so that false 'closed' indications could note be given, and that the floor strength should be increased.

But no Airworthiness Directive was issued. The modifications were only carried out slowly at a time when the aircraft were grounded for other maintenance. Aircraft do not make a profit when they are on the ground. What airline would voluntarily ground its aircraft when, after all, a method of operation to ensure safety had been devised?

It was not until February 1973 that the Federal Aviation Administration, from which Shaffer had now resigned, began to urge stronger flooring to prevent de-pressurisation of a DC-10 resulting in a downwardly bent floor distorting and/or breaking control rods. Also, as an extra precaution, they advised that the control rod route should be transferred further up the side of the fuselage to be away from any such damage.

No such modifications had been made to DC-10-10 TC-JAV of Turk Hava Yollari (Turkish Airlines) as it alighted at Paris Orly en route Ankara–Istanbul–Paris–London on 3 March 1973. The 345 seat capacity airliner was on time with 168 persons on board. Fifty of these were to disembark at Paris.

The arrival of the giant THY machine must have seemed a godsend to staff of British European Airways. Their ground engineers were on strike, and that weekend the English had fought a Rugby Union match against the French. There were an estimated 30,000 English fans in Paris, and many of them were milling around the BEA check-in looking for a flight home. Now there was the prospect of some two hundred or so seats on the final leg of THY Flight 981.

The ramp servicing for THY at Orly was subcontracted to Samor Company. This firm's personnel were supposed to be familiar with the troublesome rear cargo doors of DC-10s. However, THY crew members were responsible for checking, via the now incorporated peephole, the locking mechanism after closure. At Orly on that fateful day the rear cargo hold was emptied and the door closed at 10.35 by Mahommed Mahmoudi, a thirty-nine year old Algerian expatriate employed by Samor. He had previously seen the normally resident THY ground engineer, who that weekend was away at a training course in Istanbul, peer through the peephole, but Mahmoudi did not know why. Mahmoudi did not look through the tiny window. Nor did the stand-in THY ground engineer or Flight Engineer Erhan Ozer. By his neglect the latter virtually signed his own death warrant.

The handle closed with ease; the flight deck indication showed 'safe' – hardly surprising really for Service Bulletin SB52-37 stipulating that the locking pin of the rear cargo doors should be extended had actually been misread, and the length had been *reduced* on this aircraft. Flying at high altitude with tonnes (tons) of internal pressure bearing on the rear cargo door, it was gripping with no more security than the fingertips of a person clawing at a cliff edge.

Flight 981 took off at 11.30 with a total complement of 334 passengers, 11 crew and a ground engineer travelling as a passenger, soaring up into clear skies. Captain Berkoz engaged the auto-pilot at 11.36 as they tracked east and then north to avoid overflying the centre of Paris. Clearance was given to climb to 7,500m (25,000ft). Pressure was building up on that clinging rear cargo door. At 11.39 Flight 981 passed through 3,450m (11,500ft) over Saint Pathus, climbing at 660m (2,200ft) per minute and at 300 knots. There was some five tonnes (tons) of pressure bearing on the rear cargo door. Like the person who just cannot cling to the cliff edge any longer the door burst, tore from its hinges and hurtled backwards in the slipstream. The rear section of the cabin floor collapsed downwards on to the control rods and hydraulic piping. The last two rows of triple seats with their six passengers still strapped in were instantly ejected into the void.

In the cockpit the throttles slammed themselves shut and the pressure warning horn blared. Captain Berhoz screamed, 'What happened?'

'The fuselage has burst!' First Officer Ulusman shouted, as if such a reply was really necessary.

Not only had the fuselage burst: the control cables and hydraulic power lines were also damaged, the tailplane controls were lost, and the rudder was seized with 10° of port turn locked on. Somewhat slower than its six unfortunate passengers, the giant aircraft nosed over and began to dive towards the ground. At 11.40, its crew screaming 'Mayday!', it passed through 2,160m (7,200ft), the speed rising to 400 knots. The pressure warning ceased, only to be replaced by the overspeed alarm.

One minute later, in a shallow descent but with 17° of port bank, she struck trees at Ermononville, cutting a long swathe through the forest as she disintegrated, her human cargo shattered, pulped or tossed to hang from the scoured trees. There could be no survivors from such an impact, despite the incredible lack of fire.

Statistically the crash had to happen. Since the advent of the Boeing 747 the world had held its breath, dreading the day one of these giant wide-bodied jets would come down with a full passenger load. Possibly there were quiet sighs of half-relief in Seattle, the home of Boeing, that morning as the wreckage of Flight 981 was shown by television to the world; the first of the 'jumbo' designs had not been the first to strike such disaster.

Speculations about whether the damage had been caused by a bomb were quickly squashed as the broken pieces of TC-JAV told their tale. She had been more at risk even than any of her sisters, because of the short-ened locking bolt; but it could have happened to any of her type. Concern to keep aircraft in the air, and the manufacturer's desire that the type should not be seen as inferior to their competitors, meant that risks had been taken that so easily could have been avoided. If Flight Engineer Erhan Ozer had taken a few seconds to look through that peephole at Paris he and 345 others just may have lived.

If Dan Applegate had been listened to long before, there would have been no DC-10 rear cargo doors clinging to their frames like victims on cliff edges. In the future the type would fly not only with modified door locking mechanisms, but also with floor strengthening that would with-stand decompression stress at any altitude. However, it was not to be the end of the tragic early history of the DC-10.

Most people believe that the largest aircraft in the world is the Boeing 747. *Hughes Hercules HK-1*, a lumbering behemoth of a flying boat flown just once by its instigator – Howard Hughes – and designed during the last war as a troop transport, used to be the largest. The biggest now is in fact the Soviet Antonov 225 military freighter, closely rivalled by the American C5-A Lockheed Galaxy, the giant utility transport of the US Air Force, able to swallow through its rear loading ramp tanks, parachutists, troops or supplies.

On 4 April 1975 one of these high-winged aerial juggernauts loaded 243 Vietnamese orphans at Saigon, along with 62 adults. They found space for themselves in the cavernous hold, bracing themselves against the fuselage sides, for there were no seats or seatbelts. The children were being flown to America to start new lives away from the war in their country. But tragedy struck en route: the Galaxy's tail loading ramp broke shortly after take off, damaging the control lines and peppering the tailplane with debris.

The pilot tried to nurse the crippled giant to an emergency landing at Tan Son Nhut Airport, Saigon, but could only bring her down in an emergency pancake in a rice paddy where the wings were torn off and the wreckage erupted into fire. Slipping and sliding through the mud, skirting around the pools of blazing fuel spreading across the shallow water came the survivors; but 190, mostly children, were killed. It was one of the worst air disasters, yet it is one of the least known.

On 25 May 1979 two air accidents occurred. Both were due to structural failure. At first consideration one seems to be an insignificant minor accident, but in fact recently its implications have become tragically apparent; the other incident was another avoidable disaster to befall that almost tragic design, the DC-10.

The four-engined turboprop Vickers Viscount is one of the classics of air transport. For over thirty years it has been a mainstay of short-haul operations throughout the world. The aircraft are elderly now and soon the very last will go to the breaker's yard, replaced by such types as the Canadian Dash 7 and British Aerospace 146. Like old cars, old aircraft, though perhaps serviceable, need careful attention. The bodywork of an old car may rust around the suspension attachment points so that a dangerous failure occurs, perhaps even causing a fatal accident. Such a simple failure on an aircraft can cause disaster horribly worse in death toll.

The first of these two accidents concerned a British Airways Viscount G-AOYS, which took off from Cardiff Airport in South Wales for a flight to Paris carrying four crew and fifty-one passengers. Through clear weather, the prevailing south-westerly wind nudging her starboard side, she droned over the Bristol Channel for a scheduled call at Bristol. There the landing gear refused to lower on the port side. Manual pumping of the gear and even its disconnection from the power so that the oleo leg could fall into place by gravity failed to solve the problem.

The captain turned her back towards Cardiff where a fly-past of the control tower enabled the staff there to confirm by radio to the aircrew that it was not a fault with the cockpit indicator light, but that the wheels were still hiding in their well.

Modern airliners are fitted with fuel dump pipes that enable most of the fuel to be pumped out into the slipstream prior to an emergency landing. Old G-AOYS had no such fitting, so she had to circle to burn off fuel. Eventually she was brought in for her final landing, as slowly as possible, her captain holding her off the runway until the last moment. She skidded along Runway 31, swinging around trailing sparks. There was no fire nor injuries to the passengers as they scuttled from her broken wreck.

Why did it happen? Examination revealed that the undercarriage's hydraulic system had been in perfect working order, but that a bolt – costing only a few pence – common to both the conventional and emergency linkage of the left main undercarriage had sheared off owing to metal fatigue, and its two halves were rolling around in the wheelwell.

All over the world old but serviceable aircraft are still flying. Indeed, ancient Curtiss C-46 Commandos and Douglas DC-3s can still be found flying as flagships for the smaller nations of the Third World; some of these have actually been crashed and rebuilt several times. Some are, like the classic proverbial 'bent' car, a welding together of the parts of several similar aircraft. Something must break sooner or later.

Structural failure on one of the wide-bodied jets that are now exceeding two decades in service is a common fear today. Such thoughts were not prevalent in 1979. The Comet disasters had largely been forgotten, and the last few members of that design were only seen on charter flights in Europe, as DC-10 N110AA, the first of its type to have been delivered to American Airlines, took off from Chicago O'Hare for a flight to Los Angeles. She was the second victim of an accident on that fateful 25 May 1979.

Flight 191 carried thirteen crew and 258 passengers as the brakes were released and she began her roll at 15.04 (Central Time). Far away, in Cardiff, Viscount G-AOYS had already made her last landing. In Chicago, Captain Walter Lux had given his co-pilot, James Dillard, control of the take off. At 139 knots Lux called vee one, the speed at which they had to decide whether or not to take off. Should an engine fail now the safe take off speed with the remaining two would be 153 knots. Just another six knots on three engines would be the correct speed for Dillard to palm the control column back towards himself so that the DC-10 pointed itself at the sky.

It was just then that horrified observers, including relatives of those on board, saw the port engine complete with its pylon detach itself from the wing, tumble backwards and strike the runway in a flash of fire.

Lux and Dillard were only aware of what seemed to be a loss of power. They were completely unaware that not only had an engine gone but that 1m (3ft) of the port wing's leading edge had been ripped away with it, tearing out hydraulic and electric lines, some of which carried stall warning instrumentation. The airspeed indicator showed 145 knots so Lux called, 'Rotate!' Dillard hauled back on the column and the DC-10 staggered into the air, but with the port wing down. The loss of hydraulic power had allowed the outboard leading edge slats to be pushed back flush to the wing by the pressure of the air. With every moment that passed that wing was becoming stalled. No indication of this was conveyed to the pilots, however, as those electrical circuits had gone. In her crippled condition the giant jet needed an airspeed of 159 knots if she were to avoid the left wingtip stalling. Dillard was trying to climb her out at 14° on two engines at 172 knots. If only he pushed the nose down, flew level, disaster might yet be avoided, but, with every moment that her nose was pointed at the clouds, speed was falling.

Flight Engineer Alfred Udovich was frantically trying to make sense of the messages displayed on his panel. Those flight instruments supplied by the generator of number one engine had gone. He was not to have time to switch to the power supply from the other generators. As Flight 191 fought to climb, the airspeed dropped, yet the 'stick-shaker' warning was inoperative, its power gone along with the engine.

Slowly, almost sedately, the DC-10 banked further and further to port, descending also. Death was to come quickly for the passengers of Flight 191; but not instantly – they did not die unknowing or unwarned. There would have been screams and panic in the passenger cabin as the aircraft heeled over, with bags, cameras, radios and bottles tumbling from the overhead lockers on to the helplessly strapped-in passengers. And passengers flying across the cabin too, for there are always those who do not believe in seatbelts and the cabin staff cannot check every one. For perhaps fifteen seconds everyone on board knew that they faced death.

The DC-10 was airborne for just thirty-one seconds before, banked over at 90° so that for her last instants she seemed like a giant cross in the sky, she plunged into a mobile home park, exploding instantly. Besides all those on board, two people on the ground were also killed in this, one of the most horrific of all air disasters.

The National Transportation Safety Board quickly concluded that the flight had taken off too slowly to counteract the asymmetrical lift provided with the port wing leading edge torn off, the slats on that side retracted and an engine gone. However, had the stall warning still been functioning, it is just possible that Dillard and Lux may have spooled up the tail and starboard engines and held the aircraft in almost level flight. In this case she would probably have achieved sufficient flying speed for her crippled condition so that a circuit and landing could have been successful.

Realistically, no blame was or should have been attached to the crew. The failure happened at the most critical moment of any flight, and they did not even have time to appreciate that an engine had actually fallen off.

Records revealed that nine DC-10s of this series (DC-10-10s, as were the aircraft mentioned earlier in this chapter) had suffered engine pylon damage. This could be traced back to instructions issued by the Douglas Corporation in May 1975 and February 1978 requiring maintenance and inspection of the wing engine pylons for possible fatigue cracking. To do this inspection the operator's maintenance teams should have in each case first removed the engines and then the pylons. American Airlines engineers had discovered in 1977 that it was possible to use a modified fork-lift truck to remove the engine and pylon as a complete unit. This gave the operator a saving of two hundred expensive man hours per aircraft to do the work, as only twenty-seven hydraulic and electric circuits had to be disconnected instead of the seventy-nine necessary were the work done as instructed.

American Airlines should not be seen as the only culpable operator, they just happened to be the airline that suffered the disaster. Continental Airlines were using the same procedure and also risking damage to the pylon mountings as they were jarred by the force of the fork-lift.

Examination of the wreckage of N110AA revealed a 25cm (10in) fracture on one flange of the port pylon. Fatigue cracking was also evident at both ends of this fracture.

Another element to this disaster was that the DC-10 as originally designed had no mechanical device to lock out the slats. Had those slats remained in the extended position after the loss of the engine, 153 knots might just have proved a safe take off speed. The machine would just have achieved this.

On 6 June 1979 the Federal Aviation Administration grounded all DC-10s. Forty-one airlines operating 170 aircraft were affected. Not since the disasters to befall the British Comets had a design so alarmed the public. After modifications the type was cleared to fly again from 13 July, but for many years, perhaps until elderly Boeings started to show a propensity for shedding parts of themselves in mid-air, there were members of the public who would avoid, if possible, flying the DC-10. Leading edge slat locks, a new rear cargo door locking bolt mechanism, re-routed control rods, cables and electrics, strengthened floors – all these modifications are incorporated in those aircraft of the type now in service. All were faults that should have been corrected during development. But all were faults that should not have led to disaster. Humans designed the DC-10 and their failings led to its downfall.

The early years of the Boeing 747 saw the type enjoy a good record for safety. True, the collision at Los Rodeos was the worst aircraft accident, to date, but the fault there did not lie with the type. The Nairobi incident could have been averted by a better warning system for the leading edge slats, but there was human culpability involved in that accident too. It was really a very good record. This achievement was to be destroyed on the slopes of Mount Fuji in 1985 when a fully loaded 747SR (Short Range) plunged down after an explosive decompression.

The eve of the three-day feast of Bon, 12 August, saw Tokyo's Haneda Airport crowded with those seeking flights home or to visit relatives for the holiday. Japan Airlines Flight 123 took off at 18.00 (Local Time) for what should have been a trip to Osaka with 509 of its 528 seats occupied, almost all by Japanese nationals. The fifteen crew were under the command of Captain Masami Takahama.

Examination of the log of this aircrafts JA8119, later revealed that it had scraped the rear of the fuselage landing at Osaka as long ago as June 1978. Naturally all aircraft with nosewheel undercarriages (almost all types nowadays) have a skidplate near the tail to absorb such a mishap, but such had been the impact in this case that the rear pressure bulkhead dividing the passenger cabin from the tail section had been cracked. This was repaired in Japan by Boeing engineers. For five years this 747 was to fly safely, but meanwhile it was carrying a fault that must one day cause disaster as surely as if the aircraft were carrying a time bomb.

Flight 123 had climbed to 7,200m (24,000ft) and was approaching the east coast of the Izu Peninsula when the aircraft was rocked by a massive

explosion towards the rear of the fuselage. The ceiling above the rear lavatory had actually blown off. Loose objects tore along the cabin as the pressurised air was sucked out into the void. Passengers who tried to scream
found themselves unable to as the oxygen was torn from their lungs.
Instead they clutched at the oxygen masks that tumbled from the ceiling,
the tubes whipping around as the last of the cabin's air rushed out in the
suction of the slipstream. Perhaps a few passengers, those with cardiac
problems, died in those seconds, their hearts unable to cope with the
abrupt change in pressure. Perhaps they were the fortunate ones.

Up in the cockpit the crew donned their oxygen masks and began their
drills by turning off the pressure warning horn. Audible now was the roar
of the engines as, unaffected, they continued to power the 747 across the
sky at over 800kph (500mph). That she was seriously disabled was obvious –
she was pitching and rolling across the sky. Takahama seized the control
column and with the automatic reflexes of a pilot would have tried to
steady the machine – and then realised that he faced the ultimate horror of
his profession: there was no response from any of the flying controls. All
four hydraulic lines had been ruptured. The 747 had become over three
hundred tonnes (tons) of totally uncontrollable mass that could at any
moment tip over into a final, unrecoverable dive. As it staggered across
Suruga Bay passenger door five on the starboard side came unlocked
owing to the flexing of the fuselage as it was twisted by terrible pressures
tearing at the damaged tail. The door was torn away by the slipstream.
Passengers seated near it must have thought that the 747 was going to disintegrate in mid-air piece by piece. The cabin crew must have tried to reas-
sure them that the captain would take them down for a landing very soon.

Descending and turning east, the aircraft passed north of Mount Fuji,
the speed rising. Takahama dropped the eighteen-wheel undercarriage
and succeeded in checking the speed as she descended through 6,000m
(20,000ft), pitched only slightly nose-down, Takahama trying to control
her by throttle alone. Then she got away from him and turned a full circle
over the city of Otsuki before again choosing to go east.

At 18.45, thirty minutes after the start of the crisis, she again turned to
the north. Mountainous land loomed ahead and she was down to 3,000m
(10,000ft) now, flying slower with the throttles eased back to prevent strain
on the damaged tail; but almost too slow as she suddenly reared up on the
verge of a stall. Takahama pushed the throttles forward and also electrically dropped 5° of flap. She ballooned back up to 3,300m (11,000ft), but
almost immediately began to lose power and fell into a dive of 405m
(1,350ft) per minute. Takahama increased the flap to 10°.

Back in the passenger cabins some were writing scribbled letters on
oddments of paper or the back of tickets; letters and notes that few of them
believed would really be necessary, for the human brain does not accept
the prospect of death easily. Somehow the pilot would get them down, and
this nightmare would be a tale to tell over and over to children and grand-
children – wouldn't it?

For almost an hour Flight 123 reeled over Japanese skies out of control but for any balance that Takahama could conjure with engine power. He tried to descend her gently to a crash landing, but just before 19.00 she put her nose down in to a final dive. She impacted 1,440m (4,780ft) up Mount Osutaka just 110km (70 miles) north-west of Tokyo, bursting into flames. In a country as densely populated as Japan it was merciful that she came down away from towns and cities.

Not even helicopters could land on the mountain amidst the trees. Aircraft overflew the site in the gathering gloom, but could see no sign of life amidst the blazing trees.

It was 09.00 the following day when firemen and abseiling paratroops reached the smouldering wreckage. Was that a faint bird call or the cry of a survivor? Yumi Ochiai, an off-duty stewardess, was actually alive, but trapped in the debris! In this, an accident that by all standards would be considered unsurvivable, a further three people were found alive: a twelve-year-old girl, a mother and her eight-year-old daughter. These had all been seated together in the centre of row 56.

Public suspicions about the cause of this disaster leapt to the conclusion that it must surely be another case of metal fatigue. But it was not so. The Boeing engineers who had repaired the damaged bulkhead had not inserted a reinforcing plate to make it absolutely stiff again. Routine inspections over the years had failed to notice this error; after all, the section was virtually inaccessible and not part of normal servicing. The aircraft's tail must have flexed in flight for seven years before, inevitably, it broke. If only the pilot landing the machine at Osaka in 1978 had not misjudged his approach and scraped the tail...

A Japan Airlines maintenance manager committed suicide after the accident. There should be no short-cuts in aircraft servicing, but today, in a competitive commercial world, every operator is looking for a way to reduce costs. As air traffic is set to double in volume by the year 2000, towards two billion passengers per year, the bulk of this traffic will be catered for by aircraft designs that are two or even three decades old in 1990. Even the Boeing 747 passed the two decade mark in February 1989 with the first production machine off the stocks, honourably registered as N747PA and named *Juan T. Trippe* after the founder of Pan American, still in service with that airline. In the depression years of the late 1970s rows of jetliners for sale littered airfields across the Western world, but times have changed now. 1988 saw the smallest number of voluntary deregistrations for many years (the *involuntary* deregistration of an aircraft means it met disaster), and as far as the manufacturers are concerned it is a seller's market. With the present boom in the business an operator would have to wait approximately four years to take delivery of a Boeing 747-400, latest version of the type with updated avionics allied to an airframe whose design commenced a quarter of a century ago. Knowing that the 747 is the only airliner in its class, Boeing have been able to reduce the options available; no more must their salesmen accede to an airline's demand for a unique exit door arrangement or lavatory layout.

No air disaster has a good aspect, but there was a small mercy in the tragedy of Japan Airlines Flight 123: examination of the wreckage revealed fatigue cracking of the forward fuselage, fatigue that did not contribute to the disaster, but which otherwise may not have been noticed in other machines. It was possible to instigate inspections by the operators, and perhaps further disasters were averted. However, the longevity of many Boeing designs may recently have led to destruction.

On 29 April 1988 a nineteen year old Boeing 737 of Aloha Airlines took off from Hilo Airport, Hawaii, on yet another short trip to Honolulu. The life of this aircraft was spent on such island-hopping trips within the Hawaiian archipelago. *Queen Liliuokalani* was off on her 89,681st flight, each trip subjecting her to vibration and stresses that wanted to tear her apart while the fuselage had each time to withstand the massive pressure that cocooned her passengers and crew in a breathable atmosphere. Since being rolled off the production line in April 1969 she had also been subjected to acidic corrosion from such sources as condensation from the toilets and galley, spilt fruit drinks seeping through the floor and the salty ocean air in which she lived her life.

Queen Liliuokalani was at 7,200m (24,000ft) over the Pacific when disaster struck: the entire cabin roof from the bulkhead at the rear of the forward passenger entrance vestibule to the hooped frame just behind the wings' leading edge sheared away, the entire semi-circular section 5m (18ft) long blew away, taking with it the air-conditioning ducting, a cabin bulkhead and the overhead lockers. Stewardess Clarabelle Lansing had been attending to passengers in the forward cabin at the time of the split. She, too, was carried away.

The remaining passengers were subjected to the tempest of a 450 knot airflow. Perhaps it was fortunate that as they suddenly had to gasp for oxygen in that rarefied air they could not at first fully comprehend that they were riding on a flexing extension of fuselage forward of the wings that could tear away at any moment; in fact the seat rails were now the main support for the forward cabin and the cockpit. To passengers at the rear the drooping cockpit was out of sight as if it had fallen off. 'Wow! Just think of that!' an investigator commented later. Only the two pilots had a roof over their heads now, the passengers in the forward cabin did not even have fuselage sides. The Pacific Ocean was a long, long way down. The rear passenger cabin was pelted by debris whipping through the fuselage.

Captain Robert Schornstheimer only had to look over his shoulder to understand what had occurred. He had already begun an emergency descent and transmitted a Mayday as the pressure warning horn blared. Now he and co-pilot Madeline Tompkins reduced airspeed to lessen stress on the remaining structure and also to take away some of the force of the terrible speed-induced gale tearing at the exposed passengers. Three had already been critically injured. Carefully, *Queen Liliuokalani* was turned to starboard towards the nearest airport at Kahului on Maui Island.

Very gently she was set down on the runway, crew and passengers expecting the forward fuselage to shear off at any instant, mangled debris at the edges of the split shaking or being torn off. Yet she held together for the wheels-down landing, emergency crews running towards her then pausing in disbelief at the sight that confronted them. The pilots helped to disentangle the passengers from seating that had been twisted, and gently slid them down the emergency chutes. Ninety-four passengers and crew lived, though fifty-six were seriously injured.

Seven years before, a similar aircraft of Far Eastern Air Transport had crashed in Taiwan killing all 110 on board, that incident being blamed on corrosion. Was this the beginning of a trend, an age of geriatric jets? The British Civil Aviation Authority ordered that country's operators to carry out checks on those Boeing 737s that had flown more than 55,000 flights.

The subject of ageing aircraft was quickly forgotten through the summer of 1988, and there were other air stories to capture the headlines: the mid-air collision of Frecce Tricolori at the Ramstein air display (see Chapter 7) and then the Lockerbie tragedy. The winter of 1988–9 provided further ammunition for horror-headlines when a Boeing 737 crashed near the East Midlands Airport in England; an elderly Boeing 707 plunged into a mountainside on the mid-Atlantic island of Santa Maria (see Chapter 6); and other aircraft, particularly those of Boeing manufacture, lost substantial portions of their structure in flight.

On 28 February 1989, twenty years to the day from the rollout of N747PA, Boeing announced that a task force of airline representatives and engineers under the auspices of the American Air Transport Association had investigated samples of long-service machines and concluded that 1,200 of the Seattle company's machines should have vital structural repairs which would cost £464-million. Boeing has become partly a victim of its own success, supplying the majority of the world's long-range machines. They had even bought back two secondhand 747s with long hours in their logs for detailed examination. With political lobbies trying to enforce mandatory retirement ages on aircraft, whether through flight time, take-offs and landings or years, Boeing and other manufacturers responded strongly and quite correctly by stating that there was no danger provided specified maintenance and renewal of components and structure were adhered to. (It is strange how the lay public will form queues for a short 'hop' in an historic DC-3 at an air show when such machines must have been constructed before the first 707!)

Boeing cited the example of *Juan T. Trippe* which in 1988 was given a $21-million refit to make her as good as a new aircraft which would have cost Pan American $150-million. Further ammunition was added to Boeing's armoury by the fact that the company had recommended inspections of elderly 737s that would have revealed the fatigue cracking of the Aloha Airlines jet, yet the Federal Aviation Administration had not adopted this policy.

Some carriers were negligent too: in January 1989 a Piedmont Airlines

Boeing 737 was climbing through 300m (1,000ft) after take off from Chicago when an engine fell off. This time a safe return and landing were made, yet over a year before the Federal Aviation Administration had instructed all operators to make regular ultrasonic checks on engine mounting bolts that were suspect to metal fatigue, and on Boeing's advice to strengthen the mountings. The carriers pleaded that in an air travel boom they should be permitted to make do with just the ultrasonic checks. The Federal Aviation Administration compromised, allowing the operators four thousand cycles per aircraft (a cycle being one flight), in simple terms up to two years, to modify each aircraft.

On 24 February 1989 a United Airlines Boeing 747 flying at 6,600m (22,000ft) over the Pacific Ocean en route from Honolulu to Auckland, New Zealand suffered a failure of the fuselage skin near the forward starboard cargo hold door. In a situation that could have been as tragic as the catastrophe to befall the Turkish Airlines DC-10 near Paris, not only did the door whip away in the slipstream but also a massive section of the skin. The hole was big enough to drive two double decker buses through. Nine passengers were ejected to their deaths.

While investigation was to reveal this failure to lie with the skinning of the machine, modifications to all Boeing 747 cargo doors had been ordered in late 1987, but the airlines were given until 1990 to complete the work.

Later the same month a Federal Aviation Administration check of maintenance records revealed that Northwest Airlines had been flying its twenty-four 'jumbos' for more than eight thousand cycles without carrying out an Airworthiness Directive to check the engine mountings. The spectacle of a wide-bodied jet smashing onto a city is amongst the most feared scenarios. At 18.22 on Sunday 4 October 1992 a Boeing 747 freighter of El Al took off from Amsterdam's Schiphol Airport with a full load of fuel, three crew and a woman passenger bound for Israel. Within minutes the pilot was reporting trouble with two engines. He was trying to dump fuel for an emergency landing. Fifteen minutes after take-off, sweeping over the east of the city and unable to maintain altitude, the giant struck the high-rise flats of Bijlmeer and exploded in a mushrooming fireball. In this semi-ghetto estate largely inhabited by illegal aliens an accurate death toll will never be known, but seventy is the estimate. And the cause? It seems that at least one engine fell off the aircraft. While investigations continued, the fuse pins (designed to break and release an engine in the event of too much stress such as involved in a crash-landing) of all 747s were to be inspected. Of 516 pins tested by United States operators, 267 were faulty, indeed 27 had severe cracks.

The number of inspectors has not kept pace with the increase in air traffic, and it is almost as if maintenance deficiencies now will only be detected by lottery. Perhaps some operators are willing to fly on a metal-fatigued wing and a prayer knowing that the regulatory authorities seem at the moment to be toothless tigers.

4
Mechanical Failure

Low down on our list of possible terrors when flying comes the possibility of engine or some other catastrophic mechanical failure. It was not always so. In the pioneering days of air travel mechanical failure was rife; unreliable engines spluttered to a halt with oiled-up sparking plugs, and fuel filters clogged with poorly refined petrol. But the pilot in the open cockpit of his de Havilland or Farman biplane could usually glide down to a field, clear the blockage or clean the plugs and take off again into skies where the buzzing of an aeroplane was still but a rare phenomenon.

The modern airliner is less than a lifetime away from such machines, but technologically it is in a different era. Its thousands of mechanical components, from gyro-compasses to slat actuators, do still fail, but every system is duplicated. If undercarriage hydraulics fail there is a back-up power supply. If this second option also fails the wheels can be gravity dropped, although this emergency procedure can occasionally also fail.

A 550 seat 'jumbo' does not have the option of setting down in a meadow. Yet the passenger should not be lulled into believing that the contemporary airliner with its computerised wizardry flies without faults. Some faults are acceptable: a generator slightly down in output, an engine burning a little too much oil, even an auto-pilot with a tendency to disengage itself. Only an optimist would believe that mechanical maintenance is always perfect. The British Airtours Boeing 737 fire at Manchester (see Chapter 2) was caused by a defect that should have been corrected during routine maintenance. In a harshly commercial world pilots are under immense pressure to get airliners airborne. There are the reams of paperwork – 'Reasons for cancellation of flight'; the possible interview with the airline's senior pilot – 'I would have taken it up, son, it was only a little fault'; and perhaps even personal pride, or conceit, or even a simple wish to get home from a foreign land. So a wing tank is leaking a little more than usual – all wing tanks leak to a degree; it will hold together for this one flight, won't it? But what if turbulence should be encountered en route that stresses and flexes the wing enough to make the fuel loss critical?

Today 'black boxes' tick away in the tail of the aircraft, recording on their magnetic tape every little waver, dip, engine surge, bank, stutter, turn, climb and g-force on the machine. 'Black box' is a misnomer: these modern recorders, such as those manufactured by Sundstrand, are almost universally painted dayglo orange. For many years regulatory bodies and a few more responsible airlines had attempted to get such recorders fitted. As long ago as 1924 a single-engined de Havilland DH34 eleven-seat biplane of Imperial Airways had been fitted with an engine revolutions recorder. It did not prove to be very valuable, however, after the aircraft plunged to the grass of Croydon Airport, as the last thirty minutes of the trace were unreadable. Nevertheless it did contradict reports that the engine had been unreliable. A housing estate now stands on the site of London's first airport, where seven passengers and a pilot perished; only road names such as Kingsford Avenue and Imperial Way recall the half-forgotten history of Great Britain's early steps in commercial aviation.

There were two attempts in the United States to make flight recorders mandatory (between 1941 to 1944 and 1947 to 1948) for aircraft over 5,670kg (12,500lb) in weight operating in passenger service above 7,500m (25,000ft). Success was not achieved until 1958. Great Britain lagged even further behind, not making such fitting compulsory until after a British European Airways Vanguard turboprop had crashed on one of Heathrow's main runways in poor weather in 1965.

Today it is often assumed that once the 'black box' has been found, any air disaster will quickly be explained by its spools of tape. This is not always so. On 31 July 1973 Flight 723 of Delta Air Lines operating a scheduled passenger service was wrecked when it hit the seawall to the right of the runway at Logan Airport, Boston after completing the short hop from Burlington, Vermont. Visibility was less than 1.6km (1 mile) as the twin-jet DC9 swooped down. The approach was too fast and too low. There was a six-minute delay before the fire alarm was sounded and the emergency vehicles rushed to the scene. Only one passenger from the eighty-nine on board was pulled clear alive, but succumbed to injuries that December. National Transportation Safety Board Hearings Officer James Kuehl summed up the incident thus: 'Some crashes are clear-cut from the beginning. We knew this one was a controversial crash and not one that could be pinned down to one cause.' The aircraft had a history of instrument failure. Was it lured too low by a faulty altimeter? We will never know, despite the 'black box'.

A flight recorder might have solved the mystery of the strange antics that a Sabena Boeing 707 performed over Brussels as it arrived from New York on 15 February 1961. At 09.00 in good weather it swooped over the light gantries at the end of the runway and had nearly touched down when the engines were spooled up, the undercarriage retracted and what seemed to be an overshoot began. The jet climbed to 90m (300ft) and banked to port. It finally reached 450m (1,500ft) where it performed three turns as if doing a second approach, but before reaching the runway it banked nearly vertical and arrowed down to explode on impact, killing all sixty-one passengers, eleven crew and an airport worker. The Commission of Enquiry could only conclude that there was a fault in the flying controls.

One mystery that was solved was the reason why a British European

Airways De Havilland Comet 4B seemed to attempt to climb vertically away from Esenboga Airport, Ankara on 21 December 1961. This was a scheduled service from London to Tel Aviv operated on behalf of Cyprus Airways. There were twenty-seven passengers and seven crew as the graceful jet screamed away from its Turkish halt in snow. A screw securing the cowling above the artificial horizon had worked loose. The captain could not get a clear reading from the dial as he hauled the aircraft aloft. He was deceived into pulling back on the controls until the aircraft stalled at just 135m (450ft). Recovery from such low altitude was impossible. The port wing flipped down and the Comet smashed to earth. Remarkably, seven passengers lived, though seriously injured. Except in visual flight conditions weather no pilot can orientate himself without the artificial horizon; that and his airspeed indicator are his bibles. If they are faulty disaster is almost a foregone conclusion.

A Trans Canada Airlines Vickers Viscount was cruising peacefully 5,700m (19,000ft) above Michigan State in July 1956 when the whine of the starboard outer Rolls Royce Dart turboprop engine went out of syncopation with its three fellows, the revolutions momentarily dropping and then surging, racing to an uncontrollable 14,000 per minute.

Detroit Air Traffic Control was contacted with the request for an emergency landing at Windsor, Ontario. The fuselage was de-pressurised as the aircraft descended so that the pressure loss was hardly explosive when the propeller of number four engine sheared off, shards striking and damaging the inner engine and one blade stabbing through the fuselage. One passenger was killed and five others injured.

With the pilots pressing against the rudder pedals to counter the asymmetric thrust, a safe landing was made on the power of the port engines. The investigation was to reveal that the bevel gears of the gearbox between the engine and the propeller had sheared. The propeller had then windmilled free in the slipstream. The pilots were rather unfairly blamed for exacerbating the problem by descending at high speed!

Fire breaking out on an airliner as it roared down the runway at Manchester had horrific results (see pp. 56–59). How much more terrifying must be uncontrollable fire inside a fuselage when the aircraft is at high altitude. Over twenty years before British Airtours' Boeing 737 was burnt out, a United Air Lines Vickers Viscount was cruising through clear summer air above Newport, Tennessee, when fire broke out on board.

This was a scheduled service on 9 July 1964 that had originated at Philadelphia and would travel south to Huntsville, Alabama. The turboprop left Washington, DC, at 17.30 with thirty-five passengers and four crew heading for its next call at Knoxville, Tennessee. Atlanta Air Traffic Control was watching it approach there when the British-built machine began an unauthorised descent through 2,400m (8,000ft). It disappeared from the radar scopes at 18.13.

It was witnessed then by observers on the ground 60km (38 miles) north-east of Knoxville. It was whistling across the sky at very low altitude with a violet glare of flames illuminating the cabin windows. Smoke was streaming in the slipstream and there were dark spots on the hull as if it was beginning to get red-hot. Then, as it came down to approximately 150m (500ft), a large object was seen to fall from the over-wing emergency exit. Horrified witnesses ran to where this fell and found the corpse of a male passenger. In his desperation to escape from being burnt alive had he believed that he could climb out and cling to the wing? Meanwhile the Viscount flew on for a short distance then reared into a stall, spinning to total destruction on low hills.

Examination of the wreckage uncovered discharged extinguishers. Those on board had tried to fight that fire. Perhaps before the end they had been overcome by fumes. The cause of the blaze was never established – perhaps a passenger smoking in the lavatory, a perennial problem, or an electrical short circuit. Sabotage was not suspected.

Although many multi-engined jetliners do still carry flight engineers, this third member of the cockpit crew is now a disappearing species. New breeds of aerial giants such as the Boeing 747-400 series and McDonnell Douglas MD-11 were conceived as two-pilot machines. Safety factors aside, the role of this third pilot in piston-engine days was more onerous. The jet (or turbofan) engine works at its best at high speed and altitude, smoothly staying in rhythm with its fellows; piston engines are wilful and cantankerous, creeping out of synchronisation at the slightest opportunity. The flight engineer had continually to adjust the fuel mixtures to maintain harmony. Quite often they failed. In that now historical era of Constellations and Globemasters it was considered almost remarkable if a trans-Atlantic or trans-Pacific flight was completed with all four propellers still turning.

Pilots' unions throughout the Western world have negotiated lucrative wages; a British pilot can add to his annual salary considerably by taking a single flight to a distant destination at short notice. Once there he will stay in the best hotels and will be given the cash for four meals a day from the à la carte menu. In such a competitive business it is inevitable that managements look at their costs and conclude that flight engineers, third pilots, are now supernumerary; and after all there are no objections now to flying without the once essential navigator.

Jet engines, too, can of course fail in flight – once every 30,000 flying hours is a statistic quoted for contemporary turbofans, a time in the air that a long-service pilot may reach during his career. There is a perennial joke about how when three out of four engines of an aircraft fail over the ocean a passenger looks up and comments: 'If the other one stops we'll be stuck up here all day!' Of course, all four engines of, say, a Boeing 747 couldn't stop – could they?

The chances of this occurring through unrelated mechanical maladies are billions to one. Yet there is another element that can stop the engines: it has been known for people to turn off the fuel supply. A leaf through the pages of the International Civil Aviation Operators' Accident

Summary reveals instances of multi-engined airliners suffering near-total or total engine stoppage. A Lockheed TriStar once scraped in to Miami with just one of its three engines working: it transpired that ground engineers had not re-fitted seals to the oil drain plugs, and the oil had leaked away. More common is the error of a crew trying to draw fuel from empty tanks. In most cases the aircraft had been flying at sufficient altitude for the pilots to select full tanks and re-ignite the engines of their 'gliders'.

Bird strikes are another cause of engine failure. On New Year's Day 1976 a DC-10 of SAS was taking off from Copenhagen's Kastrup Airport when there was a loud thump and the port engine flamed out. After a successful circuit and landing it was discovered that some fifteen birds had passed through the engine; others had struck the starboard engine, and more were dead having hit the hull. Bird strikes have not yet however been recorded for the loss of a jetliner, although they have brought down propeller aircraft as large as Lockheed Electras and Viscounts. The greatest danger of a bird strike is that the cockpit crew will be injured or killed by one coming through the cockpit canopy. A modern windscreen can withstand the impact of a 1.8kg (4lb) bird at 750kph (470mph). At a certain aircraft manufacturer's, frozen chickens are being catapulted at a fighter aircraft's cockpit to test impact resistance.

Most bird strikes occur below 600m (2,000ft), and especially on the runway. The rumble of aircraft attracts worms to the surface, which then of course attract the birds. Bird-scaring vans are common sights on the world's airports.

It was only when night-flying became regular during World War II that it was realised that, contrary to popular belief, birds (other than owls) often fly at night. They certainly accounted for the downfall of some military aircraft at the time. Subsequently it has also been discovered that birds fly higher than was ever believed. In autumn 1988 a Pan American 747 was flying at 9,300m (31,000ft) over the Atlantic when the radome was dented, possibly by a goose. The 'jumbo' landed without problem, but it is unlikely that the same can be said for the goose! A 747 or other wide-bodied jet can expect to be struck by a bird approximately every one thousand flying hours. If a bird is ingested into an engine usually no more happens but that it gets plucked, gutted and ejected cooked.

Faulty maintenance, empty fuel tanks, bird strikes – what else can cause multiple engine failure? Volcanoes can!

The folklore of Java tells of how King Raja Galunggung retreated to the volcanic mountain that bears his name and buried his weapons after being defeated in battle. There he plotted his revenge. Galunggung is a smaller sister to Krakatoa, the latter lying between Java and Sumatra in the Sunda Strait. In that most destructive of all recent eruptions Krakatoa blasted out eight cubic miles of ash on 27 August 1883, killing 36,000 people. This is the Pacific 'Ring of Fire', where the earth vents the pressures of her inner core. The greatest volcanic eruption ever recorded was when Mount Tambora in Lombok ejected over sixty cubic miles of ash in

1815, killing 12,000.

Mount Galunggung, on the island of Java and some 190km (120 miles) south-east of Jakarta, had erupted in 1822 devastating 114 villages and killing 4,000 people. There were further minor eruptions in 1918 and again in 1958–9.

In 1982, pretending to be hermits, a group of men climbed to the summit to 'meditate'. This actually involved three months of searching for and then digging up the treasures of Raja Galunggung. Almost as soon as they had left the volcano, on 5 April, it began to rumble. The 'hermits' took the treasures back to appease the spirit of the warrior. But the rumblings continued. On 20 May villagers ritually slaughtered a cow and twelve sheep at midnight in the hope of quelling the anger of the gods. Still the mountain growled, sometimes throwing rocks for up to eight kilometres (five miles). Thirty thousand people were evacuated, and breaches in the south-east face had bled lava that buried homes and bridges up to eight kilometres (five miles) away.

Like a safety valve on an over-pressured boiler, the top of Mount Galunggung blew just after 19.00 on 24 June. At about he same time the British Airways Boeing 747 *City of Edinburgh* took off from Kuala Lumpur. This was the once-weekly through Flight 009 to Auckland, New Zealand via India, Malaysia and Australia. A fresh crew had taken over at the Kuala Lumpur halt under the command of Captain Eric Moody. There were 247 passengers as it flew south-westerly away from Singapore to touch the south-east coast of Sumatra and then approach Java from the north. It overflew Halim Airport at 20.34 on a course of 160 at 11,100m (37,000ft). Captain Moody glanced at the weather radar. It had a range of 480km (300 miles), some forty minutes' flying time. The scope seemed clear. Captain Moody carefully eased himself from his seat and over the centre console and went back to the lavatory. Just after he had gone Senior First Officer Roger Greaves first noticed something odd: it seemed almost as if tracer fire was rushing towards the windscreen, an effect quite unlike the common St Elmo's Fire which can dance over and around an airliner. 'Could be ice cloud,' Greaves commented. As *City of Edinburgh* approached the south coast of Java the 'Fasten Seat Belts' sign was illuminated in case of turbulence and the de-icing and engine igniters turned on.

At about the same time a few passengers noticed what seemed to be smoke wafting around the cabin. When this was mentioned to a stewardess she and a couple of colleagues began quietly looking for its source without alarming those oblivious to it. Many of the passengers were asleep with their porthole shutters drawn down.

Captain Moody was called back to the flight deck. He noticed smoke seeping out of the floor level ducts of the empty upper cabin as he passed through there. From the cockpit something peculiar could be seen happening within the starboard outer engine: the giant Rolls Royce RB211 was illuminated as if a searchlight inside it was beaming out. The wing leading edge too seemed to be glowing with a magnesium white light. Also noticeable now was an acrid smell as if electrics had fused some-where. The cabin crew suspected the common problem of a cigarette smouldering somewhere. They were calmly walking the aisles and peeking into the lavatories. At 20.40 the suspicion that something was wrong was confirmed by Flight Engineer Barry Townley-Freeman: he saw the 'valve closed' indicator for the pneumatic supply from number four – the star-board outer – engine flicker as he was about to start the air conditioning smoke drill. The engine surged and then flamed out.

'Fire action number four,' Moody called out. With the practice of simu-lator drills he flicked through the procedure: throttle closed, fuel off, fire extinguisher handle pulled to arm the bottles, but the final step of discharging it was not taken.

A child was looking out over the port wing. Curious lighting effects were happening around the inner engine on that side, too. 'Dad, the engine's on fire!' he said. His father looked, then closed the blind.

But others had heard. There is always someone quick to panic. 'Oh God, we're on fire!' a woman screamed. The exhaust from the inner port engine was a vivid pink. The cabin crew began to stow loose items, walking slowly, not to panic the passengers. 'We're going to die!'

Number two engine surged seconds after the cockpit crew had completed the drill for number four. Then the impossible happened: before the drill could be repeated for number two, engines one and three surged and flamed out. *City of Edinburgh* became a 300 tonne (ton) glider!

At 20.44 Moody declared 'Mayday' to Jakarta Air Traffic Control on 120.9MHz. 'Speedbird 9, lost four, out of 370.'

The incredible response from Jakarta was: 'Speedbird 9, have you got a problem?' It seemed that Jakarta either did not understand (the language barrier again) or could not hear properly. However, flying lower but not far distant was Garuda Indonesian Airways Flight GA875. The crew of that service could relay the 'Mayday' clearly to Jakarta.

Townley-Freeman was doing his 'loss of all generators drill', reducing the required electrical loading as much as possible – the batteries would be needed to attempt to re-ignite the engines. Unpowered, the aircraft would descend at 600m (2,000ft) per minute. She would have 23 minutes to fly, a ground distance of 224km (140 miles). Moody maintained the southerly heading for the moment, whistling almost silently over the Indian Ocean and leaving the 3,450m (11,500ft) high peaks of Java behind.

Crackling through unexpected 'static' came a request from Jakarta Air Traffic Control: 'Speedbird 9: radar cannot see you. Squawk Alpha 7700.' But hitting the button to transmit the international distress code had been one of the first actions of the crew! Their second priority was of course to re-light those engines. For there to be any hope of this the aircraft had to be travelling at 250–70 knots. Now a discrepancy in the airspeed indicators was noticed: Greaves' reading 320, Moody's 270. Moody began to nose the 747 up and down to vary the airspeed.

Back in the passenger cabin the lights were flickering. Not everyone realised that all the engines had stopped. Particularly in the front of the 747, some people slept through the entire incident. Others panicked. A stewardess told a nervous passenger who enquired what the problem was: 'When you see the flight crew heading for the rear carrying parachutes you'll know we've got problems!'

Others wrote last messages to loved ones. Strangers held hands, sometimes unable to speak to one another through language barriers. Generally they were calm, soothed by an experienced crew. This was one of those times when a brave cabin staff, themselves aware of the danger, remained calm and poised.

There was now less air coming into that cabin than was leaking out; the cabin pressure altitude equivalent was climbing. As the Boeing dropped through 6,000m (20,000ft) the flight deck pressure warning horn blared. The crew donned their oxygen masks; Moody pushed the nose forward to increase the rate of descent to 2,100m (7,000ft) per minute, and turned back towards land.

Jakarta was barely able to contact *City of Edinburgh* and still could not see her on their radar scope. They were trying to pass signals via Singapore Airlines Flight 27 now, without success. Then the Boeing descended through 5,400m (18,000ft), raising the cabin pressure as it did so. The oxygen masks dropped from the ceiling. In the strength of desperation one passenger pulled a yellow mask completely from its mounting! The cabin crew gathered their portable masks and toured the cabins to assist the passengers. With the 747 falling rapidly, the oxygen supply would shortly shut down anyway as the inside and outside pressure equalised at lower altitudes.

When *City of Edinburgh* came down another 600m (2,000ft), Moody told his fellow pilots that at 3,600m (12,000ft) he would turn back out to sea to attempt a ditching. Meanwhile the Chief Cabin Service Officer was confused. Moody had tried to phone him but this was not working. The captain instead used the public address system: 'Ladies and gentlemen, this is your captain speaking. We have a small problem, all four engines have stopped. We are doing our best to get them going again. I trust that you are not in too much distress.' Not everyone in the passenger cabin heard the further announcement, 'Will the Chief Cabin Steward report to the flight deck.'

The CSO climbed the spiral stairs to the top deck and entered the cockpit. There he saw frantic attempts being made by Townley-Freeman to re-ignite the RB211s. Time and time again the switches were re-set and the igniters pressed, without success. Through his oxygen mask Moody shouted his intentions to the CSO who did not hear clearly. Seeing the frantic efforts being made to re-ignite the engines the CSO withdrew without clearly understanding. On his way back down the staircase he decided that he would tell the cabin crew to inform the passengers that they were trying to bring the aircraft in for a landing at Jakarta, but to be prepared for a ditching if that could not be reached.

Life jackets were donned at this news. Some even inflated the vests. They thought of being trapped, drowning in the hull as it slipped beneath the ocean. The fears of others were that they would be eaten by sharks. Some prayed, some cursed. Then, at 4,050m (13,500ft) in a descent of 90m (300ft) per minute the starboard outer engine restarted. The pilot's cry of joy was tempered by the realisation that this was not quite enough to power them for a safe landing. The rate of descent could be checked, though. A minute and a half later number two the port inner, also flamed into life again. Now the 747 could level off at 3,600m (12,000ft). Within seconds the other two engines burst into song again. Moody eased back on the column and pointed the aircraft's nose up again, climbing to 4,500m (15,000ft). One staunch Roman Catholic claimed that she had seen the Holy Trinity repairing one of the engines.

Jakarta could suddenly see the 'jumbo' on radar again as if the aircraft had suddenly revealed itself from behind mountains. Moody now steered her towards Jakarta. Just as all seemed well again the St Elmo's Fire effect flickered around the cockpit windows once more and number two engine flamed out again. Although the cause was a mystery, the pilots knew now that this strange pyrotechnic display was related to the engines' failures. Moody pointed the nose down again to 3,600m (12,000ft).

Jakarta is one of those airports that would earn a black mark in most pilots' safety books; one not to have a crash at, the kind of place where air traffic controllers tend to be unwilling to take responsibility, runway lighting may be faulty and emergency procedures virtually non-existent. Flight 009 was informed that the glide slope path was unserviceable as it tracked towards land. Swooping in for landing Moody and Greaves noticed that something peculiar had happened to the windscreens: they were clouded so that it was like looking forward into fog as they swooped towards the runway, massaging the controls so that they could see the correct red-over-white formation of runway lights. Both airspeed indicators were now reading the same.

The landing was smooth but hardly silent: British Airways' crockery bill increased as the things which had been hastily stowed by cabin staff at the beginning of the crisis broke.

The emergency evacuation that the cabin crew had been primed for was unnecessary as the 747 sat at the end of the runway, Moody calling for a 'Follow Me' van owing to the semi-opaque cockpit windows. It was some time before an exasperated Moody could make the tower operator understand that it was unsafe to taxi.

The 747 was finally guided to the ramp, and most of the passengers were coached away to hotels for the night (though a few nationalities the Indonesians were not on diplomatic terms with were forced to spend an uncomfortable time in a humid and dirty terminal). The crew were at last able to examine *City of Edinburgh*.

They found a fine layer of black ash on the floor and ledges of the interior. And not only were the cockpit windows semi-opaque as if they had been scoured by grit but so were the landing lights on the wing leading edges. It was Townley-Freeman who first voiced what was in fact the truth 'That's volcanic ash!'

Indeed it was. The annoyed spirit of Raja Galunggung had nearly wreaked his revenge on one of man's most modern and sophisticated machines. Explained, too, was the difficulty of contacting Jakarta and the disappearance of the aircraft from radar. The ash that had been blown up to 16km (ten miles) high and into which the airliner had unwittingly been flown had veiled it. Although the eruption had been photographed by weather satellites no one had thought to warn aircraft of the possible danger of flying into the choking particles. An airliner's weather radar is tuned to reflect off water droplets, not dry particles such as ash, so could not warn of the volcanic dust.

Nineteen days after the events of Flight 009 they were repeated when a Singapore Airlines Boeing 747 flew into ash that was still circulating in the atmosphere and suffered the failure of three engines. It, too, landed safely at Jakarta.

City of Edinburgh remains in the British Airways fleet. To crews she has been dubbed 'the flying ash tray'.

So well known in aviation circles are the events of the Mount Galunggung eruption that we could reasonably expect that there could never be a repetition. How wrong we would be. Early in December 1989 Mount Redoubt in Alaska erupted. This time, the satellite images were indeed observed and the air corridors were closed for one week. On 15 December these were re-opened, just in time to allow a Dutch KLM flight from Amsterdam to Tokyo via Anchorage to wing through those far-northern skies.

But just one hour before the almost-new Boeing 747-400 arrived in the area the mountain erupted again, throwing dust and ash high into the stratosphere. At ten minutes before midnight, as the airliner was descending through 31,000 feet, the giant turbofans sucked in the fine particles and were choked. The flameouts came almost simultaneously. Just like Moody before him, Captain Karel van der Elst was flying a 300+ ton glider. She nosed down towards the icy sea. Down to 13,000 feet she plummeted before two engines relit, another 7,000 feet was lost before the others came to life again. The ash-scoured Boeing landed safely at Anchorage.

In British public houses, shops and newspaper columns talk was still centred around the Lockerbie disaster as 1988 ended. In the post-holiday hangover period airports were crowded with holidaymakers arriving home or departing from the British Isles. Amidst partings to friends and relatives, it was a subdued and quiet throng who gathered at Heathrow's Terminal One and checked in at the British Midland Airways desk for Flight BD092 to Belfast on Sunday 8 January 1989. For many people, the next day would be the first day back at work after the extended holiday.

Armed police and plain-clothes Special Branch officers mingled with passengers to the strife-torn Northern Irish city.

Outside, bathed in floodlights, their aircraft was being inspected and prepared for its seventh flight that day. The Boeing 737 was now the most popular airliner of all time. For a quarter of a century airlines have built up fleets of them. This is not to say that the type is obsolescent. While the 737 incorporates many parts that go back to the Boeing KC135/707 of the 1950s, a policy of standardisation that has been the key to Boeing's dominance, it has been constantly updated during that time. In 1988 the 737-400 series was introduced with computerised cockpit instrument layout and a radical change in external appearance: the engine cowling had become almost triangular in shape to incorporate the General Electric designed, French-manufactured CFM56-3C engines. These 10-tonne (ton) turbofans were much larger than the JT8D fitted to the British Airtours Manchester disaster aircraft, and without the cowling modification could not have fitted between the underside of the wing and the ground.

It was 19.52, nearly half an hour late, when Flight BD092 took to the air. The passenger cabin still smelled new. This aircraft had logged a mere 518 hours; just over one more should see the 118 passengers safely in Belfast. Captain Kevin Hunt took her over Slough at 1,800m (6,000ft) then turned north/north-west, climbing to 9,300m (31,000ft) on a course parallel to but often some thirty kilometres (twenty miles) west of the country's principal motorway, the M1.

Pork salad was being served high above the mid-shires of England just after 20.00 when passengers noticed smoke seeping into the cabin through the air conditioning ducts. Some later claimed that sparks were seen coming from the port engine at that time. However, that engine was not worrying Captain Hunt just then – the starboard one was. He reported severe vibration to air traffic control and then contacted British Midland's operations centre based at the East Midlands Airport, Castle Donington, between Leicester and Nottingham.

Few passengers had started their meals when Hunt switched on the intercom to tell passengers that the starboard engine had failed and that he had shut it down. To passengers it was described as a 'precautionary landing' at East Midlands Airport; to the crew and air traffic control it was an emergency landing. There should be no problems, as the chances of both engines failing on the same flight are millions to one, and the 737-400 was capable of taking off and landing on the power of one engine alone. Cabin staff collected the meals, moving with proficient calmness, reassuring passengers.

Leaving 900m (30,000ft) at 20.15, Hunt swung the crippled jet to starboard to circle the city of Nottingham before approaching the East Midlands Airport from the east. Two other airliners approaching the airport were turned away.

At approximately 390m (1,300ft), as the undercarriage was lowered, the almost impossible happened: when the port throttle was pushed forward for a little more power to counteract the drag of wheels and flaps there was nothing there. It was 20.25, the runway lights were clearly in sight straight ahead. But the gleaming new Boeing did not have the power to reach them. It skimmed low over the village of Kegworth where villagers were used to the sound of airliners on their landing approach. Few were roused from their homes as the Boeing swooped over.

However, watchers outside on that slightly misty night had their eyes drawn to the sky by a streak of red: the port engine, the only engine, was on fire. Just the M1 motorway lay between the village and the runway of the East Midlands Airport. If Captain Hunt could just extend the glide by a few hundred metres (yards) the Boeing could settle down on the runway threshold and rumble along to where the fire tenders were waiting.

But dragged down by the hanging wheels and the very flaps that were keeping her aloft at slow speed, the law of physics dictated that the glide slope had to meet with the ground where the motorway slashed through the landscape. In the final seconds the port engine fire warning clanged. The mainwheels struck the central crash barrier and were torn off. Throwing up sparks the rear of the fuselage underside slammed on to the northbound carriageway. There was a grassy strip ahead and then a low embankment. It was into that that the front of the machine smashed at 240kph (150mph) as vehicles on the motorway skidded to a halt, remarkably without hitting either each other or wreckage (one newspaper report of a family whose car was very lightly damaged by hitting the wreckage is believed to be untrue).

The fuselage split and then telescoped, the tail section rearing up and almost somersaulting. Fuel spilled from the ruptured tanks; people ran over from their vehicles on the motorway, and the wail of emergency tenders cut through the darkness as they made their way towards the scene in response to the last panic-stricken message from Flight BD092: 'Now we've lost the other one!' Moments later the Boeing had disappeared from the radar scope, hidden by the side of the motorway cutting.

Some passengers remarkably staggered quite uninjured from the twisted wreckage. Others were pulled clear. One of the miracles of this disaster is that the massive quantities of fuel lying on the ground did not ignite. If this had happened the death toll could have been hundreds with would-be rescuers as well as passengers caught in the inferno.

The final death toll was forty-seven. Once again, as they had been just days before on the Scottish hillsides around Lockerbie, police, army and the Air Accidents Investigations Branch were picking up the pieces of a Boeing, and zipping corpses into plastic body-bags.

A distasteful aspect to this accident was that one day a leading British tabloid newspaper was hailing Captain Hunt as a hero who had tried to stretch the glide to the safety of the runway. The next day – after assuming that he had switched off the good engine by mistake – the same paper effectively accused him of being the cause of the disaster. Meanwhile the captain lay seriously injured in hospital.

There are precedents for a crew of a twin-engined aircraft turning off the wrong engine after a failure. Ironically, a British Midland BAC One-Eleven pilot once made that mistake taking off from Milan. Luckily, the twenty passengers all got out safely.

This trial by media was quashed by Donald Cooper of the AAIB, who announced that both engines 'may have suffered a related failure'. Meanwhile other Boeing 737-400s were being carefully checked before each flight and their wiring was being inspected. There was a possibility that fire warning circuits had been reversed. Soon the plane-makers were on trial. Some of Boeing's own workers claimed that in the rush to complete bulging order books quality control was being allowed to lapse; panels that had been dropped from cranes were being incorporated into airliners, and untrained staff were drilling holes inaccurately. A Boeing 767 of Japan Airlines was discovered to have crossed wiring so that a fire in one cargo hold would register in the cockpit as being in the other.

Investigation was later to reveal that indeed the crew *had* isolated the wrong engine, the ICAO Summary listing the errors as:

1) The combination of heavy engine vibration, noise, shuddering and associated smell of fire were outside their (the pilot and co-pilot) training experience.

2) They reacted to the initial engine problem in a way that was contrary to their training.

3) They did not assimilate the vibrations on the engine instrument display before they throttled back the number 2 engine.

4) As the number 2 engine was throttled back, the noise and shuddering associated with the surging of the number 1 engine ceased, persuading them that they had correctly identified the right engine.

5) They were not informed of the flames which had emanated from the number 1 engine which had been observed by many on board, including three cabin attendants in the aft cabin.

That the lower echelons of the media who had cried 'pilot error' were to be proved right does not excuse their lynch-mob attitude.

Before looking briefly at other incidents in the wake of the Kegworth crash the implications for future safety arising from this incident should be addressed.

The Kegworth crash was a survivable accident, yet it took a heavy toll of life even though fire was not involved. Criticism was directed towards the aircraft seats. Forty years ago an airliner's seats would be bolted to the floor (as indeed pilot's seats still are), but today airlines want to change their cabin layouts even during turn-rounds. Seats now drop into rails and locking lugs secure them in place. At Kegworth the seats were torn from the rails and squashed together, crushing passengers. Passengers are now usually stronger than the seats: the human body can withstand a momentary force of 30g, yet a seat may be ripped from its rails at just 9g. There was also a call for seats to be rear-facing, a policy adopted by the Royal Air Force's Transport Command. Most of the survivors in the Manchester United football team's crash at Munich were seated in rear-facing seats that were secured to the floor. If this policy was to be adopted the seat backs would have to be a little higher, but the weight penalty would be minimal. However, would passengers accept rear-facing seats? Many are used to this for rail travel, but might find it rather uncomfortable being tipped forward while the aircraft is taking off at 320kph (200mph).

One valuable improvement to passenger security during emergency landings might be the addition of a diagonal strap to the seat belts, a modification most people would readily accept from familiarity with car travel. Another suggestion was that a video camera with a wide-angle lens should be mounted high on the tail fin of airliners to allow the crew to see what is invisible from the cockpit. If indeed sparks were streaking from the port engine early on the flight of BD092 perhaps Hunt would have diverted to Luton Airport (approximately sixty kilometres – forty miles – north of London) before total failure. The DC-10 incident at Chicago, and the Boeing 727 of Piedmont Airlines that lost an engine on take off there within days of the Kegworth disaster, are just two other incidents where such a fitting may have averted disaster or fed valuable information to the crew. Video camera fitting was one of the recommendations in the AAIB report into the Boeing 737 fire at Manchester Airport.

By June 1989 five British airlines were operating a total of twelve Boeing 737-400s. Surely it could not be coincidence, but had to be a design fault, when on another Sunday evening, on 10 June, the same British Midland Airways service to Belfast had to divert to East Midlands Airport. There had been what sounded like a loud crack and then severe vibration was set up in the starboard engine of the destroyed aircraft's twin. This time the emergency landing was successful. A broken fan blade was sent to the AAIB.

Meanwhile a Dan-Air 737-400 had suffered a similar failure. The Civil Aviation Authority cried 'enough'. The twelve aircraft of the type flying under British registry were grounded from 12 June 1989. In the United States, however, the type was to remain in the air subject to the fan blades and turbine discs being replaced and the maximum power limited. It was thought possible that the problem lay with engine vibration when subject to maximum thrust. Restricting the total power effectively converted it to a CFM56-3B-2 engine as used in Boeing 737-300s.

On 17 June Christopher Tugendhat, the Chairman of the Civil Aviation Authority, condemned the Federal Aviation Administration's refusal to join in the grounding decision. 'Three engine incidents have occurred after a very limited exposure. We are worried about an incident involving the failure of two engines on one plane,' Tugendhat commented. That very day a Britannia Airways Boeing 737-300 charter flight carrying 150 holidaymakers from Manchester to Corfu had to divert to East Midlands

Airport when the instrument panel warned of vibration on both CFM56-3B-2 engines.

Some airlines have fought for many years to get permission to fly scheduled twin-engined trans-ocean flights (considered to be more than 120 minutes flying time from the nearest airport). Permission had always been refused until 1 February 1985, when T.W.A. inaugurated Boston–Paris service with a Boeing 767, under a special 75-minute-to-alternate exemption from the Federal Aviation Administration.

5
Ice and Tempest

The most powerful force on earth is the weather. It makes our most powerful nuclear weapons seem little more than toys; it can flatten cities not just with the storm of its winds but also with its ability to suck seas into tidal waves. We have all heard of 'air pockets', but in fact these do not exist. The expression was probably originally the invention of a pulp-fiction author and somehow it has entered the vocabulary of the layman. It is also a convenient term for aircrew to use when trying to explain a bumpy flight!

The meteorological phenomena that aircrew learn to ignore at their peril are such fickle tricks of nature as pressure gradients, jetstreams and turbulence that can tear the most carefully designed and strongest of Man's flying machines to pieces.

Even close to the ground nature's cauldron can mix up a sudden witches' brew of destruction. The phenomenon of wind shear is one of her most potent fickle mixes. This is a sudden change in wind speed or direction that is usually allied to a blast of air, termed a micro-burst, which most commonly occurs in the middle of a thunderstorm. Here, the wind can blow straight down out of low-level cloud, so that when the pressure wave strikes the ground it spreads out in all directions, producing severe buffeting as air streams fight each other. A pilot in such conditions may experience a strong headwind as he flies into the storm, followed by an almost instant change to tailwind. His machine's speed over the ground in such conditions is meaningless; it is the speed of the air over his wings that is crucial. If this airspeed is below the aircraft's stalling speed as the pressure of the wind shear overcomes the prevailing wind and the airflow, then the aircraft will crash if there is insufficient height to recover from the resulting stall. It is also possible for an aircraft to literally be swatted to earth like a fly should a downdraught of wind shear strike it directly from above.

There is a roll of honour of the war dead in London's Westminster Abbey. Inscribed upon it are the names of forty-five men, women and children killed when a four-engined B-24 Liberator bomber of the US Army Air Force plunged down on to the village of Freckleton in Lancashire during a thunderstorm on the morning of 23 August 1944. It is believed that this warplane was forced down by wind shear, almost as if it were struck by a giant invisible hand.

Great Britain may have been an island under siege during World War II, but the aircraft that flew from these shores did not always do so without objections from those living beneath the flight paths. It is not just residents living near the runways of modern airports that complain to their political representatives of noise and danger. Such wartime complaints were not always without foundation. Combat aircraft were flying often overladen, and with inexperienced crews, sometimes in weather conditions that would have seen traffic grounded in peacetime. Bombers used to spin to earth shortly after take off, and young men were horribly injured and maimed in crippled machines that crashed in flames before pilots found the safe sanctuary of an airfield. Naturally, many of these crashes killed and injured civilians, too. Freckleton was the worst such incident in those terrible years.

It is a small village in England's north-west. It would have seemed very distant from the war, but for the presence of circling aircraft from the US Army Air Force's huge Air Depot 2 at nearby Warton. This was not the base of an operational squadron, but a store and repair complex to service the air force.

B-24H 50291 had already seen action with the 490th Bomb Group. She had visited Warton for a complete refurbishment and at 10.30 that morning was ready for an air test before being handed over to the 2nd Combat Division for further operations.

Even as test pilot First-Lieutenant John Bloemendal taxied the high-winged bomber out for take off, one of the short but violent storms characteristic of an English summer was sweeping its way across Lancashire. He took off less than five minutes before the storm warning was telephoned to Warton. She flew in company with another Liberator piloted by First-Lieutenant Peter Manaserro. As they circled the gently undulating countryside the pilots saw the great solid mass of cloud sweeping towards Warton. There was thunder and lightning in that boiling mass. Lightning is one of the weather phenomena most feared by pilots. It can rip great holes in the thin shells of an aircraft's structure, and then wreak havoc with the complex electrical wiring inside or even ignite the volatile fuel sloshing in the tanks.

The two Liberators flew back towards Warton, but when they reached the airfield the storm was at its height there. Both B-24s radioed that they were going to circle away to the north to await the weather's clearing.

Meanwhile the rain began to beat down on the little village of Freckleton. In Trinity School teacher Jenny Hall, who had begun work there only the day before, tried to recapture the attention of the thirty-eight children in her class as their eyes were drawn to the blackened sky where thunder and lightning railed. Out in the winding High Street civilians, RAF and American personnel scuttled to the warm glow of the Sad Sack cafe for shelter. The downpour was so heavy, witnesses later recalled, that it was impossible to see across the road. The wind ripped up young trees and smashed hen houses on a nearby farm. The fury of the storm drowned the roar of 50291's four Pratt and Whitney engines as she climbed away from Warton. Then, just as she crossed the heart of Freckleton, the wind shear caught her and flung her down on the village.

The aircraft totally destroyed the Sad Sack, and scythed across the road into Jenny Hall's infant classroom. Petrol from the smashed fuel tanks instantly burst into flame, running down the narrow street.

Horror-stricken villagers, many of them parents of children inside the school, with American personnel from Warton and the civilian fire service fought the flames and tore at the wreckage. Only three children were pulled alive from the rubble of the classroom; thirty-five others, Jenny Hall and another teacher perished. From the Sad Sack they pulled corpses of four RAF and six American personnel, along with several civilians. John Bloemendal, his co-pilot and flight engineer also died.

The majority of the civilian victims, including the children, were buried together in a communal grave in Freckleton's Trinity churchyard. Today a brass plaque in a large block of concrete, forming the centrepiece of an ornamental garden in a memorial playground built by American personnel, commemorates the victims of the worst air accident during the last war to involve civilians. A memorial fund established by the village's Parish Council was mishandled; some factions wanting the funds to be used for a new school, others favouring a memorial hall for the community's use. The bitter wrangle was not resolved until the mid-1970s when the trustees finally donated the money towards a community centre, a new school already having been built by the County Council. Inflation over thirty years had devalued the money so that it only provided a tenth of the £60,000 cost of the centre when it was opened in 1977. By then Warton airfield and its bombers were just a fading memory from a distant war.

The wartime Liberator was viewed in its time as a giant aircraft, although compared to the contemporary Lockheed L-1011 TriStar it would seem almost puny. Each of the three engines of Lockheed's wide-bodied airliner has almost the combined power of the engines of a Liberator. Yet nature is still more forceful than these giants of modern technology, and the Lockheed TriStar must obey the same laws of physics as the obsolete Liberator. One of these powerful aircraft was apparently destroyed in just the same way as that B-24 at Freckleton.

An L-1011 of Delta Air Lines was approaching Dallas-Fort Worth Airport through the midst of a storm on 2 August 1985. Incredibly, and fatally, they had elected to make their approach through cumulonimbus cloud that they did not know harnessed lightning. The pilot was probably staring out past slapping windscreen wipers for the first glimpse of the runway while the co-pilot checked the glide slope and scanned the gauges. Below, cars swept through the rain lashing down on a highway. In the blackness of the storm few drivers saw the glow of the aircraft's lights until the last moment; they probably heard the roar of her engines first.

The airliner's passengers were strapped in, some surely wishing that they could get down out of this turbulence, the less nervous possibly thinking about their business after the imminent landing. Suddenly the

wide-bodied jet plunged down. Perhaps a few had time to think that this
was one of the air pockets that they had heard of before oblivion came to
them.

The huge airliner crashed on to the highway 1,800m (6,000ft) short of
the runway, striking two cars, shrugging them aside like children's toys,
and killing one driver. In that moment she became a fireball as the fuselage slammed into a water tower. The tail section complete with the last
ten rows of seats sheared off. Three stewardesses and twenty-six passengers
here survived, crawling away or being pulled from the mangled wreckage
clear of the flames by drivers who had skidded their vehicles to a halt.

The death toll in this accident totalled 135, two more than the number
that perished when a Boeing 727 of All Nippon Airways on a flight from
Sapporo crashed into the sea approaching Tokyo International Airport in
March 1966. At that time it was the worst-ever air accident and one that
was never explained. The almost new, three-engined Boeing was seen by
witnesses on ships in Tokyo Bay approaching the airport and was just
minutes from landing when it plunged in flames to the sea.

By 1985 a death toll of such a high figure was accepted by the public as
normal; after all, aircraft now were capable of carrying five hundred
persons. What the public would not accept were frequent disasters with
such a heavy toll of life. 1985 was one of the worst years. A Boeing 747 of
Air India had already been destroyed off the Irish coast by a bomb planted
on board (see Chapter 9), and just eight days after the loss of the Delta Air
Lines TriStar a Japan Air Lines 747 crashed near Mount Fuji (see Chapter
3). The total death toll for 1966 had exceeded four hundred passengers.
In terms of distances/passengers flown, however, the two years were
comparable; in fact 1985 can be seen as a better year, in that the statistics
were distorted by the death toll of 349 on board the Air India jet who were
murdered through a bomb on board, hardly a case of culpability by the
manufacturer.

1966 and Mount Fuji featured in another accident. Brief storms, such as
those that apparently destroyed the B-24 over Freckleton and the TriStar
near Dallas, are sometimes experienced; hurricanes may raze towns and
villages; droughts may bring starvation; floods might bring devastation;
but generally the wind is no more than a gentle breeze. It is hard to believe
that the sky holds jetstreams and conflicting air currents that can whip up
a maelstrom of turbulence strong enough to twist and tear an airliner to
destruction.

Such a fate befell British Overseas Airways Corporation Flight BA911
from Tokyo to Hong Kong on 3 March 1966, killing all 11 crew and 113
passengers. The Boeing 707 had taken off at 13.58 flying, rather incredibly
at such a late date, under Visual Flight Rules. The 3,700m (12,400ft) peak
of Mount Fuji was clear of cloud, an ominous warning if only the pilots
had known it. Passengers would have been crowding to the starboard side,
staring through the windows there to the snow-capped volcanic peak

sliding past and looming above them. Some would have been taking photographs, blessing their luck that for once the peak was not veiled by cloud. At least one passenger was using a cine camera – the film survived, ending in a whirl of carpet as the Boeing disintegrated.

Atsugi Tower had heard nothing from the airliner after the Boeing had radioed climbing through 600m (2,000ft). Air Traffic Control kept calling, but the airwaves were silent. However, near Mount Fuji there were witnesses to the fate of Flight BA911 who saw the pieces of an aircraft, trailing what they thought was smoke, tumbling from the sky.

Search planes soon found the wreckage 88km (55 miles) west of Tokyo and on the south-east side of the mountain. This was one of the earliest accidents where flight recorders helped establish a cause of disaster that might otherwise have remained unsolved or with conclusions that were unproven. In this instance it might have been supposed that there had been a catastrophic structural failure. Indeed, the aircraft did break up, but it was not through design weakness. The Boeing was twisted apart by the very air through which she flew.

At between 4,200 and 5,400m (14,000 and 18,000ft) the giant royal blue fin had broken away after first being twisted violently to port and crumpling down to strike the tailplane on that side. The tailplane's main spar had then fractured to allow the starboard tailplane to shear off. Such damage as this was sufficient to throw the airliner out of control, but she was to be torn further apart before plunging to earth. As the tailfin had broken away the airliner was swung to port. The five hundred knot airflow now hammered against her starboard side while the engine pylons were quite unable to withstand this sudden strain and, led by number four, the starboard outer, the engines quite simply broke away. In the same moment the forward section of the fuselage sheared off, while simultaneously the starboard wing twisted upwards and snapped as if it were a mere twig. All these events happened in less time than it takes to read this account.

In broken pieces the airliner plunged to earth, trailing not smoke, as the eyewitnesses had not unnaturally assumed, but fuel vapour. Only the forward section of the fuselage caught fire and that was as a result of impact. The cause was determined to have been clear air turbulence; the wind whipping over the crater of Mount Fuji had been compressed into pressure waves strong enough to pound any aircraft to pieces.

Conditions near Mount Fuji that day are known exactly, for one pilot at least was to encounter the invisible storm and live to tell the tale. Walt Fink was the pilot of a US Navy Douglas A4 Skyhawk requested by Atsugi Tower to search for the missing Boeing. This is his description of how his nimble jet fighter was affected:

I soon discovered why the 707 went down. It had run into severe clear air turbulence at a low altitude and, from what the later reports said, it broke up in mid-air. I flew into the same turbulence and truly thought the airplane was going to come unglued. My oxygen mask was pulled loose on one side, my head was banging off both sides of the canopy, the instrument panel was unreadable, and the controls were just about useless. Somehow I managed to get the nose pointed up more times than down and eventually climbed out of the turbulence. When I got back to Atsugi the A4 had registered plus 9 and minus 4 G's. Needless to say, it was grounded for inspection, but good old Douglas engineering came through without a hitch.

That buffeting felt by passengers as their jetliner soars above the Rocky Mountains or the Alps, that sensation of riding a rocky road, bounding from bump to bump, the reassuring voice of the captain on the intercom and the 'fasten seat belts' sign flashing on, that is probably clear air turbulence. It is mostly encountered in the lee of mountains, caused by the very peaks that the air streams over. Pilots learn when and where they are most likely to encounter this invisible killer; yet their best protection from it even today is a report from another aircraft that has already flown through such conditions – and survived to tell the tale.

We have already seen how the build-up of ice on the wings of an aircraft can deprive it of lift so that it fails to become airborne or is dragged down shortly after take off. But ice on the flying surfaces is not just a problem before take off. Modern airliners operate at heights where the temperature is constantly below freezing. Cruising at 9,000m (30,000ft) the sky may be cerulean blue with brilliant sunlight, but no one could survive more than seconds in the temperature of that inviting scene, even if there were oxygen to sustain them. Icing may not in fact be a problem at such altitudes. Ice can only form where there is moisture. To reach this dry air, however, our aircraft may have to climb through cloud, where the killer ice may form and aerodynamic lift can be destroyed in seconds without a counter-measure to deter it.

On 5 January 1977 a Vickers Viscount of Falconair was approaching Stockholm's Bromma Airport when it abruptly pitched down into a vertical dive five kilometres (three miles) from the runway threshold. All twenty-two on board were killed instantly.

The investigation was conducted by the Flight Safety Section of the Swedish Aeronautical Research Institute, who concluded that the uncontrollable dive began at 345m (1,150ft) at the time when the flaps were pumped down from 32° to 40°, their maximum, during the landing approach.

The flight recorder trace suggested that there was a substantial accumulation of ice on the tailplane. This conclusion was reached by considering how the auto-pilot had been compensating for an apparent increased weight at the tail of the aircraft. This probable icing had built up because the anti-icing temperature was operating too low, partly owing to the reduced power for it being taken from numbers two and three engines – those inboard on each wing – if it was operating at all. The electrical switches of the system were discovered in the wreckage to be in the 'off' position.

Perhaps the pilots were not anticipating icing problems. No specific warning had been given about the risk of icing that day in the Stockholm area. They probably died believing that some catastrophic structural failure had occurred at the tail of their turboprop airliner.

It emerged during the investigation of this accident that contemporary British practice with Viscounts was to use no flap at all when icing was a possibility, compensating for this with a slightly higher landing speed. If this was considered safer practice by British European Airways which had been operating the type for almost thirty years, why had it not become universal practice?

There is no worldwide flight safety incident reporting procedure that can guarantee that airlines and flying crews are specifically informed of potential hazards and experience with particular types of machine unless there is a design fault. If an accident investigation reveals a defect in a type's design and construction this can, although as in the instance of the DC-10 rear cargo doors is not always, be corrected and all operators informed. Incidents due to causes other than design or manufacturing faults however are bound in the International Civil Airline Operator's Accident Summary, and it is then usually the prerogative of airlines to memorandum their crews, or for the aircrews themselves to read the reports (including details given in journals such as *Flight*) and absorb information that could save their lives.

As early as 1955 a similar incident had happened to a Vickers Viscount in America. The deaths of twenty-two people near Stockholm could have been avoided if the relevant information had percolated through to the Linjeflyg crew. There was an additional factor in this disaster, however: the anti-icing operating instructions in the airline's operations manual for the Viscount were incomplete, an error traced back to the British manufacturer's official flight manual. The villain of the Stockholm disaster will always be recalled as the killer ice that can creep so insidiously over flying surfaces, but in this instance it was assisted by faulty and missing information.

Wind and rain was sloughing over New York on 24 June 1975 as Eastern Air Lines Flight 66 came in over Rockaway Boulevard to land at Kennedy International Airport. The triple-engined Boeing 727 was carrying a crew of 8 and 116 passengers. Perhaps one of them glimpsed a flash of lightning seconds before the jetliner smashed on to the road, for this was the likely reason given for the cause of this disaster in which all but two crew and nine passengers died.

Lightning strikes on aircraft are in fact not at all unusual, and only rarely disastrous. They may have accounted for many unsolved disasters. Lightning may have even struck the B-24, that plunged on to Freckleton, and the Delta Air Lines TriStar near Dallas-Fort Worth. It will never be known. When investigators have pursued every likely clue in their search

for the cause of a mysterious crash and the only possibility left is that it was
flying through storm cloud at the time of the disaster, it will always be
tempting to record the possible cause as 'struck by lightning'.

On 8 December 1963 a Pan American Boeing 707 was cruising over
Elkton, Maryland when a lightning strike caused an explosion in the port
wing's outer fuel tanks. All eighty persons on board died as it crashed in
flames and out of control.

Modern meteorological forecasting and the development of weather
radar, both ground-based and as on-board aircraft equipment, have
enabled airliners to avoid most storms. However, light aircraft flying under
Visual Flight Rules still often fall foul of the elements. Over Great Britain
weather fronts from the Atlantic average a speed of 48kph (30mph) and
are 72km (45 miles) deep. It is easy for a weekend flier to take off into
clear weather then suddenly find himself or herself embroiled in a storm.
Many have died; many more have been severely frightened, learning the
hard way that any aircraft can seem puny when pitted against the might of
nature.

The thermals, updraughts and downdraughts of storms and weather
fronts can not only toss tiny Cessnas or vintage Tiger Moths around, but
even 'jumbo' jets, throwing them up and down and tearing them apart.
There are many tales of the flying pioneers feeling their way through
storms, blinded and lost, desperately seeking the light of a landing field.
Stories of storm-bound destruction, such as befell the *Shenandoah* and the
R101, are not associated with the modern jetliner. They carry weather
radar, they can detour around storms or even climb above them, and can
'home' in to sanctuary through the technical wizardry of radio and
beacons. Yet as recently as 4 April 1977 a modern, rugged and fully-
equipped airliner did meet its fate through a storm.

Southern Airways Flight 242 was a scheduled service from Muscle
Shoals, Alabama, to Atlanta, Georgia. It flew into a storm of such ferocity
that it was first incapacitated and then brought down. The twin-engined
Douglas DC-9 jetliner took off from an intermediate call at Huntsville,
Alabama at 15.50 Eastern Standard Time with just a twenty-five minute
'hop' to Hartsfield Airport, Atlanta, remaining. There were eighty-one
passengers and four crew on board.

Foul weather swept across the southern states that day; storms seemingly closing in like a coven of vengeful witches on this puny machine that
dared to intrude upon their domain. At 15.58 Memphis Centre, which
had taken over traffic control of Flight 242, broadcast an open message to
all aircraft in range: 'Hazardous weather in vicinity of Tennessee, southern
Louisiana, Mississippi, northern and western Alabama, and adjacent
coastal waters.'

By 16.00 the DC-9 was into such severe turbulence that the captain
elected to hand-fly the machine at the drastically reduced airspeed of 285
knots. Behind him the passengers were strapped in, being airsick,
resolving that if only they could survive this they would drive or take the

bus next time. Even the roar of the engines was drowned by the ululation of the storm. Hail beat on to the thin shell of the Douglas's fuselage, while lightning lanced through the early darkness. Then the cabin lights flickered and a few cried out in alarm. A generator had failed. It took half a minute for the co-pilot to tap power from the other generator, but even as he did so utter disaster was only moments away.

Just before 16.10 the windshield actually cracked, probably owing to being struck by gigantic hailstones. Almost in the same moment the tail-mounted port engine 'flamed out'. As the co-pilot reset the switches ready to press the igniters in the hope of bringing it to life again, the starboard engine, too, failed.

At 16.13, powerless, with the two pilots desperately trying to get the engines to fire again, the aircraft was 30km (20 miles) west of Dobbins Airport and descending in a bucking ride through 2,100m (7,000ft), the crew trying to stretch out the glide path for an emergency landing there.

But the battered DC-9, little more now than an overweight glider, was not to reach suitable land. The law of gravity that her engines had enabled her to disobey was now dragging her down on a glide path that fell far short of any runway. Still feverishly trying to get power back from at least one of the jets, the pilots stared through the cracked windscreen and the lashing rain for a clear space below where an emergency landing might just be possible.

The DC–9 swept out of the lowest layer of cloud above State Highway 92 which bisected New Hope, Georgia. Vehicles ploughed slowly through the rain and the spray, their headlights on. The DC-9 captain elected to try to land on that highway. Sweeping silently in, landing lights cutting a glowing swathe through the rain, the airliner attempted to touch down. A petrol station loomed ahead. It was impossible to avoid it.

The petrol station erupted in flames as the airliner ploughed through it. Now the DC-9 itself was in flames as it swept on, striking a truck and five cars as it began to break up, spilling out passengers and cargo. Drivers swerved aside as the blazing comet that moments before had been a sleek airliner screamed towards them.

Eventually the broken and twisted pieces of the DC-9 came to rest. Fire was everywhere. Screams came from the shattered fuselage and from crumpled vehicles. It was the kind of crash when survivors would not be expected, yet twenty-two passengers were pulled or crawled out of the wreckage, though one died later. One member of the cabin crew also survived, but eight road travellers were killed on the spot and another died later in hospital. Red hot metal hissed as it was slaked by the rain while emergency vehicles burst through the pandemonium to take away the dead and the injured.

Perhaps this accident was avoidable. It is easy in hindsight to say that the aircraft should not have taken off again from Huntsville until the weather had cleared. In the United States, though, the airliner is a normal mode of travel over the country's vast distances. All the airlines face massive competition from other operators. Just to financially survive they must, whenever possible, arrive at their destinations on time. To err too much on the side of caution may result in financial ruin.

Even had the passengers of Flight 242 been told just how serious were the storms closing in, how many of them would have left the aircraft and waited for a later flight in clearer weather? We do not expect the expensive technology of the modern airliner to be destroyed just by the weather. But it has happened many times before, and it is impossible to say that it will not happen again.

6
Beware the High Ground

In the early days of 1989 after the Lockerbie disaster the fiery fate of a 1968-built Boeing 707 of the Tennessee-based charter company Independent Air was not relayed as a major news story in Great Britain. On the afternoon of 8 February with 137 Italian passengers en route from Bergamo in Northern Italy to the Dominican Republic it was coming in for its refuelling halt at Santa Maria in the Azores, a single-runway airport that many years before had been the last glimpse of land for the passengers of another flight (see pp 144–146).

The airport is on the west coast of the island so that the track of the Boeing would bring it in to approach over land that reached up to 540m (1,800ft). Cloudbase that day was at 360m (1,200ft) with a further (broken) band at 150m (500ft). At 13.56 the co-pilot contacted Santa Maria tower reporting leaving Flight Level 200 (20,000ft) for Flight Level 40 (4,000). The controller radioed: 'You are cleared to 3,000ft.'

In the kind of language confusion we have witnessed at Los Rodeas the co-pilot read back: 'Re-cleared to 2,000ft.' The Boeing struck Pico Alto Mountain at 1,730ft. The passengers and seven crew perished instantly. Investigators later found the altitude alert warning (a radio altimeter) set for 2,000ft and the barometric pressure set at 1027; yet the latter should have been at 1018.7.

The contemporary fears of 'geriatric jets' and sabotage could be discounted. The story fell from the headlines; it was just another aircraft that had flown into a hill, a fate to befall nearly 700 machines since the last war. In any year collisions with high ground can account for up to ten per cent of disasters, usually with terminal effects to both aircraft and all on board. To a pilot height is safety – the greater the altitude the more time there is available to deal with any crises. Most high ground tragedies happen close to airports – and all too many airports are surrounded by high ground. In the event of an 'overshoot' – that is, an aborted landing – all aircraft must climb away to a specific height and heading relayed to them by air traffic controllers as they approach for landing.

Dirk Parmentier was one of the few pilots who was almost a legend among his peers (see pp. 35). As the Germans invaded Holland in 1940 Parmentier escaped from Schiphol Airport with a KLM aircraft and flew to

Britain. The summer of 1943 found him flying the perilous route between neutral Portugal and England with an unarmed DC-3. Over the Bay of Biscay his flight was 'jumped' in daylight by six Luftwaffe Junkers-Ju88 fighter-bombers. In a classic piece of airmanship Parmentier escaped. Six weeks later another unarmed DC-3 on the route was shot down. Among the dead was popular actor Leslie Howard.

Parmentier had amassed over 16,000 hours of flight time as 20 October 1948 found him revving up the four piston engines of KLM Constellation *Nijmegen* at Schiphol. At almost the last minute a consignment of freight for Iceland was loaded on to this New York bound flight, so that the silver airliner was an hour late as it lifted itself into the low cloud of the early autumn darkness. Prestwick on the Ayrshire coast of Scotland was a sched-uled halt before the long haul across the Atlantic, but should this be unap-proachable because of bad weather Shannon Airport in Eire was the alternative. *Nijmegen* carried enough fuel to fly to Shannon and return to Schiphol if a safe landing could not be made. Just after 21.00 Prestwick transmitted a warning that a cloud base of 80m (600ft) and rain were fore-cast for that airport by 23.00. *Nijmegen* was still on the ground at that time. The warning was not repeated, so as Parmentier overflew the rolling hills of the border country between England and Scotland, hills that in years to come would reverberate to the roar and destruction of Pan Am Flight 103 at Lockerbie, he expected poor, overcast conditions on the western coast of southern Scotland, but not severe weather that would force diversion.

Shortly before 23.00 First Officer Kevin O'Brian established contact: 'Prestwick Approach Control from Tare Easy Nan, do you read me? Over.' Now the Constellation just needed guiding down. 'Is GCA serviceable?'

Nijmegen would be guided in by radar, the ground operator reading off the height and distance from his cathode ray tube. 'GCA is set up on Runway 32. The runway in use is Runway 26. GCA can give you overshoot on Runway 32.' So the Ground Controlled Approach would bring the Constellation in over Runway 32 from where it should be possible to visually overshoot that main runway, over which a cross-wind of up to 32kph (20mph) was blowing, and perform a left-hand loop downwind on to the shorter Runway 26.

Parmentier was flying on the assumption that the cloud base was no less than 210m (700ft). When a morse radio signal was broadcast at 23.06 informing traffic that the cloud base was deteriorating, it was not received by the crew of *Nijmegen* who were now concentrating on voice radio. The only useful information they did get was that the wind on the main Runway 32 had dropped to below 32kph (20mph). Parmentier himself had always recommended that KLM pilots should accept a cross-wind of up to 24kph (15mph) on the main runway at Prestwick rather than looping around to Runway 26. He elected to attempt a landing on Runway 32, but with the clearance to overshoot to Runway 26 if he encountered gusts of wind that he considered would make the former strip hazardous.

The approach was made form the north-east, Parmentier's and O'Brian's eyes flicking from the instruments to the impenetrable cloud they were rushing through. Back in the passenger cabin thirty passengers fastened their seatbelts, noting the change in the engines' note. 'If you lost contact on this approach fly at 1,200m (4,000ft) and call Prestwick Approach Control,' the GCA operator instructed, a standard warning to ensure that the aircraft would climb safely away from the hills that surrounded the airport. 'I am advising you of a strong cross-wind from your left on this runway. Do not acknowledge any further instructions.'

Nijmegen and her fragile human cargo were at the mercy of the ground operator and his flickering screen. No more than thirty seconds would ever elapse between guidance from the ground. 'Heading 295. Three miles [five kilometres] to go.' The airliner was being pushed to starboard by the wind.

'Hello, controller, I shall overshoot on this approach and land on Runway 26.'

'Roger. The surface wind is 15mph [24kph]. Give me a check call when you are downwind for Runway 26.' In the van parked to the side of the main runway the controller could hear the roar of the airliner's engines now as it swooped down between those hills.

Through the cockpit windows the clouds parted like veils being drawn apart. There below was the main runway, its beckoning lights seeming to converge. Parmentier let *Nijmegen* descend until she was 60m (200ft) above the threshold of Runway 32 then gently tweaked the four throttle controls forward and applied port bank as he climbed away in the turn that should bring them back to approach Runway 26 from the west. 'I have overshoot. I am going to do a visual circuit for landing on Runway 26.' The airfield and its guiding lights should not disappear from view. Visibility was three kilometres (two miles), but there was slight drizzle. The lights of Runway 32 were switched off, those for Runway 26 on. It must have been at that moment that a cloud swept over the airfield, obliterating the lights. This can only be hypothesis; the certainty is that *Nijmegen* overflew the runway even as Parmentier and O'Brian gazed out of the port windows expectantly. Pushed now by a tail wind, every moment was taking *Nigmegen* towards high-tension electricity cables. O'Brian had a map of the Prestwick approaches balanced on his knee. The cables were shown on it, but had been incorrectly indicated as being at 13m (45ft), not their true 135m (450ft). It was only one error on an inaccurate map – the ground contours showed the maximum ground to be no more than 75m (250ft), not nearly 150m (500ft), as they really were. Parmentier had flown into Prestwick many times before, O'Brian sixteen times. Surely they were aware of those cables in their path. Or were they preoccupied with an emergency? Afterwards the crash investigation raised the possibility that the port inner engine had been shut down. Were the pilots diverted by having to deal with a fire in that engine? To shut it down, turn off the fuel supply, discharge its fire extinguisher and feather the propeller (turning its blades edge on to the slipstream to reduce drag) would take perhaps one minute, time enough for the Constellation to cover the distance to the lethal cables. Even now just a tug on the control column would nose her up enough to clear them.

No tug came. *Nigmegen* sliced through the three 132,000 volt cables. The lights of Prestwick Airport and in the villages around flickered. 'We have hit something!' Parmentier called. The fuel in the airliner's tanks ignited and the electrics fused. Yet she still flew, a fireball racing across the sky. 'We are climbing!'

Parmentier still had some degree of control over this burning mass. He tried to climb clear of low ground and turn back for an emergency landing. The GCA operator could see her: she was eight kilometres (five miles) east-north-east. The turn to port became uncontrollable, the Constellation turned a full circle over the village of Tarbolton, rousing the population from their beds. They watched aghast as the airliner reeled, a flaming torch, across the night sky.

'Have you any idea where we are?' Those were the last words from the doomed airliner before she ploughed into the hillside near isolated Auchinweet Farm. Medical aid did not reach that bleak spot for over ninety minutes. By then only six people were still alive. They all died during the next day. Ironically the fire did not totally destroy that inaccurate chart – the charring stopping just short of that inaccurate 13m (45ft) spot height.

Airlines produce their own maps for pilots' use. While no pilot can fly into an airport without first having completed a familiarisation trip as co-pilot first, there will often be times when he must rely on that aerial navigation map with its crucial ground height information displayed in both plan and horizontal elevation. It is vital that the information is accurate. Unlike many everyday maps where high ground is clearly shown by shading, the normal pilot's map only has a dot and a spot height marking. In the years since the *Nijmegen* disaster many airlines, but not all, have modified their maps to have a shading around treacherous high land. Such a simple thing can save lives.

Many sites on this earth have more than once witnessed the carnage and horror of air disasters. Parmentier's *Nijmegen* is not the only aircraft to have ploughed into the bleak hills near Prestwick. The most chilling coincidence happened just below the 4,810m (15,781ft) peak of Mont Blanc in the Alps, where two Air India airliners were lost. The first disaster befell a Constellation on 3 November 1950. Eight crew and forty passengers, all on board, perished instantly. Sixteen years later the growling 'Connies' (Constellations) had given way to the screaming Boeing 707s. On 24 January 1966 VT-DMN was making its approach to Geneva on the same track as its piston-engined ancestor. This would be the final halt before London's Heathrow for a service that had originated in Bombay. As the light of dawn glared off the jagged peaks Captain J. d'Souza called Geneva Air Traffic Control reporting the flight as being over Turin and estimating arrival over Mont Blanc summit at 07.02, the turning point for the final approach to Geneva. Clearance was given for this Flight 101 to descend to 6,000m (20,000ft). Minutes later, being buffeted in the mountain air, d'Souza reported that he was approaching 6,300m (21,000ft) and requested clearance to descend through cloud to 5,700 (19,000). It was 07.00 when he reported reaching that height. He was told to maintain it. 'I think we are passing abeam Mont Blanc now,' d'Souza radioed, but was he totally sure of his position? His arrival over Mont Blanc's summit should have been indicated by a cross-bearing from Lyon VOR beacon some 151 nautical km (82 nautical miles) distant. However, the terrain caused notorious reception difficulties. Was the signal lost that morning?

On his radar screen the air traffic controller could see the true position of the Boeing. 'You have eight kilometres (five miles) to Mont Blanc,' he warned.

'Roger,' d'Souza replied. But 'roger' to what? Did he understand the warning? Just moments later he radioed that he was leaving 5,700m (19,000ft) and descending. The horrified air traffic controller could only watch as the blip representing the Boeing and the 117 people on board became stationary and then slid backwards.

The impact was almost in the very same spot as the Constellation all those years before. Once again the shattered pieces of an airliner and its passengers rolled and tumbled down the ice-scoured mountain. The red-hot engines melted the snow, the meltwater dripping down while fire blazed as a beacon to disaster near the summit. The tragedy had been at 4,680m (15,585ft). Just another 60m (200ft) higher and she would have cleared the summit. Pieces of her must still lie up there now.

On 29 February 1964 a British Eagle Airways Bristol Britannia left Heathrow, London, with a scheduled flight to Innsbruck. It was flying at 3,600m (12,000ft) and descending towards its destination when contact was lost. The wreckage was not found until the next day. All seventy-four passengers and eight crew were dead, their pulped and burnt corpses strewn over the eastern flank of Glungezer Mountain only some 75m (250ft) from the summit.

The cause was never positively ascertained, though it is disturbing that the airliner should have been flying under Visual Flight Rules at such a late date. And there perhaps lies the key. It can only be conjecture, but perhaps the mountain was invisible to the pilot of the four-engined turboprop. A gleaming white snow-draped peak can become camouflaged against a similarly coloured sky to form a totally disorientating 'whiteout', a phenomenon known to pilots in the polar regions. US Air Force pilots flying from McMurdo Field in the Antarctic first had to fly in company with experienced colleagues to learn of such hidden perils.

The Antarctic is perhaps the last romantic wilderness on earth, a great glittering wasteland of ice-glazed mountains and creeping glaciers. It is a sobering truth that above this land Mankind's use of chloro-fluorocarbon gases has torn a hole in the ozone layer. The atmosphere on which all life depends is barely thicker than the coat of paint on a child's toy globe. On 28 November 1979 an Air New Zealand DC-10 swept over the ocean towards that breathtaking land. It came on a day's outing so its passengers could photograph the landscape then return home – non-stop airborne tourists.

But the 257 people on board that day met their deaths high up on the ice-covered slopes of the volcanic Mount Erebus. Little did they know their aircraft had been programmed for destruction eight hours before take off. The brain of the inertial navigation system computer was remorselessly, with its unerring accuracy, taking the aircraft to destruction as it screamed above the broad ice plain of McMurdo Sound.

This scenic tour had become a regular operation for Air New Zealand. A fortnight earlier Captain Simpson had taken command of the trip. Flying in clear weather he had disengaged the auto-pilot to swing his DC-10 manually over Victoria Land where the passengers could gasp at glaciers that had scoured the mountains for millions of years. He was some 48km (30 miles) west of the inertial navigation system track when controllers at the US Air Force McMurdo base gave him clearance to descend to 600m (2,000ft) and then fly visually across McMurdo Sound. Flying east he was surprised at the distance, expecting it to be just 16km (10 miles), but his distance measuring equipment recorded 43km (27 miles). Was there an error in the navigation programme loaded into the computer?

The following day Simpson phoned Captain Johnson, Air New Zealand's Flight Manager for their DC-8 and DC-10 fleet, and mentioned the possible anomaly. Johnson claimed after the disaster that his fellow pilot requested that the airline's navigation section should look at the position of the McMurdo waypoint. He alleged that he did not recall Simpson specifically mentioning a 48 nautical km (26 nautical mile) discrepancy. Johnson asked the navigation section to check the McMurdo position and report back.

Doomed Captain Jim Collins spent his last evening on earth poring over his airman's maps of the Antarctic with his teenage daughters. As he went to bed at 22.00, ten kilometres (six miles) away in Newton, a suburb of Central Auckland, lights were burning that Tuesday night as Air New Zealand updated the information in the company's central computer.

The superintendent of the navigation system, Laurence Lawton, and his chief navigator, Brian Hewitt, retrieved from the electronic brain what they believed was the current printout of the track south of McMurdo Sound and saw the final waypoint given as 77° 53'S, 166° 48'E. However, this was not the current flight path, but one last used fourteen months before. These men were unaware that fourteen months previously the operator had punched a '4' instead of a '6' (48'E instead of 68'E). This was technically an error, but it had not been noticed as fortuitously it had diverted the airliners safely over McMurdo Sound. Now Lawton and Hewitt looked at the flight plan used in the eighteen months before the airline had instituted computerisation. The final waypoint given then was taken from the intersection of two runways on the US Air Force's Williams Field, an ice-strip used by ski-fitted aircraft. This waypoint would give a direct track that passed over Mount Erebus. They also noted that the Americans had corrected this position by 10' or 3.9 nautical km (2.1 nautical miles). The earth's magnetic field is in constant flux.

Hewitt and Lawson decided to make the final waypoint the nearby USAF TACAN (Tactical Air Navigation Station) military aid, a beacon Air New Zealand's DC-10 could 'home' to. This new position would be at 166° 58'E. This was printed on to Collins' flight plan as he slept. In the morning he would programme that, and his own death, into the INS computers of his aircraft. A resumé of the catalogue of errors is as follows:

1 A silly error is made – the airline's navigation section routes flights over the 4,027m (13,211ft) high peak of volcanic Mount Erebus to Williams Field on the south side.

2 A typing error is made – the destination point thus moves 48 km (26 nautical miles) and functions well for fourteen months. Had this error not been made, any flight before the fatal one could have flown into the side of the volcano.

3 A message is garbled – a comment to advise checking of the Antarctic flight plan is taken as a mistake concerning the waypoint to be amended.

4 A mistake within a mistake is made – the earlier typing error is not noticed and a fatal shift takes place, routing aircraft over Mount Erebus.

Programmed for disaster, Jim Collins brought the sleek DC-10 down to 5,400m (18,000ft) as land approached. Visibility was estimated at 48km (30 miles). Over the ice continent an airspeed of 260 knots had to be maintained as this flying was performed 'clean' – that is, the flaps and slats must not be used because if they should fail to retract after low-speed flying their additional drag would burn up so much fuel that the long haul back to New Zealand would be impossible.

The majority of the passengers were New Zealanders, but there were also twenty-four Japanese, ten Americans, two Britons and an Australian. Many of them were making a final check of their cameras as Collins was trying to establish VHF radio contact with McMurdo base; but he didn't have any success. The signals were being blocked by the towering mass of Mount Erebus. Contact was briefly made once as the DC-10 circled to lose altitude, descending down to just 450m (1,500ft), the cockpit crew looking out for the huts of McMurdo Base. Below lay just the dazzling clear ice sheets of the frozen sea, yet land was rising up on both sides of the aircraft's path. Back in the passenger cabin shutters began to click. **See Map 5.**

'Actually these conditions don't look very good at all,' Collins commented. 'I'll have to climb out of this.' That was when the radar altimeter showed a sudden drop in altitude: 210m (700ft), then 150m (500ft). The terrain warning light blinked on and an electronic voice warned: 'Whoop! Whoop! Pull up! Pull up!'

'Go around power please,' Collins instructed. First Officer Greg Cassin pushed the throttle levers gently forward. We can only assume that the crew thought that it was a false warning, but they correctly acted as if doing an overshoot following an attempted landing approach with the undercarriage retracted.

Flight Engineer Brooks was calling off the ground clearance: 'Five hundred... four hundred...' The engines were spooling up. Collins palmed the control antlers back. Death was instant for all on board that airliner. Camera shutters clicked in the instant of their owners' deaths. Film that survived the impact and fire showed the pieces of disintegrating airliner and passengers splashed outside the cabin windows.

The two underwing engines struck first, tearing the wings off. The fuel tanks were ruptured. Sixty (tonnes) tons of fuel exploded in a fireball as the nose section, the top of the fuselage and the tail continued on, spinning and rolling, finally telescoping. The rear engine seared over the top of the fuselage panels, delivering power for some seconds before coming to rest ahead of the main wreckage. There was silence but for the crackle of flames.

Soon American helicopters came to begin the gruesome task of bringing the remains down from their 450m (1,500ft) high point of impact. The last body found was that of a stewardess lying in an icy hollow, her corpse almost unmarked as though she were asleep.

Tom Chippindale, the New Zealand Chief Inspector of Air Accidents, flew to the scene as the bodies were being hauled down the ice-glazed lava slopes. At first he put forward a theory of the DC-10 having been flying in cloud. This was quickly overturned when surviving exposed film was developed revealing clear air and glimpses of land. He amended his theory to 'flying towards cloud'.

Back in New Zealand Captain Gordon Vette and other shocked friends and colleagues of Jim Collins were unwilling to accept this 'pilot error' charge. With journalist John McDonald of the *Auckland Star*, Vette set out to prove otherwise. Meanwhile the widowed Marie Collins was being visited by senior management of Air New Zealand who, under the pretext of offering their condolences, tried to instil in her a belief that the accident had been her late husband's fault. Yet these people must have known within days that their navigation section had been in error. The homes of Vette and Collins were even burgled in an attempt to steal back incriminating documents. Vette was risking his own career to prove the truth.

The Royal Commission of Enquiry sat for seventy-five days under the Honourable P.T. Mahon QC. The judgement was that the main cause of the disaster was the personnel of Air New Zealand's Flight Operations Division altering the latitudinal and longitudinal co-ordinates of the destination point without the knowledge of the crew, failing to ensure that the pilot in command had previously flown the route under the guidance of another pilot, and failing to provide a topographical map on which the programmed flight path was displayed. Chippindale's final conclusion, delivered on 30 June 1980, also had some credence after his earlier false assertions: that Collins had been flying towards an area of poor surface and horizon; it was a 'whiteout', Mount Erebus invisible against the surrounding landscape. Air New Zealand was ordered to pay NZ $150,000 contribution towards the cost of the enquiry. Justice was done, but could not resurrect the 257 people who flew to their deaths in the cold wastes of a frozen continent.

7
The Crowded Sky

The sky seems so vast that it is almost inconceivable that two aircraft cruising in it could collide. How could two machines on different routes be in the same place at the same instant when there is so much space? It is often easier at night to appreciate how many aircraft are flying, when their winking lights can be seen. Occasionally these lights may be a shooting star, a minor pebble of space debris that is usually small enough to burn up as it enters the earth's atmosphere, or one of the many satellites – telecommunications, or space probes. These satellites eventually re-enter the earth's atmosphere. Like meteorites, they usually completely burn up, but some pieces get through to lower altitudes. There is no record of an aircraft having been struck by either a meteorite or a piece of falling space junk – yet.

If it seems incredible nowadays that aircraft can collide in mid-air, how much more unlikely it must have seemed in 1922. Yet that year, in the infancy of airline travel, two civilian planes collided over France. A Farman Goliath of Grands Express Aèriens and a de Havilland D.H.18 of Daimler Airways were cruising north of Paris. They were navigating by the usual rudimentary method of simply following a road – but in opposite directions and at the same height. They collided head-on and fell to earth in a burning tangle of fabric and wood. All seven on board the biplanes died. Now there is a rule to advise those using such basic navigation: 'When in flight, stay right.'

Just before World War II the problems of too many aircraft in too little sky were becoming apparent near American airfields as the pilots of DC-3s and other pioneering airliners were the first to experience the now so familiar 'stack' of aircraft waiting to land. No longer was it possible for a pilot to just glance around to check that there were no other aircraft on the circuit, turn into wind and then sideslip down to a grass strip.

By 1944 the Atlantic had been air-bridged. Less than twenty years had passed since the era of Lindbergh, Amelia Earhart and other pioneers, and now not only US Air Force bombers and transports were plying the route, but also the Boeing 314 Clipper flying boats of Pan American and British Overseas Airways Corporation. The latter could have been flying the route for civilian passengers, were it not for war. Clearly, there was going to be an explosion of civil airline travel soon.

Already, combat flying had shown that crowded skies seemed to attract aircraft to one another in a terrible kind of destructive magnetism. For

RAF machines the danger lay in the dark above enemy Europe as the bombers flew singly to their targets, converging there. The shadow that passed them by in the night could be a night-fighter, could be another bomber. Many saw no shadows, just felt the crunch as they struck. They died not knowing whether their machine was being raked by cannon shells or by impact with another aircraft, friend or foe. For the US Air Force the danger lay over eastern England as the mighty squadrons rose up from airbases all over that flat landscape to form groups before setting off for Europe, many never to return.

Representatives of fifty-two allied and neutral nations met in Chicago during 1944 to discuss the future of civil aviation. From this meeting, remembered to this day as the 'Chicago Convention', the International Civil Aviation Organisation was born to regulate and mediate between the commercial airlines of the world.

Great Britain was one of the original signatories of the Chicago Convention. As the war in Europe drew to its end Britain set about building its own organisation to control and regulate aviation. Initially the approach was cautious with no government keen to relinquish a tight hold. Until 1967 the control of air transport passed variously through the Ministry of Transport, the Ministry of Transport and Civil Aviation, the Board of Trade and the Department of Trade and Industry. For two years from 1967 a committee under Sir Ronald Edwards looked at the problem of regulation and recommended a Civil Aviation Authority. This new body was to bring under one umbrella the confused aviation functions of the Department of Trade and Industry, the Air Licensing Board and the Air Registration Board. It was also to undertake a positive role in the economic and safety regulations.

Full responsibility came to the Civil Aviation Authority in April 1972, including the task of managing the National Air Traffic Control Service jointly with the Ministry of Defence. This authority now employs over seven thousand people from offices in Kingsway, central London. Three-quarters of these staff are with the National Air Traffic Control Service. None of them are civil servants, although the authority is a government adviser. It formulates and publishes its own air transport policies, including those relating to noise problems near airports, development, the ever-increasing fight against terrorism by better security, and accident enquiries when necessary, following investigation by the Air Accidents Investigation Branch, the latter being totally independent.

One of the greatest problems facing the Civil Aviation Authority in recent years has been complaints of near-collisions over Great Britain. There have been many near-misses (this is the accepted description but is really a misnomer – near collisions would be a more accurate phrase) but not, to date, a collision over the country despite the ever-growing traffic converging on the four airports serving London: Heathrow, Gatwick, the now-expanding Stansted and the new City Airport in the revitalised ex-docklands of the capital's east end.

It is to be hoped that one never happens for the scenario of, say, two Boeing 747s colliding over the densely-populated suburbs of London is horrifying to contemplate.

Near-collisions are not recorded in the accident bulletin of the International Civil Aviation Organisation. They can, however, be reported to the authorities either by aircrew or an air traffic controller. As far back as February 1961 the pilot of a United Arab Airlines Comet 4C reported a near-collision with a Trans-Canada Airlines DC-8 jet over Epsom, a busy town beneath Heathrow's flight path. Even then the Ministry of Transport, the regulatory body of the time, declared: 'It is not normal practice to publish the findings into this type of incident.'

Sufficient press coverage had been given to this incident however to force more information from the bureaucrats. It emerged that the Douglas DC-8 had been cleared to climb to 1,200m (4,000ft) but that instead of then levelling off it had continued to soar through 2,500m (5,000ft) where the Comet was, quite correctly, flying. The DC-8 pilot had simply misheard the controller's instructions.

Two matters arise from this incident: Is it right that the regulatory body should investigate itself (a system still pertaining, the Civil Aviation Authority both investigates such incidents and manages the National Air Traffic Control Service) and should aircraft separation rely on the linguistic abilities of pilots and air traffic controllers? The latter problem is now being tackled electronically and an explanation of developments will be given later in this chapter.

The greatest threat to airliners, however, comes not from others of their own type, but from light aircraft, especially the most basic types without radios and with pilots qualified only to fly under Visual Flight Rules in clear weather at low level, which can blunder into their path. The problem is not new.

On 30 January 1949 two pilots from Meriden in Connecticut decided to fly south to look at New York from the air. They had filed a flight plan (itself not mandatory – it mainly ensures that a search will be instigated if the aircraft goes missing) to say that they would be flying at a maximum of 900m (3,000ft). At 16.20 they were heading back north having had a clear view of the city. It is presumed that they were gazing down at Long Island for they apparently did not see, at least until it was too late, the Pan American Lockheed Constellation looming up from their left. It was climbing from La Guardia Airport bound for Shannon, Eire.

The airliner was cleared to climb to 5,100m (17,000ft) under Visual Flight Rules. But the 'Connie' crew did not see the little Cessna 195 until it was almost on top of them. The light plane's wheels just missed the Lockheed's cockpit smashing into the fuselage just behind the navigation astrodome (now an anachronism!) The little aircraft's propeller ripped into the Constellation's skin before it disintegrated, tumbling to earth with its pilots perhaps knocked unconscious, perhaps already dead. The undercarriage and twisted propeller remained embedded in the Pan

American machine as the pilot brought her down to an emergency landing with no injuries to the thirty-three on board.

Another light aircraft joy-ride became a nightmare in the summer of 1956. The owner of a Cessna 170 was approaching Bartlesville, Oklahoma, at the same time as a scheduled Tulsa to Kansas City flight of Continental Airlines whose DC-3 pilot was in touch with Bartlesville tower and making his pre-landing checks. Thus occupied neither he nor the co-pilot saw the little aircraft first approach from the right and then turn north flying directly ahead at a slower speed. The Cessna pilot heard a rumbling sound and looked down to see the silver shape of the DC-3 sliding just beneath him.

With a sickening but not severe crunch the two aircraft became interlocked. As the pilots recovered from the shock and the passengers of the Douglas gazed up in horror at the wheels that had suddenly appeared in what had been the roof it became clear that the aircraft were in fact fused together! Though badly crippled none of the flying controls of the DC-3 were damaged and, carrying the Cessna piggyback, the airline pilot managed to land without injury to anyone on board this flying union. Both pilots were later blamed for the collision: 'Failure to maintain adequate look-out'.

A few years later over Hickory, North Carolina, another Cessna, this time a model 310 twin-engined machine, also struck the top of an airliner, but this time the incident would not pass without fatalities. The thirty-seven year old private pilot had 2,250 total hours logged, some 130 in multi-engine machines, as he took off from Grand Rapids with three passengers on 20 April 1960. Meanwhile, airborne was a Fairchild F-27 twin-turboprop (the licence-built version of the Fokker F-27 Friendship) of Piedmont operating from Cincinnati, Ohio, to Fayetteville, North Carolina, with a call at Hickory. There was no control tower here but the Federal Aviation Adminstration had a flight service station which was in touch with the Cessna. Fifteen minutes before the crash and while fifty-four miles nor 'nor' west of the airport, the Cessna pilot reported that he was continuing to land there under Visual Flight Rules.

The Fairchild F-27 was almost down to one hundred feet when the pilot was warned by his company radio that there was: 'An aircraft right of the runway.' The pilots scanned the clear sky but could not spot it. 'Approaching Runway 19, looks like he's right behind you. You'd better go around.'

Just as the First Officer of the airliner retracted the undercarriage and pushed the throttles forward the impact occurred.

Witnesses on the ground saw the Cessna above and behind the Fairchild, where the airliner's pilots could not possibly see it. The light aircraft struck the propeller and port wing of the airliner. As the overtaking craft the Cessna pilot was at fault. He paid the price with his life as his aircraft spun to destruction, killing, too, his three passengers. The Fairchild F-27 completed a successful emergency landing on one engine

6 May 1937 Lakehurst, New Jersey: The stern of Hindenburg, having lost its buoyancy, settled to the ground. Pointing to the sky for a moment, the forward section settled too, burning like a furnace. (Popperfoto)

(Above) John Derry's DH110 disintegrates at the Farnborough Air Show, 6 Sept 1952. (Popperfoto)

(Opposite inset) These people queuing at Llandow Aerodrome, near Cardiff, did not know that tragedy lay ahead. They were supporters of the Welsh Rugby Team about to fly to Ireland for the International Rugby match against Ireland at Belfast. On the return trip all but three of them lost their lives when the plane, a Tudor V, crashed 14 miles west of Cardiff. 13 March 1950 (Popperfoto)

(Opposite) Llandow, South Wales: A picture taken from the air of the wreckage of the Avro Tudor V in which 80 people were killed. The aircraft was carrying 78 passengers and a crew of five. The crash occurred when the aircraft 'overshot' Llandow airport.

(Below) All but one passenger survived when this Armagnac Airliner was wrecked at Orly Airport on a scheduled flight from Tunis. 31 Jan 1957. (Popperfoto)

(Above) Gloucester, England. Chance in a million brought this twin engined Varsity, operated by the Ministry of Supply, down right on top of the house, when the live engine failed during a single-engine flight test. Test pilot and assistant were killed, but they avoided a school of 1,000 children and other houses. Three women in this house escaped unharmed. 28 March 1963 (Popperfoto)

(Opposite, above) Idlewild, New York: One of the engines and propeller of the Eastern Airlines DC-7B which crashed and caught fire as it attempted to land in thick fog at Idlewild Airport, New York 30 November 1962. 25 of the 50 persons aboard were killed. Some of those who lived walked from the flaming wreck. Others were hurled out with their clothing ablaze. (Popperfoto)

(Opposite, below) A tyre is the biggest part visible of the Turk Hava Yollari DC-10 that smashed into the Ermenonville Forest near Paris on 3 March 1974 following a cargo door blow-out. (Popperfoto)

(Above) The scene at Riem Airport, Munich shortly after the Elizabethan aircraft carrying the Manchester United team back from Belgrade had crashed on take-off on 6 Feb 1958. It killed 21 persons including seven 'Busby Babes'. (Popperfoto)

(Right) Austrian mountain troops trudge through deep snow to reach the tail section of the ill-fated British Britannia airliner which crashed into the top of 8,500-ft high Mount Glungetzer on 29 February 1964, whilst on a scheduled flight from London to Innsbruck. The 75 passengers aboard the aircraft – all Britons except one – and eight crew members died in the crash. (Popperfoto)

(Opposite) A police helicopter attempts to rescue survivors from the Air Florida Boeing 737 which plunged into the frozen Potomac River, Washington, on 13 Jan 1982. (Popperfoto)

The wreckage of a JAL DC-8 which plunged into Tokyo Bay is hoisted onto a salvage barge. (Popperfoto)

(Opposite, above) The tail-plane of the United Air Lines Douglas airliner lies in the middle of a street in the residential section of Brooklyn, New York. The Douglas aircraft, with 84 people on board, collided in mid-air with a TWA Constellation airliner, with 44 passengers on board, in open country over Staten Island on 17 December 1960. 134 died. 11 year old boy Stephen Baltz survived the crash but died in hospital of burns. (Popperfoto)

(Opposite, below) A New York-bound Spanish DC-10 jetliner carrying 380 passengers and a crew of 13 crashed on 13 September 1982 on take-off at Malaga, skidding across a road, and trapping people in flames. Authorities said at least one passenger on the charter flight had died. (Popperfoto)

without injury to the thirty-six passengers.

Less than one month later the pilot of another light aircraft would also perish after a collision with an airliner, this time whilst flying a Stampe biplane near Paris. He collided with an Air Algérie Caravelle jet. On 19 May 1960 the Caravelle was on its final approach to Orly. The Stampe was skirting to the south of Orly and heading for Saint-Cyr airfield. It carried no radio, yet was at 1,200m (4,000ft) and crossing directly over the Orly approach flight path, passing from right to left in the path of the twin-jet. A literal interpretation of the then applicable rules of the air stated that the Stampe had right of way. This is akin to the maritime rule of 'steam gives way to sail'. Just as a massive supertanker cannot possibly halt or change course when a sailing dinghy appears in front of its bows, so the Caravelle, flying at nearly 400 knots, could not possibly swerve. In the horrendous impact the little biplane was smashed to pieces, but not before it had ripped open the top of the jet's fuselage. Debris slammed backwards in the slipstream to damage the rudder and be swallowed by one of the rear-mounted engines, causing it to stop. Nineteen of the thirty-four passengers were injured, one fatally. As the pieces of the Stampe cascaded to earth along with its lone pilot, Captain Moussov fought for control of his airliner. He achieved a remarkable landing at Orly.

Had the airliner passed the collision point in the sky five seconds earlier or later it would have been a near-collision; a very frightened and wiser private pilot would have lived and the incident would merely have been logged as just one of the hundreds of such occurrences. Two people had to die to prove that the old rule of 'give way to traffic from the right' could no longer be applied where high-speed jets were concerned. Light aircraft just had to stay away from commercial air corridors. Equally apparent was that modern airliners, particularly jets, could no longer cruise the skies under the old Visual Flight Rules. Sadly this lesson was not learnt quickly enough (see p. 123).

Today, any semi-skilled person can build an aircraft in a garage, then the machine can join the ever-growing ranks of potential aerial perils. US airline pilots dub the lower flight levels 'Indian country' because of the dangers there, and also the manufacturers' habit of naming their light planes after tribes. In Great Britain phrases such as 'Biggles buggers' are used by some airline pilots to describe amateurs with cavalier attitudes not unlike the fearless fictional pilot hero created by W.E. Johns. In Britain it can take approximately forty hours of instruction and cost £3,000 to get a 'ticket' – a private pilots' licence. Five hours of flying time logged every thirteen months is enough to keep it valid, and such weekend pilots are never tested again. In fact, with no air police there are no inspections of licences, so anyone who has been instructed by a friend or relative can be at the controls of an aircraft with little risk of being penalised unless disaster should strike. Such basic pilots are of course restricted to fair weather flying, though many of their breed do not look at a meteorological forecast before taking off and find themselves embroiled in storms that pound their little craft to pieces. Another £12,000 or so will gain an 'instrument rating' allowing the potential 'accident looking for some-where to happen' to fly into airports instead of airstrips and through foul weather and darkness.

One is forty-six times more likely to be killed in a light aircraft than an airliner. Now there are also microlight aircraft buzzing around the skies; nothing more than powered hang-gliders, flying umbrellas, 'Mary Poppins machines', but they can nevertheless attain many thousands of feet altitude. More than one airliner pilot has reported that he has flown *beneath* one of these machines; the consequences should one of these 'aerial motorcycles' smash into the cockpit of an airliner are horrific to imagine.

Nowadays a secondhand piston-engined helicopter can be purchased for the same cost as a 'performance' sports car of the ego-chariot rather than practical variety. The flying machine still has more kudos than the horseless carriage. One Los Angeles manufacturer of such machines advertises that in a helicopter the busy executive can soar over the noto-rious freeway traffic snarl ups, flying from home to office. Imagine the chaos and potential carnage if everyone took to the skies! The barely regu-lated free-for-all of the light aircraft is an ever-growing problem that will have to be tackled soon.

It seems incredible that as recently as 1956 two long-range airliners with over 120 people on board could cruise over America's breathtaking Grand Canyon with only the eyes of their aircrews to prevent collision. Heavy clouds enshrouded the Californian coastline that day as the United Airlines DC-7 was bound for Chicago from Los Angeles International. The DC-7 could trace its ancestry back to the DC-2, but it was the last of an old order. The four-jet DC-8 was on the horizon to doom the long-range piston-engined airliner to early obsolescence.

The Douglas took off just three minutes behind a Trans World Airlines Lockheed Super Constellation bound for Kansas City. With over fourteen thousand horsepower of Wright turbo-compound engines, the DC-7 cruised northwards at 6,300m (21,000ft). There were fifty-three passen-gers on board, with three cabin crew to serve their needs. In those days fresh food would be prepared and cooked on board; no tasteless cook-and-chill pre-packs then to reheat in a microwave for seconds. The pilot would go back into the passenger cabin, strolling between the aisles and talking to each passenger. Only emergencies make long-distance and trans-ocean captains leave their cockpits now. Fears of skyjackings and of leaving, in many cases, just one pilot at the controls to deal with possible crises have seen the end of the practice, the end of an era. The modern pilot sits cocooned and almost imprisoned in his little capsule, food brought forward by a stewardess. Both pilots do not eat the same meal in case the food is poisoned. The pilot boards before the passengers, and leaves after them, his life spent in a tiny world of humming electronics so divorced from the passenger cabin that often it must seem that the rest of the aircraft does not exist.

Back on that fateful day in 1956, the Trans World Constellation was flying ahead of the United DC-7 but the latter was gaining. Their flight paths would cross over the Grand Canyon. So far all was safe and in order: a lapse of time and 600m (2,000ft) would separate the machines at the intersection of their courses. However, what is now impossible if regulations are observed and radar is reliable, came to happen as the Lockheed pilot cleared the cloud veiling the coast and radioed air traffic control for permission to climb to 6,300m (21,000ft). This was refused as the tracks of the two airliners were converging and the DC-7 was already at that altitude. Soon afterwards the Trans World captain amended his request. He was flitting in and out of the cloud tops; he asked to fly 300m (1,000ft) above the top strata of cloud under Visual Flight Rules. Whether he now flew the airliner at 6,000m (20,000ft) or slightly above will never be known. However, very soon afterwards the DC-7 captain also requested permission to change to Visual Flight Rules. Air traffic control at Salt Lake City estimated that the Constellation should cross the path of the Douglas with three minutes to spare and a vertical separation of 300m (1,000ft), a margin that was perilously close. At 10.31 the operators at Salt Lake City picked up two fragmented messages: 'Salt Lake City, United 718...' and then a horrifying, 'Up, up... We're going in!' **See Map 6.**

Only silence then greeted the calls from air traffic control.

The wreckage was easy to find from the air, the glittering fragments of the aircraft scattered over five square kilometres (two square miles) of that great rift in the earth's crust. Mountaineers from Europe were called in to help recover the bodies. They laboriously hauled up much of the wreckage too, though a great deal had slipped into crevices.

The position of the wreckage allowed investigators to deduce what had happened, though the conclusions cannot be assured of being totally accurate. It seems that the airliners were on almost parallel courses at the time of impact, the Constellation flying at 416kph (260mph) just below and ahead of the Douglas. Approaching 32kph (20mph) faster, the DC-7 crew might just have seen the triple tails of the Lockheed before their aircraft sheared into them. They could have been flitting in and out of thin cloud at the time, the passengers on both airliners peering out and down at the magnificent landscape far below. Perhaps the passengers on the Constellation heard the roar of the Douglas as it came upon them. It was common practice for pilots flying in the area to cruise slowly over the canyon, perhaps even circling it under Visual Flight Rules.

The crash ended those days. With jets on the horizon, the era when pilots could dance with the cloud at whim had to end. The modern airliner is less than a lifetime but a quantum leap away from the juddering biplane that could roam between the clouds with just the pilot's eyes to protect it from collision.

New York was lashed by rain on 16 December 1960. Pilots trusted to radar to guide them in to the safety of La Guardia and Idlewild International airports. Once again aircraft of United and Trans World were involved in a disaster, a four-jet DC-8 of the former and another Lockheed Constellation of the latter.

The La Guardia approach controller was horrified to see another blip appear on his screen and advance across it on a track that would merge with the return of the Trans World Constellation. Watching radar screens it is often hard to realise that the little blips that creep across them represent massive fast-flying aircraft. The controller looked on horrified as the two blips merged, flared for an instant, then separated again.

The collision happened at 1,500m (5,000ft), the jet scraping over the top of the Lockheed almost directly above Miller Army airfield on Staten Island. There were thirty-nine passengers and six crew on the Trans World flight. Possibly many of them were still alive as the disintegrating airliner dropped vertically to explode on the Army base.

The United DC-8 kept flying for another minute or so, screaming on towards the heart of New York. It was mid-morning. Brooklyn Square was crowded. A few looked upwards, unperturbed at the sound of a jet approaching, until the shriek of the engines became a screaming wail. A shadow passed over the square, then the DC-8 impacted with the devastation of a huge bomb. All seventy-six passengers and seven crew were killed, along with six New Yorkers who had had no chance to run to safety.

Even as the streets were being wracked by exploding debris the air traffic controllers were trying to contact the aircraft and their dead pilots while staring horror-stricken at their radar screens not wanting to believe the evidence they told.

Two days after the accident and before the official investigation, as the implications of this crash and its death toll became clear (a total of 134, the worst-ever at the time), E. Quesada, then head of the Federal Aviation Administration, took the unprecedented step of releasing a transcript of the conversations between air traffic controllers at the time of the crashes. It now reveals the horror that swept over normally calm controllers as realisation came to them.

The La Guardia approach controller was the first to voice his fears. At 10.34 he contacted the control centre:

La Guardia: I think we got an emergency. Nobody declared anything, but who is that jet or fast-moving aircraft that went from Preston towards Flatbush?
Control Centre: From Preston towards Flatbush?
La Guardia: Yes. He's at Flatbush right now.
Control Centre: Er..., a fast-moving aircraft going where? Do you know his destination?
La Guardia: I don't know. I think he may have – now listen to this – he may have hit one of our aircraft. We're not sure.
Control Centre: All right, stand by.

Now they checked their screens. Perhaps it was just a fault on the radar – a glitch. The La Guardia controller was trying to call the Constellation. There was no answer. There had merely been twelve seconds of humming after the blips had converged. He called the Control Centre again:

La Guardia: All right, now we've got troubles, but we're not sure of it. We lost contact with a Connie, 266 I believe his number is. He was on a collision course with an aircraft, an unknown aircraft, heading north-east from Preston towards Flatbush. That aircraft is now a mile outside the La Guardia outer marker, heading north-east bound.
Control Centre: The unknown, you still have the unknown in radar contact?
La Guardia: No, we're not talking to the unknown, but we see him, yes.

The DC-8 was still flying then, diving down to the heart of the city, pieces falling off and fluttering to the streets below. The La Guardia controller called the airport's tower:

La Guardia: I think we have trouble with a Connie. There's something wrong. He's not moving or anything. He may have got hit by another airplane.
Tower: Uh, OK.

Meanwhile the Idlewild approach controller had realised that a United Airlines DC-8 had gone off the air. He was now called by his compatriot at La Guardia:

La Guardia: Uh, is that your traffic at Flatbush?
Idlewild: Just a minute... No, it's not our traffic, La Guardia.

But it was. The DC-8 had been approaching New York at 1,800m (6,000ft) and had been instructed to descend to 1,500m (5,000ft) before it reached the beacon at Preston, a small township just outside the city. The crew of the United Air Lines jet acknowledged this instruction with the response that they would try. Soon afterward the DC-8 contacted control to confirm that its altitude and position was correct, but the pilot was wrong, they had already overflown Preston and were seventeen kilometres (eleven miles) to the north-east, just moments away from impact with the Constellation. The DC-8 crew had been doing their own navigation, inconceivable in an airliner today, with the radar being used as an adviser only. The La Guardia controller spoke to Idlewild again:

La Guardia: Well, now we lost communication with an aircraft and, ah, something may be wrong with him.
Idlewild: Just a minute. It could be ours on approach control, New

York.
La Guardia: Yeah. Well, what type of aircraft is that?
Idlewild: A United DC-8.
La Guardia: And what, and what's his altitude?
Idlewild: He was last cleared to five thousand.
La Guardia: Oh boy! Our man was at five too. We lost one aircraft. I don't know where he's at now.

The Constellation had disappeared from the radar, its vertical dive taking it below the level of the 'ground clutter'. One can imagine the terror that the La Guardia and Idlewild air traffic controllers must have felt, thinking back, checking, trying to convince themselves that they had not made some catastrophic error.

The controllers were to be vindicated but the accident had ramifications that shaped air transport policies for the next three decades. The United DC-8 had overshot the position it had been cleared to, probably partly because the crew had been distracted by doing their own navigation at a critical time. A system of dual responsibility – an air traffic controller allocating height but not being able to insist on position – was an operating practice fraught with the possibility of error. Prime responsibility for avoiding collisions would now rest with controllers with pilots' eyes as the last line of defence; and a poor last protection. The field of vision from an airliner's cockpit is very restricted. For much of the time the pilot's attention must in any case be directed at his instruments, scanning the array of figures and dials by the reflex of habit, perhaps not even seeming to pay much attention to them, but just one dial showing a reading at odds with what he expects should galvanise him (or her) to full alertness as surely as a red light glowing on a car's dashboard.

Aircraft can become almost invisible in the sky. A glance at military aircraft recognition silhouettes reveals that it is difficult for the human eye to perceive whether an aircraft is flying towards or away from the observer, if it is viewed at an oblique or obtuse angle. A jet pilot has only instants to make such a decision. Impact will probably come before his hands can even pull at the antlers. A jetliner is in any case not a manoeuvrable little Tiger Moth; it travels one and a half kilometres (a mile) at cruising speed before even beginning to turn.

Back in 1960 one other truth was also realised; that the new jetliners were travelling at almost double the speed of the piston and turboprop machines they were supplanting. The DC-8 had difficulty in descending to 1,500m (5,000ft) in the time allowed, and to overfly the marker by seventeen kilometres (eleven miles) took only a minute or so.

1960 was a black year for air safety. Some four hundred passengers were killed, an accident rate of 1.0 per 160 million passenger kilometres (100 million passenger miles). Even then the saying 'the drive to the airport is more dangerous than the flight' had been coined, yet in 1960 it was hardly true. The possibility of being killed in an air disaster was almost as great as that of being killed on the roads. It was predicted that by 1969 there would be 244,800 million kilometres (153,000 million miles) flown. Assuming an average of twenty-five fatalities per disaster compared with an average of fifteen in the years just prior to 1960 when aircraft were smaller, there would be a civil air disaster approximately every six days. Luckily, it did not happen that way. In fact, the distance flown in 1969 approached 320,000 million passenger kilometres (200,000 million miles), with a death toll of lower than three hundred.

Commercial air travel came of age in 1960. Better radar, guidance by air traffic controllers at almost all times, stronger aircraft, the development of inertial navigation systems, the realisation that at least 1,600m (1,000ft) of space separation should be maintained at all times – all these factors contributed to an improving safety record. The pilot was becoming the observer of instruments, a passenger for most of the time, but still responsible and capable of taking control of the aircraft when the mechanical and electrical complexities failed. The cynical pilot declares that he is the only component that can be manufactured by unskilled labour!

Civil airline pilots still term the skies above Germany's River Ruhr 'fighter alley', not in memory of the great air battles that took place there half a century ago, but because of the perceived danger of collision with one of the NATO aircraft patrolling and training in that zone where the Eastern Bloc faced the West. 'I'm always looking up for the F104 coming down!' a pilot once said. These are the home skies of the still futuristic-looking but obsolete Starfighter, of which more than two hundred have been lost in accidents, giving rise to much black humour such as *Q –* What's the definition of an optimistic F104 pilot? *A –* One who doesn't take out an insurance policy before take off; Notice to Starfighter pilots – would they please ask their wives not to keep phoning the squadron office to see if they're still alive; *Q –* How does one get an F104 jet? *A –* Buy a field and wait!

Collisions between military and civilian airliners have frequently happened. In 1949 the US government was still trying to dispose of its war surplus military aircraft to lesser powers. The Bolivian Air Force showed an interest in the twin-boomed P38 escort fighter and sent their Captain Eric Rios Bridoux to the United States to test one. Bridoux was performing aerobatics with one of these twin-engined fighters over the outskirts of Washington, DC, on 1 November as an Eastern Air Lines DC-4B was approaching to land at National Airport with a flight from Boston. Bridoux requested permission to land, but was told to hold at 1,500m (5,000ft). Perhaps he misunderstood, or perhaps his approach seemed clear to him. The air traffic control radar revealed his aircraft on a collision course with the civil flight. The pilots of the four-engined Douglas were warned to look out for traffic converging with them, but they did not see the P38 as the heavy fighter slammed into the top of the Douglas' fuselage.

The airliner was cut in two and crashed in the Potomac River with its tail section on the bank, killing all four crew and forty-nine of its passengers. One woman survived for a few hours before succumbing to her injuries. Bridoux died shortly after being pulled from the wreckage, his fighter also having plummeted into the river. The Bolivian Government did not purchase any P38s.

The greatest problem with the mix of civil, military and private light aircraft in the skies is that air traffic controllers may not be able to converse with all parties, sometimes being confronted by an unidentified blip on their radar screens. In the West military and civil air traffic controls liaise to regulate the flow of military traffic through civil air lanes, while certain zones are permanently set aside for air force training. However, mistakes do happen and the different breeds do encroach upon each other's domain. A light aircraft pilot, his machine not even radio fitted, once landed at London's Gatwick Airport, one of the busiest in the world, believing it to be Biggin Hill forty-eight kilometres (thirty miles) away. One can imagine the terror of the air traffic controllers as they had to scatter intercontinental airliners across the sky to avoid the unidentified blip on their radar screens. Most airports can relate similar experiences.

Military aircraft have the greatest destructive record, which is hardly surprising considering that airliners do not fly in formation, intentionally perform aerobatics, or hill-hop beneath radar to practise bombing.

On 6 June 1971 a US Marine corps F4 Phantom was at 4,500m (15,000ft) over Duarte, California. It was 'hot-dogging', the pilot flinging the heavy two-seat fighter-bomber around the sky. Only the observer saw the Air West DC-9 appear alongside. The fighter-pilot lived, ejecting to safety; fifty-one people on the DC-9 died.

Only weeks later, on 30 July, Sergeant Yoshimi Ichikawa of the Japanese Air Self Defence Force was flying his F86 Sabre jet fighter in formation with an instructor in a similar machine. Too late the latter cried out: 'Climb and turn right!' All 162 on an All-Nippon Airways Boeing 727 bound from Sapporo to Tokyo were killed 7,800m (26,000ft) above Shizukuishi. Ichikawa ejected to safety as the pieces rained down. He was later charged with involuntary homicide, but acquitted.

It is not even necessary for aircraft to collide for disaster to result: near collisions can prove fatal, too. In the fading evening light of 8 February 1965 a Douglas DC-7B of Eastern Air Lines took off as Flight 663 from John F. Kennedy (the renamed Idlewild) Airport, New York, bound for Richmond, Virginia. As it climbed out over the Atlantic a Pan American Boeing 707 was in-bound for JFK from Puerto Rico. The required 300m (1,000ft) altitude separation did exist between the two airliners as they converged on each other, but when air traffic control told the DC-7 crew to turn to a heading of 170°, the same as the 707, they became like two people on a street who in trying to avoid one another keep simultaneously moving to the same side. The airliners could not stop, and one too high, one too low, they almost collided. Perhaps the slipstream of the jet tore at the elderly piston DC-7 hard enough to damage its controls; perhaps its pilot overstressed it in taking avoiding action: in any event, the Eastern Air Lines machine plunged into the ocean ten kilometres (six miles) off Jones Beach, Long Island. All eighty-four on board died as the Boeing crew looked down and the pilot radioed control: 'It looks like he's in the bay then, because we saw him. He looked like he winged over to miss us and we tried to avoid him, and we saw a bright flash in the sea about one minute later.' The Boeing landed undamaged.

New York air traffic control required 600m (2,000ft) separation for a time afterwards, although it has returned to 300m (1,000ft) now that there are far more planes in the sky to keep the traffic moving, trusting to better radar and altimeters.

Mid-air collisions are survivable. In the same year as the events described above, on 4 December, an Eastern Air Lines Lockheed L1049C Constellation and another Boeing 707, this time of Trans World Airlines, came together over Carmel, New York State. Bound for Boston with five crew and fifty-one passengers, the Lockheed was flitting in and out of the cloud tops at 3,000m (10,000ft). The Boeing formed Flight 42 which had begun at San Francisco and would terminate at John F. Kennedy Airport. It had a crew of seven, fifty-one passengers, and was bearing south-east at 3,300m (11,000ft).

The south-west bearing Constellation crew saw the jetliner ahead in the two o'clock position as their courses converged. It seems that the Lockheed pilot was drawn to climb too high by an upward slope to the carpet of cloud beneath him. The jet crew spotted the sun glinting off the fuselage of the Constellation and performed an emergency 2.5G climbing turn to starboard, pandemonium breaking out in the passenger cabin as everything loose, including those standing at the time, hurtled to the port side. The Eastern Air Lines crew performed a similar manoeuvre with the same effect on its passengers, but to port. Had either crew noticed the other aircraft just a moment earlier, the incident might yet have been just another near-miss. However, the port wing of the 707 sliced into the star-board fin and tailplane of the Constellation, snapping off the number one engine and part of the 707's wing.

The 707 pilots discovered to their amazement that not only were they still alive, but also that the jet could actually fly with one-third of a wing and an engine missing. To the gasps of astounded onlookers and the prayers of its passengers it landed safely at John F. Kennedy Airport.

The Constellation was not so fortunate. With the tailplane damaged, the pilot's only means of control was by adjusting the power of the engines. An emergency landing in a field was attempted and through brilliant airmanship was almost successful. At the last moment the port wing struck a tree, swinging the airliner around as fire broke out. When the bone-jarring, metal-rending slide ceased those on board scrambled to escape from the flames. The captain was asphyxiated by choking fumes as he tried to rescue passengers. One passenger died from the same cause, and two later succumbed to injuries, but a total of fifty lived.

Pilots term a cloudless blue sky burnished by summer sunlight CAVU – ceiling and visibility unlimited. These were the conditions high above Yugoslavia on 10 September 1976, a day when pilots could look around and see the silver specks of other airliners spearing through the stratosphere around them; a day when a collision between two airliners might be thought impossible, but the day the worst mid-air collision so far occurred.

Cruising through the sky, sunlight glinting off its wings at 9,900m (33,000ft), came a British Airways Trident 3 bound for Istanbul. It was lightly loaded with fifty-four passengers and six cabin crew. In the cockpit there was a friendly atmosphere: voice recorders had become standard by then so we know what conversations were exchanged in the final minutes.

Flight Engineer Brian Helm was reading a newspaper. 'Listen to this,' he said. 'Eight people injured in an air crash on Tuesday were killed when a helicopter taking them to hospital crashed.'

'Yeh! How unlucky can you get?' commented forty-four year old pilot Dennis Tann. Little did they know it was their own last day on earth.

The Trident had taken off from Heathrow at 08.32 for the three and a half hour flight as BE476. At 10.04 it entered the upper sector of Zagreb Air Traffic Control and came under the responsibility of twenty-eight year old controller Gradimir Tasic.

Unable to find any other accommodation, Tasic was forced to live in a wooden hut within the perimeter of Zagreb Airport with his wife and baby. His shift of duty had begun only minutes before. As he had walked across the grass to the control centre he must surely have gazed up to that azure sky trying to relate the aircraft that arrowed through it to the blips that he would shortly see on his screen. His first contact with the traffic in the skies was to request Flight BE476 to squawk for identification: a transponder on the Trident relayed a signal that shot to earth with the echoing radar beam that positively identified the aircraft by displaying its flight number alongside the glowing return of the bounced beams on Tasic's console.

Tasic later claimed that the Trident entered his airspace at 10,050m (33,500ft). If this was true he should have contacted Captain Tann to warn of altitude irregularity, but he did not. The Yugoslav should have had an assistant, but this individual had not reported for duty. Tasic was trying to contact him via the telephone.

Approaching Zagreb on an almost reciprocal course to the Trident was a DC-9 of Inex-Adria, under the command of fifty-one year old Captain Joze Krumpak. It was carrying 107 West Germans and a Yugoslav from Split to Cologne, package tourists returning from holidays on the islands of Hvar and Brac on the Dalmatian coast. The twin-engined jetliner was densely-packed, the seats fixed at close pitch, passengers squeezed in to keep the price low.

At 10.06 the DC-9 as Flight JP550 was approaching Zagreb at 7,800m (26,000ft). Krumpak called control asking for permission to climb higher.

The middle sector controller, Erjavec, seated across the room from Tasic and operating with the aid of an assistant, radioed back: 'JP550, Flight Level 31 is not available, 32 also. Are you able to climb maybe to 350?'

After Krumpak's affirmative Erjavec sent his assistant, Pelin, across the control room to inform the busy Tasic. Distracted by the traffic on his screen and his search for assistance, Tasic allegedly took little notice of Pelin. The latter later claimed that he asked Tasic's permission for Flight JP550 to climb upwards from Erjavec's height band to 10,500m (35,000ft) where Tasic would assume control of it. He alleged that he pointed to the screen indicating the glowing blip of the DC-9 that was closing on the track of the Trident, but was still safe, separated by a thousand metres (several thousands of feet) of altitude even if their horizontal paths were to converge.

Pelin later testified that Tasic gave assent for JP550 to climb. Tasic denied this. It was an arrangement in any case made mainly by gestures, so there is no tape recorded evidence to ascertain the truth. The Inex-Adria DC-9 pointed its long snout towards space, clawing higher.

At 10.14, climbing steeply, Krumpak contacted Tasic for the first time. 'Good morning Zagreb, Adria 550.' On Tasic's console the DC-9's blip was closing fast on that of the Trident, and the former was climbing up to the flight level of the British machine. '325 crossing Zagreb at one four,' continued the transmission from the DC-9 – it was at 9,750m (32,500ft) and crossing the Zagreb navigation beacon, the VOR needle in the cockpit swinging around to point at 'FROM' instead of 'TO' as the signal fell behind, a buzz on the crew's headphones informing them aurally and nudging them to make the position report.

Did Tasic then glance at his console and see the closing blips, or did he realise from the confused picture he must have had in his mind that not only would the blips intersect but also that they would do so at the same altitude? He called out to JP550: 'What is your present level?'

'327,' came the reply. It was at 9,810m (32,700ft) and still nosing up to the approaching Trident at 9,900m (33,000ft). Reverting to his native Serbo-Croat in his panic, Tasic yelled: 'Hold yourself at that height and report passing Zagreb!'

The DC-9's pilot and co-pilot must have gazed at each other in confusion: they had just reported passing the Zagreb beacon, so what was the crisis? We'll never know if either crew saw the other aircraft. Tasic was still shouting, trying to warn them, but his voice was almost incoherent in his terror now. 'Aircraft in front of you passing left to right!' And then the blips flared on his screen before separating again into two images.

CAVU (clear air, visibility unlimited), flying twenty-four kilometres (fifteen miles) behind the Trident, the pilot of a Lufthansa Boeing saw the accident happen. At a combined speed of over 1,600kph (1,000mph) the Trident and the DC-9 met almost head-on. Like a knife through butter the DC-9's port wing slashed through the fuselage of the Trident from just below the base of the cockpit and into the passenger cabin, cutting through metal, cables, hydraulics, plastic trim, seats and passengers. Debris slammed back into the rudder, breaking it away. The DC-9, too, was mortally wounded.

The port wing of the Inex-Adria machine erupted into flames then most of it sheared off, cartwheeling in the rarefied air of that altitude like a catherine wheel as it tumbled towards the earth. Meanwhile the port engine exploded as debris was ingested into it. The detonation sheared off the tail of the machine. Pitching down, it began to roll with the asymmetrical lift of the starboard wing. The pilots tried to hold her, but the DC-9 was beyond control. Thirty seconds after the collision, spinning, it disintegrated in mid-air, spewing out its passengers. They were at least unconscious as they began the long drop to earth, most of the fuselage plummeting down ahead of them to explode in woodland, igniting seventy square metres (eighty square yards) of trees.

Farmworkers did not hear the collision and in the glaring sun few could have seen the silver, almost wingless, forward fuselage of the DC-9 spinning down to destruction. The first that most of them knew of disaster was when a nightmare hail of bodies crashed to the fields around them – passengers still strapped in their seats, with luggage, pieces of fuselage, and the fireball that had been the port engine.

Tasic was still calling out to the aircraft even as the first fragments of it struck the ground. 'Adria 550! Bealine 476!' he kept repeating, praying for an answer, praying that it was another of the hundreds of near-collisions that happen each year. There was only silence on the airwaves. There may still have been life in the Trident cockpit – it was never discovered whether or not anyone had any kind of control over the British jet as it speared down, the wings level, to smash tail-down into a field. By then fifty per cent of its passengers had been sucked out into the void through the gashes in the fuselage. The Trident's impact was so great that anyone left alive in it would have died then. The cockpit section was severed by the crash, shooting forward to come to rest three hundred yards (two hundred and seventy metres) further on, its crew dead inside.

Clouds veiled what had been a clear sky that night, rain dripping on the would-be rescuers as they shone flashlights into trees, hoping that someone was alive; climbing to see if flapping cloth was just luggage, pieces of humanity or maybe by a miracle someone whose drop had been softened somehow. One child who had fallen strapped to a seat was said to have shown signs of life; a woman had lived for ninety minutes. But there were to be no survivors of the 178 people who had been on board the two jets.

Tasic was tried for manslaughter. Found guilty, he was sentenced to seven years' imprisonment. He was released in November 1978 after serving twenty-seven months in K.P. Dom Zabela prison. Nothing could ever punish that unfortunate young man more than the mental image of the destruction that occurred which will haunt him for the rest of his life. There is not one member of his profession who could not say: it could have been me.

The peak holiday season of 1988 saw British airports thronged with passengers waiting to get away. Some of them had to wait for a day or even more as 'flow management' was enforced, no aircraft being allowed to take off from foreign parts unless there would be space for it in British skies. Passengers fumed and complained. In that pre-Lockerbie disaster summer air safety was not in the forefront of their thinking; they were victims of their own demand to fly, having been drawn by cheap flights. But did they think of safety when comparing the various prices? Much of the passengers' criticism was aimed at the main British air traffic control centre at West Drayton near Heathrow: its computers kept failing, grounding aircraft until the technicians could coax it back to life, and forcing controllers to revert to card indexes to bring down those aircraft airborne at the time. But new computers cost money.

In the next few years microwave landing systems (MLS) will be introduced. These will allow aircraft to approach runways from a clover-leaf pattern, instead of the rigid stack and long straight final let-down that is the present norm. To instigate such a system will require the co-operation of the airlines, who will have to fit the necessary equipment to new and long-service older machines and will of course pass these costs on to their customers. Most mid-air collisions happen on final approach. MLS offers the prospect of safer flying, yet it will not be introduced without objections.

In 1989 the radar control area of West Drayton was expanded to offer greater radar coverage for the Dash 7 aircraft flying from London's Docklands Airport. Light aircraft instructors claimed that the new control area forced them and their students to overfly forty-eight kilometres (thirty miles) of the Thames estuary before they could reach uncontrolled airspace to perform practice spins.

The disaster to John Derry's D.H.110 at Farnborough (see p. 61) seems a long time ago now. Perhaps that's why the lessons of what had been the worst airshow accident have been forgotten. The public's appetite for such aerial carnivals had grown over the years, despite a succession of catastrophes. The bi-annual Farnborough event has witnessed accidents to a twin-engined Breguet Atlantic which stalled in a turn after a low-level fly-past, and at the press preview of the 1974 show, on 1 September, the pilot of a Sikorsky Blackhawk assault helicopter entered a second roll at less than 120m (400ft) when the nose of the machine dropped and, too low to recover, it smashed down on the grass, killing the co-pilot on the spot. The pilot died nine days later. It was an example of 'grandstanding', showing off, the temptation of any pilot before a crowd.

The Soviet Union's version of supersonic civil transport was to be destroyed at the Paris airshow of 1973. The Tupolev Tu-144, dubbed 'Concordski' in the West and with a design similar to that of the Anglo-French trailblazer, had completed its display on 3 June and was about to land when pilot Captain Koslov was informed that he was approaching the wrong runway. He commenced a steep go-around which put him on a collision course with a Dassault Mirage fighter aircraft. Now he pushed his aircraft down.

The co-pilot had been operating a ciné camera on behalf of French television. Not being strapped in, the negative gravity of the sudden descent threw him up and forward from his seat to land across the centre console. As the pilots recovered themselves Koslov made a hasty recovery from the dive that the structure just could not withstand: the right wing fractured.

The wreckage hailed down on the town of Goussainville. Eight people on the ground and six on board the Tu-144 perished. At the same airshow in June 1989 a Soviet Mig 29 fighter also came to grief. A symbol of the end of 'the cold war', this state-of-the-art warplane had already thrilled crowds at Farnborough with seemingly impossible slow-speed, near-stalled fly-pasts. It was repeating this feat when the starboard engine ingested a stone (most probably) that had been in the intake, possibly sucked in during take-off. Crippled in a near-stalling point turn there could be no recovery. Just an instant before the Mig exploded on the ground in open space the pilot ejected, landing just bruised although his canopy had not opened fully from such a low-level escape.

In May 1988 a valuable relic of the early jet age was lost at an airshow at Coventry in the English Midlands. The Gloster Meteor Mark VII twin-jet fifties fighter dived to fiery destruction just outside the airfield perimeter because its RAF pilot, Flight Lieutenant Peter Stacey, had left the airbrakes extended after speed had fallen below 170 knots, contrary to safe practice with the type. As he lowered the undercarriage, the machine was thrown into a dive from which recovery was impossible. It was the type of accident that could so easily have involved fatalities to those on the ground just as horrendous as those at Farnborough in 1952.

Such incidents do not seem to affect attendances at air displays, however. Crowds flocked to the Ramstein airshow in Germany on 28 August 1988. One of the highlights of the display was to be a performance by the Italian Air Force's aerobatic display team, Frecce Tricolori. All major air forces have such a team; the Red Arrows in Great Britain; the Thunderbirds in the USA; and Patrouille de France in France. All have suffered fatal accidents in practice yet are maintained as aerial flagships to show the public what their taxes purchase in terms of military hardware.

The Red Arrows pioneered the use of 'singletons' breaking away from the main formation to perform hairraising passing manoeuvres. Frecce Tricolori had evolved a variation on this theme whereby the ten-aircraft team would divide into five-ship and four-ship wings which would cross while a singleton flew beneath them. The manoeuvre required split-second timing. On 28 August, however, it went catastrophically wrong.

The multiple flights successfully crossed as they overflew the runway but singleton pilot Giorgio Alessio swooping down found himself flying towards rising ground, low embankments where hundreds of members of the public were watching in awe. Instinctively, Alessio pulled back on his control column, he also deployed the airbrakes of the Aeromacchi MB-339A jet.

Two seconds later the singleton struck the aircraft of team leader Mario Naldini at the head of the five-ship formation and became a cartwheeling fireball bearing straight for the public enclosures. Naldini's plane veered into that of his wingman, Ivo Nutarelli. Both crashed and perished just off the runway.

Sixty people, including the three pilots, died on the spot. Others, some badly burned but in temporary shock that dulled the pain, milled around in disbelief. Many will live for the remainder of their lives horribly scarred. The death toll eventually reached seventy.

In the wake of such a disaster airshows were banned in Germany for the foreseeable future. It is hard to believe that such a ban will be in force for very long. On the same day as the Ramstein horror a Finnish Valmet Redigo crashed at an airshow at Kleine-Brogel, Belgium, killing the pilot who had tried to perform a loop at low level.

Just days after the Ramstein tragedy the Royal Air Force's Red Arrows display team were permitted to overfly the crowds gathered at the Farnborough Air Fair in England on the basis of their experience. Obviously, merely preventing overflying of public enclosures cannot be total protection against tragedy: high speed aircraft at just 300m (1,000ft) could veer towards a town or grandstands should there be an incident.

That most terrifying of all scenarios – two wide-bodied airliners colliding over a city – has not happened, yet. Modern technology has given us a new weapon in the armoury of protection: TCAS (Traffic Alert and Collision Avoidance Systems). The system works simply by means of an on-board computer which interrogates signals from all other airliners so fitted. If this electronic brain computes that a collision is imminent, automatic avoiding action will be taken.

The United States took a unilateral decision that all aircraft with more than thirty-one seats would be fitted with TCAS from 1 January 1992. The passenger may take comfort from this policy, but there are those in the air transport industry who feel that insufficient thought has been given to its introduction. In May 1989 the Secretary-General of the British Air Transport Association wrote to that most august journal *Flight International* saying that should there be a high number of 'nuisance' commands (ie false warnings), there could be a lack of confidence in the system. Certainly, a warning that 'cries wolf' too often, in the manner of the Trident stick-push low pressure caution encountered in Chapter 2, may be over-ridden when it is telling the truth. Will an airliner whose TCAS has been triggered be sent lurching across the sky so that others, too, are diverted, swamping the electronic brains? 'In such circumstances there is always the danger that an aircraft could end up in a more difficult situation than that which originally pertained,' W.H. Davies wrote.

Only time will tell if some people's fear of airliners careering across the sky in avoidance manoeuvres will trigger the TCAS of others until their systems become swamped with information and 'trip out' come true. As yet of course, TCAS cannot prevent that greatest peril: the prospect of light aircraft colliding with airliners. An example of the tragedy that waits in the airways occurred over Eggenfelden, Germany, on 26 July 1989 when a Luftwaffe Panavia Tornado collided with a microlight machine. The heavy fighter-bomber landed safely, the 'flying motorcycle' pilot perished. Suppose the microlight had collided with the windscreen of an airliner...

8
Without Trace

In the scale of air disasters the loss without trace of a single-engined Norseman utility aircraft of the US Air Force over the English Channel on the night of Friday 15 December 1944 with three people on board is no major incident. But that Norseman which took off from Twin Woods Farm near Bedford on that foggy winter's day was carrying a musician who even then was a legend: Glenn Miller.

Born in Clarinda in America's Mid-west of Iowa in 1905, Miller milked cows to pay for his first trombone and then through college pursued his ambition of creating an orchestra with a new and distinctive sound. In the 1930s he specialised in arranging, finally getting the opportunity to organise Ray Noble's big band. In 1937 he formed his own first band, but the sound was neither particularly good nor commercially successful. He tried again next year and this time, by increasing the clarinets and blending these with the saxophones, he found that distinctive mellow Glenn Miller sound.

He soon rose to the peak of his profession, and when war came Eisenhower chose him to lead a band that would entertain the Allied Expeditionary Forces for the invasion of Europe. This American band of the AEF arrived in England shortly after D-day and was billeted in London's Lower Sloane Street. They spent their first night cowering in the basement – the V-1 'doodlebug' flying bombs were coming over. Alternative accommodation for the orchestra was hastily found in Waterloo Road, Bedford, one-time home town of the R101.

The sixty-two piece band performed almost constantly through those autumn months as the AEF broke out from their Normandy bridgeheads and began to surge towards the heart of Nazi Germany. Now Miller dreamt of broadcasting from Paris at Christmas. He first had to meet his commitments to the British Broadcasting Corporation, which involved recording six weeks' programmes in advance. Working long, long hours this was achieved, leaving just one programme to perform – the special Christmas show that it was hoped to broadcast live from Paris.

Originally, Miller's executive officer, Lieutenant Don Haynes, was scheduled to fly to Paris to make the arrangements, but Miller, the perfectionist, decided that he would fly over ahead of the band itself. It had been planned for the bandleader to take a Douglas C-47 transport to the liberated city on Wednesday 13 December, but the weather conditions that day were so bad that the flight was grounded. The next day dawned similar. In

Bedford Don Haynes had lunch with Colonel Norman Baesell. The colonel was intending to fly to France and invited Miller to join him.

So, on 15 December Haynes drove Baesell and Miller out through the centre of Bedford, passed the statue of John Bunyon in the town centre and headed east for a little over a mile to the airfield that had been built around the farmhouse at Twin Woods. Waiting there was the C-64 Norseman and its pilot: Flight Officer John Morgan from the 35th Depot Repair Squadron, Abbots Ripton.

The weather was wet, bitterly cold and foggy. The very basic Norseman aircraft, a type that had originally been designed principally for transport around the backwoods of Canada, could not climb up to clear air – it would have to fly through it in conditions that made icing a probability. The Norseman had no de-icing equipment. Neither did the little aircraft carry any parachutes and, in common with most planes of its type at that time, its radio transceiver's reliability was suspect. Don Haynes stood and watched as the puny Norseman took off. It was almost two days, when the other members of the band arrived in France aboard a C-47, before it was even realised that Glenn Miller was missing.

It has been generally assumed that Don Haynes was the last person to see the aircraft. But this may not be so. At that time the RAF's Bomber Command was able to carry out some raids in daylight. On this particular day 138 Lancasters were to be escorted by 100 Mustang fighters which were to group over Bury St Edmunds in Suffolk and then fly to bomb the German town of Siegen, some eighty kilometres (fifty miles) east of Cologne.

This intended raid became an abort when the fighters were unable to take off from their bases owing to fog. The bombers however did form up, but on receiving the recall signal were unable to turn back for an immediate landing with their bombs on board: every aircraft carried an 1,800kg (4,000lb) blast bomb, or 'cookie', and at least 3,600kg (8,000lb) of other bombs, mostly incendiaries. To return to land with a highly unstable 'cookie' on board was perilous in the extreme, so they had to be dropped somewhere safe.

One of the three prescribed jettisoning areas was in the English Channel. A squadron that had been recalled early winged away to distribute its bombs in the North Sea off the Wash, but most headed for the Channel and point 50.15N, 00.15E. There was a 16km (10 mile) radius exclusion zone around this grid reference into which shipping and aircraft should not intrude unless engaged in bomb jettisoning.

Flying Officer Victor Gregory decided to dispose not only of his 'cookie', but also all the incendiaries as his Lancaster tracked towards the jettisoning zone. Such are the financial wastes of war. The bomb aimer, Flying Officer Ivor Pritchard, glanced through the bombsight to ensure that there were no aircraft or ships flying below before pressing the releases. 'They're going off,' he commented over the intercom as he saw the waterspouts of other aircraft's bombs exploding.

Pilot Officer Fred Shaw, the navigator, climbed from his position in the cabin and came forward to the flight engineer's station on the starboard side of the cockpit to look at the scene through the small blister window there. He was gazing at the shivering shock waves of exploding 'cookies' when he saw another aircraft coming towards them at a much lower level. 'Hey, there's a kite down there!' he yelled into the intercom. He identified it as a Norseman. Shaw had trained in Canada, home of the little plane's design, so it is unlikely that he was mistaken. It was flying at approximately 450m (1,500ft) towards France, some 900m (3,000ft) below the Lancaster.

Even as Shaw watched, the Norseman dipped its port wing and dived into the sea. In the rear turret of the Lancaster, Flight Sergeant Harry Fellows caught a glimpse of the olive drab aircraft just before it disappeared in a fountain of spray. 'There's a kite gone in! Did you see it?' The Norseman's position made it invisible to Gregory and the upper turret gunner, while the other crew members were engrossed in their work. Shaw and Fellows believed that blast waves from exploding 'cookies' brought down the Norseman. This is very probable. Even the far larger Lancaster could be destroyed by the blast effect of such a bomb if dropped from below 900m (3,000ft).

Also possible is that the little utility aircraft was peppered with small incendiary bombs. Even dropped from low altitude, these could penetrate two storeys of a house. These projectiles were raining over the Channel that day as the Lancasters disposed of their loads.

Because the raid was not completed, there was no debriefing of the bomber crews when they landed back at their bases. The fate of the aircraft that flew into the sea was discussed briefly by the aircrews of 149 Squadron and then forgotten – this was wartime, such incidents happened daily, and there could be no hope of survivors in that chill sea. Search and rescue operations were only instigated if survivors were likely or distress transmissions received.

If the routes and timings of the Lancaster and Norseman are examined the evidence seems conclusive that Shaw and Fellows did indeed witness the death of Glenn Miller. The Norseman took off at 12.55 GMT. The rain of flying bombs launched from the ground and in mid-air by converted Heinkel bombers meant that the British had moved all their anti-aircraft guns to the coast after the missile assault began that June. Royal Air Force fighters patrolled the skies over Kent's 'Garden of England' and to the capital. Most of the flying bombs were destroyed by the late-mark Spitfires, Typhoons and Tempests. This was not an area of the sky that the Norseman would want to stray into! Morgan would have set course to cross the coast over the area of Eastbourne, not many miles west of R101's last glimpse of England. From there he should have steered slightly easterly, for the Southern Jettison Area lay in mid-Channel directly south of Eastbourne. It would only take a minor error of navigation to stray into the exclusion zone. **See Map 3.**

Gregory's Lancaster settled back on to its runway at Methwold in

Norfolk at 14.20 GMT. Assuming normal cruising speed for the two aircraft it is very likely that they could have intersected over the dropping zone.

Post-war scrutiny of Germany records show that their aircraft did not operate near the English Channel that day. Allegations that Miller is alive but insane or that he was a spy, whether for the allies or Germans, are absurd. It was a foolhardy decision by the trio who stepped into that Norseman. The genius musician was a man of incredible drive and ambition. Like many with such a personality he died young while the more cautious live on.

One of the more popular legends of the sea is the mystery of the *Marie Celeste*, a brigantine found drifting and abandoned by its crew between the Azores and Portugal in 1872. Yet there never was a ship *Marie Celeste*! The saga as it is usually recounted originated from a short story published in *The Cornhill Magazine* written by a young Arthur Conan Doyle. His information was gleaned from the true story of the vessel *Mary Celeste*.

This ship was indeed found drifting and abandoned, but not shipshape with still-hot meals on the tables and lifeboats still slung in their davits, as is usually recounted. In fact, it is quite possible that the brig was abandoned by its crew during a storm when they thought that it was about to founder. Such events resulting in drifting, abandoned ships have happened before and since.

The loss of five Grumman Avenger torpedo bombers of the US Navy is often tagged as the *Marie Celeste* of the air. Like the sea saga (and the loss of Glenn Miller), to present the story in such a way would be erroneous. This mystery is not inexplicable and has never needed the investigative skills of Conan Doyle's later creation: Sherlock Holmes.

As the Avengers took off from Fort Lauderdale Naval Air Station at 14.10 Eastern Standard Time on 5 December 1945, four of the single-engined machines carried the normal crew complement of three men, while the fifth was one man short, making a total of fourteen men in the training flight. The operation was led by Lieutenant Charles Taylor, a flight instructor. The prescribed course was to be out over the Atlantic on 091° East, North at 346° over Grand Bahama Islands and back to Fort Lauderdale on 241° West.

The first indication that Flight 19 was in trouble came at 15.40 when Lieutenant Robert Cox who was circling Fort Lauderdale heard someone transmitting on 4805Kcs calling 'Powers'. This was the name of one of the pilots of Flight 19. This voice on the airwaves was asking what his compatriot's compass reading was. Cox then heard: 'I don't know where we are. We must have got lost after that last turn.'

Cox informed Fort Lauderdale control tower that some aircraft or boats seemed to be lost. He also radioed out: 'This is FT-74; plane or boat calling 'Powers' please identify yourself.' There was no answer to this request. Some time later and after repeated attempts Cox received the call: 'FT-28 to FT-74, both my compasses are out and I am trying to find

Fort Lauderdale. I am over land, but it's broken. I'm sure I'm in the (Florida) Keys, but I don't know how far down and I don't know how to get home.'

Cox advised that this lost pilot should put the sun on his port wing. He added: 'I will fly south to meet you.'

The FT-28 (Taylor's call sign) said: 'I know where I am now. I'm at 2,300ft (690m). Don't come after me.'

'I'm coming to meet you anyway.'

Shortly afterwards FT-28 called again, asking if Miami or any other station could turn on radar to pick them up and relay an accurate bearing. Radio reception then virtually broke up. There was considerable static that day and 4805Kcs was also getting interference from a carrier wave and Cuban broadcasting. Port Everglades was able to contact Taylor at 16.25 and advised: 'Suggest you get another plane in your flight to take over lead.'

Five minutes later Taylor called back: 'One of the planes thinks that if we went west we would hit land.'

Port Everglades and Fort Lauderdale air stations held a telephone conference and their joint conclusion was that Flight 19 was in fact on course and over the Bahama Bank.

At 16.45 Taylor managed to contact Port Everglades again with the message: 'We are heading 030° (north-east) for forty-five minutes, then we will fly north to make sure that we are not over the Gulf of Mexico.' The naval air stations were attempting to get radio bearings from these transmissions, but without success.

Lieutenant-Commander Donald Poole, the Flight Officer at Fort Lauderdale, instructed his control tower to tell Flight 19 to fly 270° (west). This transmission was not acknowledged by Flight 19, but a few minutes later a brief clip of conversation broke through the airwaves: 'If we would just fly west we would get home, dammit!'

Just minutes later, at 17.07, Taylor was heard to radio his flight: 'Change course to 090° (east) for ten minutes,' yet just seven minutes later Port Everglades heard: 'We are now flying 270° (west). We will fly 270° until we hit the beach or run out of fuel.' At 17.22 Taylor called: 'When first man gets down to 10 gallons (45 litres) of fuel we will land in the water together.'

Port Everglades was trying to get Flight 19 to change frequency to 3000Kcs, the emergency channel. At last they got a response from Taylor: 'I cannot change frequency. I must keep my planes intact. Will stay on 4805Kcs.'

It was dark now and the wind was whipping the waves into whitecaps. Clearly Taylor was afraid that all five Avengers would not be able to re-establish contact with each other on the new frequency. At 18.00 an approximate fix was at last obtained. This placed the flight within a 160km (100 mile) radius of 29° 15'N, 79° 00'W – over the Atlantic north of the Bahamas and east of Florida.

Fragments of messages still came through. At 18.02: 'We may have to ditch any minute,' and at 18.15: 'What course are we on? We are over the Gulf. We didn't go far enough east. I suggest we fly east until we run out of fuel. We have a better chance of being picked up close to shore.' But flying east would take them farther out over the Atlantic. The last fragmentary message picked up was at 18.37: 'What course are we on now?'

Flight 19 could have been airborne until approximately 20.00. At some time the pilots of the five torpedo bombers had to face the terrifying prospect of attempting to ditch in that storm-lashed ocean, an almost impossible achievement in the dark. Even if any of the aircraft made a successful landing on the water, they would be dragged down in seconds by the weight of their Pratt and Whitney engines. It is likely that all fourteen men died together.

At 20.37 the coastguard radioed all ships east of Florida to 74° to be alert for five aircraft considered to be down, but before then search and rescue aircraft had been despatched. From Banana River Naval Air Station north of Fort Lauderdale two Martin Mariner flying boats were sent out. One was directed to fly direct to 29°N 79°W, the other under the command of Lieutenant Jeffrey was to fly up the coast to 29°N and then east to 79°W where the two aircraft should rendezvous and commence a square search if neither had found any trace of Flight 19 by that time.

The Martin Mariner had a bad reputation with its crews. Dubbed 'a flying gas tank', fuel vapour tended to penetrate the interior of these aircraft. It was not the kind of machine in which an airman should sneak a surreptitious cigarette. We will never know if that was the reason that Lieutenant Jeffrey's machine was seen by the cargo steamer *Gaines Mills* to explode in mid-air at 28° 59'N, 80° 25'W at 19.50. Like streamers of blazing phosphorous the burning wreckage plunged into the turbulent sea. There had been thirteen crew on board.

So what should have been a routine training flight had led to the deaths of twenty-seven airmen, directly or indirectly. No wreckage or bodies were ever recovered. The stormy sea had many hours to disperse the traces before dawn. And that day came with such high winds and tremendous seas off Florida that it was actually dangerous for search aircraft to fly – but they did.

Flight 19 is often considered to be a victim of the fictitious 'Bermuda Triangle', a somewhat undefined area around that island where, according to various writers, aircraft and ships vanish mysteriously, perhaps abducted by flying saucers or lured to the sea-bed by rays from the sunken continent of Atlantis. But the only real mystery surrounding the events of Flight 19 is why on 14 October 1947 after a prolonged enquiry the US Navy absolved Taylor of all responsibility for the loss. We must believe that the aircraft ditched in formation – one for all and all for one. The pilot who'd said: 'If we would just fly west we would get home, dammit!' had been right.

The United States's need of long and medium-range transport aircraft to supply the Pacific war was to give that nation a lead in commercial aircraft design and manufacture that has not truly been usurped since (although the British Comet nearly gave Great Britain a lead in jet transports). Just before war broke out Lockheed was developing the Constellation as an intercontinental airliner for T.W.A. in competition with Pan American's Boeing 314 Clipper flying boats. Such machines, along with Douglas's DC-6 series, were to pioneer post-war routes after serving as military transports through the war years.

Great Britain was not going to watch the U.S. industry take the lead without a fight. A wartime committee chaired by Lord Brabazon had drawn up specifications for commercial aircraft to serve the routes of the Empire when peace came.

One design that emerged from these deliberations was the Avro Tudor. Powered by four Rolls Royce Merlin piston engines (a development of those which had powered combat aircraft such as the Spitfire, Hurricane, Lancaster and Mosquito), it was a workmanlike design marred by a dated tailwheel undercarriage; but an aircraft almost obsolescent on introduction to service, a last fling of the piston engine before turboprops had their brief heyday.

The Tudor was to prove ill-starred: a crash of one of the prototypes took the life of its designer, Roy Chadwick (who was also responsible for the Lancaster), and the loss without trace of two British South American Airways Corporation Tudor IVs cast doubts over the type that were never lifted.

All aircraft are fitted with control locks. These may take the form of tabs (almost like clothes pegs) to hold the control surfaces to rigid sections of the structure, or actual locks that prevent the control column and rudder pedals from moving more than a fraction when the aircraft is on the ground so that winds cannot move them. Maintenance engineers do not need unnecessary wear to contend with.

Pilots should always ensure, by moving all the control surfaces, that the locks are off and all clear of jamming before taxiing from the hardstanding. We must assume that Test Pilot Sydney Thorn of Avros did this before taxiing the first prototype Tudor II at Woodford Airfield, Lincolnshire on Saturday 21 August 1947. What he clearly did not do is look out of the cockpit windows to see what the aileron controls were actually doing. If he had done so, he would have noticed that the port aileron was going down when his hands were guiding it to go up; the starboard aileron was similarly reversed. The wiring had quite simply been crossed.

Two hundred and seventy metres (three hundred yards) after take off the starboard wing dipped. Thorn moved the control antlers to the left to counteract an unbalance that was perfectly normal. But with crossed controls his instructions merely pushed the starboard wing further down. He can barely have had time to comprehend what was happening when the airliner struck the ground and became a fireball. Besides Thorn and

Chadwick, two Avro technicians on board were also killed.

Thorn's mistake (and that of fitters in wrongly wiring machines in the first case) is not unique. In a far more serious incident on 20 December 1952 a US Air Force C-124 four-engined Globemaster captain actually forgot to release the knob locking the rudder and elevators. The double-deck troop transport took off from Larson Air Force Base, Washington State, with 131 soldiers and crew on board. Just two minutes after take off it smashed into a snow-carpeted field. The tail section broke away, but the front wreckage caught fire. Eighty-seven died, and many of the survivors were seriously injured.

On 27 January 1948 under the command of former RAF pilot Captain Brian McMillan, British South American Airways Corporation Tudor IV *Star Tiger* lifted off from London's new airport at Heathrow with twenty-five passengers bound for Havana. Captain McMillan and his crew of five would be in command of *Star Tiger* as far as Bermuda, from where a relief crew would take over for the final leg to Cuba. The passengers suffered extreme discomfort on the first leg to Lisbon when the cabin heating failed; the cabin temperature was only just above freezing as *Star Tiger* overflew the Bay of Biscay. One of the gyro-compasses also failed. During the overnight halt in Portugal the faults were repaired.

Trouble with the port inner engine delayed take off by two and a half hours the following morning. As *Star Tiger* ascended for the next leg to the Azores, almost immediately both the compass and the heating system failed again.

Star Tiger skirted the high ground to the east of the Azores airport, Santa Maria, landing safely on the single runway in mid-afternoon. Waiting there was a BSAA Avro Lancastrian freighter under the command of Captain Frank Griffin. Both aircraft were scheduled to fly on immediately to Bermuda, provided the meteorological conditions were satisfactory.

The leg from the Azores to Bermuda was then one of the longest ocean crossing plied by commercial aircraft – three thousand kilometres (two thousand miles) of featureless sea against a prevailing west/south-westerly wind. There were no weather ships in that vast tract of Atlantic, and weather forecasts for the route were little more than educated hunches.

To cross this daunting spread of sea the Tudor, with its booked passenger complement, had a maximum endurance of sixteen hours. However, this might not be enough: twice in the previous three months since the service had been inaugurated, *Star Tiger* had had to divert to Newfoundland when the headwinds had increased during the flight, making continuation to Bermuda either hazardous or impossible. Another BSAA Tudor had landed at Bermuda with the fuel gauge needles flickering against their stops.

Pilots and navigators planned their Azores–Bermuda flights in three stages. Before take off they computed a 'point of no return' from where the aircraft would have insufficient fuel to return to the Azores and was committed to onward flight. They revised these calculations in the air. The second stage saw the aircraft able to divert to Newfoundland should the winds prove stronger than originally estimated. In the third and final stage the aircraft had no option but to press on for Bermuda, as no other land would be in range.

Captains McMillan and Griffin consulted in the Santa Maria meteorological office: there was a strong wind blowing from the west, that seemed to increase with height. Furthermore, thick layers of stratocumulus were expected to obscure the stars for at least 1,600km (1,000 miles). Aircraft on this route then relied on astro-navigation, obtaining their bearings with a sextant. It seemed that a late-afternoon take off from the Azores that day – so that darkness would overtake *Star Tiger* within three hours – risked the hazard of navigator and Second Officer Cyril Ellison being unable to get an astral fix before the point of no return.

Griffin felt that he could make the flight that night with his Lancastrian, but that had a nineteen-hour endurance and besides, there was little point in the transport leaving ahead of the Tudor as it was carrying freight that would be transferred to *Star Tiger* at Bermuda, weight that the airliner would be able to carry unassisted on the final shorter leg to Cuba.

The captains decided on a day's postponement. The crews and passengers were booked into the airport hotel.

The meteorological forecast the following afternoon seemed far more favourable: westerly winds as usual and heavy cloud for the first 1,280km (800 miles), but clearer skies were predicted from that point which should enable Ellison to obtain astral fixes well before the point of no return was reached.

Griffin with the Lancastrian took off at 14.30 GMT (12.30 Local Time), about an hour before *Star Tiger*. This would enable the longer-range transport to pass warnings of any weather deterioration back to McMillan en route. The two aircraft would be able to maintain radio contact with each other throughout the flight.

Before he took off Captain McMillan ensured that the fuel tanks of the Tudor were 'full to the gills'. Actually, this meant that he was taking off with a 450kg (1,000lb) overload. The options had been to leave two or three passengers behind or reduce fuel by 689L (150gall). Mindful of the vast distance ahead and the airline's economics, McMillan took the overload – it would rapidly be used. The Tudor took off safely; if the weather forecasts proved correct *Star Tiger* should reach Bermuda in approximately twelve and a half hours, leaving a fuel reserve of three and a half hours.

At 16.11 GMT *Star Tiger* and the Lancastrian made radio contact with each other for the first time. Griffin was encountering headwinds in excess of those forecast: 55 knots instead of the anticipated 30–40. Shortly afterwards he requested a forecast for the latter stages of the flight, this request being directed via the Azores. No answer was received and for a while he became uneasy. However, just before 18.00 his radio operator made direct contact with the US Air Force base at Kindley Field, Bermuda. The information that he received was that the winds on his planned route were indeed stronger than had been predicted by Santa Maria, but that they seemed to be lessening in force near Bermuda. It cannot be known whether or not *Star Tiger*, then flying about 320km (200 miles) behind the Lancastrian, heard this broadcast. However, logged radio messages reveal that shortly after this McMillan in the Tudor amended his flying time to thirteen and a half hours. The safety margin still existed, but it was being eroded.

At 21.30, when the aircraft was almost halfway along its route, the navigator of *Star Tiger* was able to find a gap torn in the clouds, allowing a starshot with his sextant. This revealed the strengthening headwinds, but McMillan, who had now been in radio touch with Bermuda for over an hour, still estimated his flight time at under fourteen hours. Very shortly afterwards *Star Tiger* passed the point of no return and was committed to onward flight, though with the haven of Newfoundland still available by swinging north.

It was 01.00 before *Star Tiger* reported another successful astro-shot. The point of no alternative was rapidly approaching. The position of *Star Tiger* at that time did not reveal what the navigator of the Lancastrian was to discover just thirty minutes later and about 240 km (150 miles) further west: the freighter had been pushed 108km (68 miles) north of its intended track during the previous hour, indicating a south-westerly wind of some fifty knots instead of the light and variable winds forecast by Bermuda for this zone.

As the crew of the Lancastrian awakened to the situation, *Star Tiger* passed the point where sanctuary in Newfoundland was an option – it was committed to flying to Bermuda; there was not enough fuel to reach any other land. **See Map 7.**

It was 02.00 before *Star Tiger* got another accurate astral fix. Ellison's calculations quickly showed that the Tudor too had been blown far north of her intended track. McMillan swung her to port, right into the teeth of what was now a gale, and reported that he now re-estimated his flying time as fourteen and a half hours. Provided there was no sudden deterioration over Bermuda he would still have a fuel safety margin of an hour or so. An hour later Captain Griffin radioed *Star Tiger* for the last time, saying that he was one hour out of Bermuda and about to contact approach control there on voice telephony. 'See you at breakfast,' was his farewell message.

At this time the Tudor was some 640km (400 miles) out from Bermuda, therefore she had not overhauled the freighter in the expected way and must have been more affected by adverse winds. Thick cloud was now rolling in towards the island, and it was unlikely that further star-shots could be taken. However, at 03.15 Radio Operator Tuck reported a satisfactory radio bearing from Bermuda. Surely now they could home in on this?

Seven hours had passed since Bermuda ground station had taken over responsibility for *Star Tiger*. The operator was supposed to contact every aircraft under his control at least once every thirty minutes, but the records show that silences of up to an hour were not uncommon. It was 03.50 before he called *Star Tiger* again. There was no response from the airliner. At this time he contacted approach control and asked if they had heard from the Tudor. They had not. Despite this, it was after 04.00 before the operator again tried to contact the aircraft. Even then, absorbed as he was by other traffic, the operator did not seem to attach any particular significance to the silence on the airwaves. Indeed, it was 04.40, over ninety minutes since the last radio contact, before the alarm was raised.

By this time Captain Griffin had brought the Lancastrian safely in and was contentedly eating his breakfast, expecting to be joined shortly by the Tudor's aircrew. Captain Geoffrey Rees, who had been waiting to take command of *Star Tiger* for the final leg to Cuba, assumed command of the freighter and, accompanied by Captain Griffin, took off to fly back along the track of the Tudor soon after dawn. From Kindley Field a radar equipped B29 also took up the search.

Flying in dreadful conditions, twenty-five aircraft took part in the first day's search; over five days 104 sorties and 882 flying hours were devoted to the hunt for survivors or wreckage from the Tudor. Nothing was ever found.

Here indeed was a mystery for the Ministry of Aviation Court of Investigation. *Star Tiger* had been fitted with two identical wireless-telegraphy transmitters with a range of over a thousand kilometres (several thousands of miles) and three wireless-telephony transceivers with a range of approximately 320km (200 miles). Power for these was supplied by duplicated generators and batteries. Total failure of all of these systems does seem unlikely, yet no distress signal was heard.

Look at the facts again, however: Bermuda was no more than a leaf in a lake compared to the vastness of the Atlantic Ocean; to miss it by 320km (200 miles) needed only for the airliner to be a degree or so off course during the last hours of its flight; *Star Tiger* could have passed by the island without ever having come within radio-telephony range. The radio-telegraphy equipment may have failed. In their report, concerning the maintenance record of *Star Tiger* Air Investigation Board investigators noted that: 'certain defects reappear regularly... indicating that major checks at the maintenance base failed to eliminate them. Secondly, the aircraft not infrequently took off on passenger-carrying flights over long distances with not unimportant defects un-remedied.'

Remember also that one of the gyro-compasses had failed twice on earlier legs of the flight. If it had failed again on this long ocean crossing reliance would have had to be placed on the two bowl compasses on board, the most basic of instruments, easily upset by turbulence. *Star Tiger* had planned to fly at an altitude of just 600m (2,000ft), low flying that would give precious little time for the pilots to pull the machine out of a dive caused by some sudden catastrophic failure. The possibility that they were so tired that they simply flew straight into the sea cannot be discounted; the Tudor had suffered mechanical failures during the flight and its maintenance was questionable – perhaps the auto-pilot too had failed.

Or was *Star Tiger*'s last hour spent struggling blindly towards that tiny speck of land, pushed north by gale force winds and never coming within voice radio range (its 320km (200 mile) range was an ideal; this would be reduced by the flight's low altitude and poor transmission conditions), finally to attempt a ditching in the turbulent ocean? The passengers would have known before the end that they were lost, bracing themselves for the ditching, perhaps escaping on to life rafts only to die later of exposure.

Just before the anniversary of the loss of *Star Tiger*, her sister plane *Star Ariel* vanished en route from Kindley Field, Bermuda to Kingston, Jamaica. Under the command of Captain McPhee Tudor G-AGRE took off at 08.41 (Local Time) on 17 January 1949 with seven crew and thirteen passengers. Ten hours' fuel had been taken for a flight with an expected duration of five and a half hours. At 09.42 *Star Ariel* radioed Bermuda to report that it was over 30°N and was changing frequency to contact Kingston.

The call was acknowledged by Bermuda, but Kingston heard nothing from the aircraft. To those in Jamaica this was hardly surprising. They knew by teleprinter that the flight had left Bermuda, but would expect it to remain under the eyes of that island's air traffic control until she was abreast of Nassau, halfway along the planned track. Thus, owing to the inexplicable decision of *Star Ariel* to relinquish radio contact with Bermuda so early in the flight, and contrary to normal practice on the route, the airliner was virtually forgotten until 13.52 (four hours and ten minutes after its last message) when Kingston asked Bermuda for information regarding G-AGRE; which by that time should have been just eighteen minutes away from landing at Kingston.

At 14.54 BSAA Bermuda declared the aircraft as overdue at Kingston and announced the emergency, immediately despatching another of their Avro Tudors from Nassau to intercept *Star Ariel*'s planned track and to fly the route northwards to Bermuda, searching along the way.

Only the storm-lashed Atlantic Ocean knows the fates of *Star Tiger* and *Star Ariel*. Perhaps as calamity struck the latter, Captain McPhee had a few seconds' realisation that this must have also been the fate of his colleagues a year before. McPhee also took to his watery grave the reason why he 'signed-off' from Bermuda control so early in the flight.

The only lesson learnt from the loss was that planes should not relinquish contact with one ground station before effective reception had been established with another.

Nothing could ever be specifically proved against the Avro Tudor design, but after the loss of the two *Stars* they were withdrawn from all scheduled passenger service. They remained in use for charter operations, however, and, regrettably, were still not immune from disaster (see p. 190).

9
Spy-Plane 007

It is a sadness of present days that we have come to accept aircraft hijackings and terrorism as regular events. Such occurrences now pass relatively unnoticed in those countries not affected unless they are as dramatic as the destruction of Air India's *Kanishka* off the coast of Eire or Pan American's Flight 103 in Scotland – incidents that are reported in the next chapter. In 1989 a Boeing 747 was hijacked by a sixteen year old boy who forced it to land at Rome. He was talked into surrendering after a few hours and it then emerged that he was not, as he had claimed, carrying explosives. It was not an incident extensively reported by the media outside Holland and Italy; we have become immune, we shrug off the news and hope that our holiday flight to the Bahamas does not include a stop-over in Beirut!

One of the most horrific recent attacks of terrorism which shook the whole world concerned the Korean Airlines Flight 007 with a total of 269 on board which was shot down by a Russian fighter as it was leaving their airspace and about to enter that of the Japanese. The USA and South Korea called it an act of murder, the Russians claimed that the ironically numbered flight was on a spying mission. Who was, and is, telling the truth?

Our story must start not on a summer's night in 1983 however but five years earlier on 20 April 1978 with a Boeing 707 of the same airline airborne over the north-west corner of Greenland. Flight 902 from Paris to Seoul via the polar route was just minutes from Canadian airspace when it sheared away from its Anchorage-bound course, instead bearing 112 degrees and flying south-east with its ninety-seven passengers. If the pilots' later tale was to believed they did not realise the significance of the sun now appearing on the right side of the aircraft.

Soon the Boeing 707 was approaching Russian airspace. Fighters were scrambled to intercept it. Sukhoi Su-15 supersonic interceptors caught up with the airliner over the Kola Peninsula only after it had flown over the headquarters of the Northern Russian Naval Fleet. Events then are somewhat confused. Captain Kim Chang-Kyu later claimed that he 'lost his head' when he realised that he was off course and made a break for the Soviet/Finnish border which lay two hundred miles south west. Perhaps he had first seen warning shots from the Russian fighters. The end came however when the Sukhois fired missiles which tore into the port wing and fuselage. The crew brought the crippled airliner down on a frozen lake near the White Sea port of Kem, 280 miles south of Murmansk. It was one thousand miles off course. Two passengers had been killed and thirteen injured by shrapnel. **See Map 9.**

The surviving passengers, the co-pilot and ten crew members were collected by a chartered American airliner two days later but Captain Kim Chang-Kyu and his navigator were held for a further week by the Russians. Particularly in the light of events about to be related, was this deviation really an accident or was the machine fitted with eavesdropping devices, a 'Q-plane' to spy on the chief Soviet naval base at Murmansk? Perhaps the thawing of the cold war may bring an answer in the years to come; and solve the mysteries of Flight 007.

John F. Kennedy Airport, New York, 31 August 1983: 23.05 Local Time (04.05 GMT), the Korean Airlines Boeing 747 roared off into the darkness, into history, bound for its first scheduled stop and crew change at Anchorage, Alaska. Here Captain Chun Byung-In, a man with 10,600 flying hours, 6,618 on the 747 type, took command. Like all Korean Airlines pilots he was an ex-Korean Air Force fighter 'jockey', a man described as an 'ace' aviator by his peers, and a personal friend of the South Korean president. In addition to his co-pilot and engineer he was in command of a flight crew of twenty stewards and stewardesses. There were also six KAL flight crew, all pilots or flight engineers 'deadheading' to Seoul.

They worked for an airline viewed by many others as a 'maverick'. KAL was not a member of the International Air Transport Association and as commercial practice it would undercut other operators' fares. Did it also take 'short cuts' across restricted airspace to save on fuel costs? If so, why did Byung-In load 119,610kg (263,700lb) of fuel at Anchorage (some 3,580kg (7,900lb) more than was needed for safety) yet claim 5 tonnes (tons) less than this on his Weight & Balance Manifest?

The flight plan across the North Pacific was via Airway Romeo 20, one of five, and the route nearest to the Russian border. This information was duly programmed into the 747's three Inertial Navigation System computers. These machines 'talk' to each other in flight; if one disagrees with its fellows it is 'snubbed' and an indicator light illuminates to show the crew that it has failed. Why then did Flight 007 radio back to Anchorage fifty minutes after take off that it was passing the Bethel VHF radio beacon, yet the US King Salmon radar station plotted the 747 as being nineteen kilometres (twelve miles) north of track? Later events seem to discount the likelihood of the crew ignoring the amber warning light of an INS failure.

At this time the Boeing was almost dawdling along while coming up fast behind it was Korean Airlines Flight 015. The airliners would by now be in VHF radio contact with each other. At 14.30 GMT Anchorage, which was still in control of both flights, attempted to contact Flight 007 for its routine report, but received no reply.

In such a situation it would be normal practice for air-sea rescue services to be alerted. The Anchorage radio operator hesitated, but did continue to try to contact the flight. Finally, at 14.44, 007's position was reported; but by Flight 015 who reported it as being on course. This report, besides being contrary to acceptable practice, was also false: 007 was north of its intended track, and this deviation was gradually increasing. By 16.00 it was 240km (150 miles) north.

Both 747s were now travelling at Mach 0.9 and their overspeed warning buzzers would certainly have been howling had they not been isolated. The Boeing 747 is not made to be hovering so close to the sound barrier. Those passengers awake must have been suffering from the turbulence created by the aircraft flying too fast.

Circling ahead of the two Korean airliners was an American Boeing RC135 surveillance plane, hovering off the coast of Komandorski Island. In truth this was an eavesdropping spy plane. The Russians were expected to launch one of their then new PL5 missiles from their nearby Kamchatka Island test site that night.

That there was a planned rendezvous between the RC135 and Korean Airlines Flight 007 seems beyond dispute. The Russians claim that Flight 007 entered their airspace *with* the RC135 at 7,800m (26,000ft) off Komandorski Island, while Flight 015 was reporting to Anchorage that 007 was 240km (150 miles) south of here. **See Map 8.**

Passengers on Flight 007 would presumably be unaware of the spy plane flying in company with them. It would almost certainly have invisibly taken station behind the 747. It is not known what messages were passing between the American surveillance plane and the 'civilian' airliner. For ten minutes the two aircraft flew in formation before, at 16.11, the RC135 banked away into the darkness, turning back towards Alaska, while the 747 tracked on towards Kamchatka Island. It entered restricted Soviet airspace at 16.20. Just three minutes later it radioed Anchorage to 'sign off' from that station and switch to Tokyo's Narita Airport Air Traffic Control; it again reported itself as being some 240km (150 miles) south of its true position.

At 16.30 the Boeing crossed over the coast of Kamchatka Island. Minutes later four Russian Mig 23 and Sukhoi Su-15 fighters were scrambled to intercept it. Later one of the pilots who caught it stated that Flight 007 was showing no navigation lights at all, and also took evasive action when it realised that fighters were around it. The Russians have continued to claim that at no time did they recognise the 747 to be a civilian airliner. It is not certain how close this first wing of fighters came to the 747. If they were particularly near to it they must surely have seen lights from the passenger cabin. It is hardly conceivable that all the window shades were down.

At this time the airliner could have been brought down by SAM 2 (surface-to-air missiles) from the batteries at Petropavlovsk. Possibly this site was not even aware of the intruder in Russian airspace if, as seems possible, the 747 was using ECM (electronic counter measures) equipment to 'blind' radar. Were all those additional aircrew really being 'dead-headed' back to Seoul to balance crew rosters, or were they playing some part in the operation of this flight? Were the Russians being lenient as they let Flight 007 leave the coast of Kamchatka at 17.08, or was this first fighter interception foiled by ECM?

As the 747 headed out over the sea of Okhotsk it called Tokyo to report its position – but it was now 290 kilometres (180 miles) north of this reported course. It did not inform the Japanese of any attempted fighter interception. At about the same time Russian Fighters were scrambled from the airbase on Paramuschiv Island in the Kuriles. Soon afterwards 007 approached Sakhalin Island and left its straight course, swinging in a northward arc even deeper into Russian airspace. This action was confirmed by the Japanese military radar at Wakkanai. 007 was now heading towards waiting Russian fighters, led by Lieutenant-Colonel Osipovich in a SU15, that had scrambled from Dolinsk naval base just north of Korsakov.

Ground radar vectored Lieutenant-Colonel Osipovich into a position behind the airliner at 18.05. Flight 007 was now on a heading of 240° and at 7,800m (26,000ft). Two minutes later this heading changed to 260° with the airliner climbing a further 300m (1,000ft) before reverting to 240°. At 18.12 Osipovich reported that he had the 'hostile' in sight. The Russians later claimed that they were trying to hail the intruder by radio and that their fighters were making flypasts of the (they claim) unlit airliner and waggling their wings to attract attention. One might say that the hump-backed profile of a 747 is unmistakable and that these Russian pilots must have known that this was a civilian machine that had strayed off course. However, the 747 does have a military use, as an airborne command post for the US Air Force, and in darkness a pilot would have difficulties distinguishing either an airline's livery or the additional small aerials that distinguish the military version.

At 18.13 Osipovich radioed his own ground control with the message, 'I see it, I am locked on target.' Now, almost as if its crew had been overhearing all the Russian radio traffic, Flight 007 burst on to the airwaves asking Tokyo if they could make an altitude change from 9,900 to 10,500m (33,000 to 35,000ft). But it hardly seems likely that 007 was even at 9,900m (33,000ft); rather that this break of silence was a ruse both to identify the aircraft as civilian and pretend that it was accidentally off course.

Far below, the Japanese fishing vessel *Chidori Maru No. 58* was thirty kilometres (nineteen miles) off the coast of Moneron Island. Shortly after 03.00 Local Time its crew heard two or three explosions in the sky and saw a flash like a shooting star streaking through the darkness. This does tend to confirm Kasmin's story that he fired tracer rounds as a warning over the nose of the airliner.

The Su-15 fighter was equipped with two Anab AA-3 air-to-air missiles, one rigged to be heat-seeking (to lock on to the hot exhaust of any target), and the other radar-guided. We do not know if both were fired, but at least one streaked away from beneath the fighter and screamed at Mach 2.5

towards Korean Airlines Flight 007 at about 18.26 GMT.

A panic-stricken message was now transmitted from the doomed airliner. Following its standard call-sign there was a disjointed eighteen-second transmission: 'Radio... Korean Air Zero Zero Seven... All engines... rapid decompression... descending to one zero... Delta...' The Japanese radar at Wakkanai reported that the 747 fell rapidly, disappearing from the radar trace at 18.29. The Americans, however, who had a separate radar at Wakkanai, claim that 007 was airborne for almost another ten minutes, descending first to 4,800m (16,000ft) at 18.30 and 300m (1,000ft) at 18.38. She was 584km (365 miles) off course.

An incident like this – a civilian airliner shot down without good cause by the Eastern Bloc – could spark off the next world war. But was there a good reason for the destruction? How would America have reacted in those cold-war years if an Aeroflot airliner had 'strayed' so far off course that it had passed over sensitive military installations and if this 'accident' had been compounded by another Aeroflot airliner passing back false position reports for its compatriots for some hours? Would the British have allowed a Polish airliner under such conditions to infiltrate the airspace over an important military exercise?

Unidentified radar blips might be a spy-plane or a nuclear bomber. In this case the tragedy is that seemingly over two hundred innocent passengers perished because American intelligence, in consort with Korean Airlines, cynically decided to use them as pawns in the spying game. Did they believe that no one would shoot down an aircraft that must surely be recognised as a civilian machine that had 'strayed' off course? What of the investigations into the incident? The Russians and Japanese searched the sea for wreckage, but without co-operating. There were many near collisions between the countries' ships as they criss-crossed the area. Meanwhile political accusations flew between East and West. Who was telling the truth?

The US and Korean version of events is that the 747's INS equipment malfunctioned to the extent that it took the airliner 584km (365 miles) north of its planned course; this would involve the failure of all three computers. In this case, why was Captain Chun in Korean Airlines Flight 015 continually reporting back 007's position reporting it to be on course, but from *notes that he was carrying*? And why did 007 fly in consort with the RC135 for ten minutes?

The wreckage of KAL Flight 007 lies in deep water. Some bodies were recovered, revealing violent explosion injuries, but the aircraft's black boxes were never found; or if they were no one has, to date, revealed their information. The United States should have initiated an investigation by the National Transportation Safety Board; indeed one was started, but the State Department ordered that enquiries should cease. The South Koreans have simply maintained that the incident was an act of murder. Perhaps one day a crewman of the RC135 surveillance plane or someone else who knows the truth may step forward. Until then it will never be discovered.

For several years the United States maintained a self-righteous stance over the events of Flight 007 and then they, too, shot down an unarmed civilian airliner.

For seven years bitter war had raged between Iraq and Iran, involving land forces as well as gunboats in the Persian Gulf. Over several years these had attacked not only the vessels of their enemies, but also neutral ships, particularly tankers, entering those waters to collect oil. Both parties were guilty of these attacks.

By 1988, tired of the loss of shipping and the deaths of so many innocent sailors, several countries including Great Britain and the United States sent warships into the Gulf to protect their merchant vessels.

On the morning of 3 July the Aegis-class cruiser USS *Vincennes* and sister ship USS *Montgomery* were on station south of the island of Qishm at the western edge of the Strait of Hormuz. The crew were at the alert, their nerves taughtened. The US Navy had already seen action in the Persian Gulf, and less than a year before sailors on board the USS *Stark* had been killed when it was struck by an air-launched missile believed to have been fired from an Iranian Grumman F14 Tomcat fighter. This supersonic jet was built in the United States and sold to the Arab nation in the late 1970s, just before the overthrow of Iran's shah by Muslim fundamentalists, perhaps a case of sowing one's own seeds of destruction?

While the grey warship ploughed a wake of phosphorescence through the gentle swell of the Gulf's waters the thermometer at Bandar Abbas Airport in Iran was nudging 100°F, the sun searing down on the concrete ramp where passengers were strolling out to board the waiting Iran Air A300 Airbus for a scheduled flight to Dubai in the United Arab Emirates on the opposite side of the Gulf. Wives enveloped in their traditional black chuddars trailed behind their husbands. Many Iranians were making this short flight purely to buy luxury gods that had become unavailable in their war-stricken country; others were emigré Iranians returning home after visiting relatives.

In the cockpit of the twin engined wide-bodied jet Captain Mohsen Rezaian was going through the pre-flight checklist. He had been in command of this shuttle trip twenty-five times before. His flight plan directed him via the 32km (20 mile) wide commercial traffic corridor Airway Amber 59, high above the warships in the Gulf.

Captain Will Rogers III of the USS *Vincennes* had been warned by his intelligence services that the Iranians might attack US shipping in the Gulf that weekend to coincide with US Independence Day celebrations. The previous night a Danish ship had been set upon in the Strait of Hormuz. Captain Rogers paced the darkened control room in the heart of his warship, the glowing display screen showed the position of shipping, the electronics humming. The operators were monitoring a dozen Iranian gunboats circling in their own territorial waters and a convoy of merchant ships passing through the Strait as Captain Rezaian was turning on the Airbus's transponder which enabled electronic signals to identify it as civilian flight Iran Air 655.

Rogers had ordered his Sikorsky Seahawk helicopter into the air to take a closer look at the Iranian gunboats. At about 10.00, not far away, the boats attacked a Norwegian oil tanker. Just ten minutes later, the Americans allege, the Iranians opened fire on the *Vincennes'* helicopter, which scuttled back to its landing pad at the rear of the cruiser. It seemed that the warnings of a probable escalation of violence were well founded.

Distracted now by the hostile gunboats, it seems that the navymen in the *Vincennes'* control room did not, as they should have done, monitor civilian air traffic control wavebands at Bandar Abbas Airport. Had they done so they could have overheard conversations between Resaian and the control tower making it clear that a civilian flight was about to depart from there. This airport also served as a base for Iranian F14 fighters.

At 10.40 the *Vincennes*, now at combat stations, engaged allegedly approaching Iranian gunboats with its 12cm (5in) gun, sinking two of them. In almost the same minute Flight 655 took off with a total of 290 on board, 60 of them foreign nationals. The *Vincennes* was steaming almost directly under Airway Amber 59.

Flight 655 was noticed by a radar operator in the *Vincennes'* control room at 10.47. The Airbus was merely a blip on his screen, but closing fast on the warship. The operator told Captain Rogers and projected the radar trace on to an overhead screen. The *Vincennes'* radar could not distinguish between military and civilian aircraft; the glowing speck on the screen was the same size for the bulky Airbus as it would have been for an F-14 fighter. Captain Rogers believed that this radar trace was outside the civilian air corridor and moving so fast that it was likely to be one of the Iranian Tomcats. He ordered that the pilot should be warned to alter course.

In the cockpit of the A300 Captain Rezaian was in contact with his air traffic control, requesting permission to climb from 2,100m to 4,200m (7,000 to 14,000ft). Rogers later claimed that the unidentified aircraft was given eleven warnings during the next few minutes. It is also alleged that the Airbus's transponder was interrogated and gave an electronic return that identified it as an F14 fighter.

There was one other way that the *Vincennes'* crew could have identified the aircraft: in the control room of the warship there was a copy of the international airline timetable. Flight 655 was flying on schedule and included in the guide. But the events took place in minutes. At 10.51 the blip was within five minutes' flying time of the *Vincennes* and Captain Rogers fully believed it to be hostile. He recalled that the USS *Stark* had been hit because her captain believed an approaching radar blip was a friendly Iraqi aircraft and had allowed it to get too close before realising that it was an Iranian F14 which had then launched two Exocet missiles, one of which had struck the ship.

Rogers now radioed the US Joint Task Force commander, Rear-Admiral Anthony Lees, whose flagship was also in the Gulf, to seek advice. Rogers was told to use his own initiative.

At 10.54, with the A300 just 14km (9 miles) away, the *Vincennes* launched two Standard surface-to-air missiles which streaked away towards the Airbus. At least one of them struck. Destruction was almost instantaneous: the Airbus disintegrated in mid-air and rained down to the waters of the Gulf. The sailors on board *Vincennes* cheered and patted each others' backs – they had revenged the attack on the USS *Stark*, and had brought down an Iranian Tomcat. Hadn't they?

Iranian air traffic control was trying to contact their Flight 655. They declared it missing as ships began to trawl debris and the first mutilated corpses from the Gulf; corpses that were clearly civilians. Within an hour, when Dubai declared Flight 655 overdue, the awful truth became clear.

The American President, Ronald Reagan, was informed at 05.00 (Eastern Standard Time) that an Iranian F-14 appeared to have been downed by missiles from an American warship on patrol in the Gulf. He was left to sleep for another two hours and then phoned by the Situation Room of the White House to be informed that the aircraft may have been a civilian airliner.

That lunchtime in the United States, the eve of Independence Day, an embarrassed President Reagan announced to a press conference that a civilian airliner with 290 on board had been shot down by the US warship USS *Vincennes*. Inevitably when people heard this comparisons were drawn with Korean Airlines Flight 007. In subsequent days the US government adopted an almost attacking stance. Why did the Iranians allow a civilian aircraft to overfly an area where their military forces were at that moment engaged in combat? White House chiefs of staff also claimed that the airliner was outside the civilian air corridor.

The Iranians, although justifiably accusing the US of an act of terrorism, took a restrained diplomatic stance. Here was an opportunity to cultivate international opinion in their favour; and television pictures of distraught relatives brought unusual sympathy to a nation almost universally despised at the time.

By Independence Day the truth began to emerge. The USS *Vincennes'* electronics could not have distinguished the size of the approaching aircraft; the radar return was the same magnitude whatever the bulk of the aircraft; and Flight 655 was on course within the civilian air corridor. It had been shot down literally 'in the heat of the moment' by navymen whose nerves were on edge.

Gennadi Osipovich and Captain Will Rogers III, the men who pressed the red buttons, must live with their consciences for the rest of their lives. However, there are postscripts to the story of Flight 655. In March 1989 Rogers' wife was driving through San Diego when smoke was seen pouring from her car. As she stopped and ran clear it burst into flames. It is believed that an incendiary bomb had been planted on the vehicle.

But even before Mrs Rogers' car was destroyed Pan American Flight 103 had been involved in cataclysm above the quiet Scottish town of Lockerbie. Was this the Iranians' retribution?

10
Malice Aforethought

This chapter concerns itself with murder. There may be some who will allege that the destruction of KAL Flight 007 and the Iran Air Airbus were also homicide but in neither of those instances was there premeditation – unless it is assumed that Flight 007 was deliberately off-course in which case perhaps the US government and South Korea should be seen as culpable rather than the Russian defences and Vassily Kasmin. Pilots and air traffic controllers may, through negligence or an uncharacteristic lapse of concentration, instigate catastrophe but there is no malice afore-thought in such a scenario; Gradimir Tasic's late realisation that aircraft under his control were on a collision course or even Captain van Zanten's decision to begin his take off roll at Los Rodeas can be viewed as involun-tary homicide – manslaughter – but from the earliest days of commercial air transport, even back to those times of biplanes and open cockpits that we revere now through the rose-tinted spectacles of nostalgia, passengers have flown at the peril of being hijacked or blown apart in mid-air by persons with malice aforethought.

Aerial crime has, in general terms, been through three distinct stages. Until the advent of the intercontinental jetliner in approximately 1960, attacks on civil aircraft were mostly made either as suicide bids or murder attempts on a specific passenger – in either of these situations the deaths of other passengers would be viewed as incidental.

The second stage of malice aforethought was the era of hijackings, a form of terrorism that became common during the 1960s, although the first such case came as early as 1930 when a Ford Tri-Motor was seized during a Peruvian revolution yet the word did not enter general vocabu-lary until much later. It had originated as the cry used by English high-waymen to halt staging coaches: 'Hang 'em high, Jack!' Only in 1958 would the phrase be transferred to represent the seizure of an aircraft; a practice that in these years was almost exclusively confined to forcing American airliners to divert to Cuba. After Castro's coup the traffic flow would be reversed with Cuban pilots escaping from his regime. In an ironic twist the revolutionary was the first to have to instigate security checks and employ skymarshalls – armed guards to foil hijackers or pilots who might otherwise deliberately deviate to an unscheduled destination. Some passengers believe that guards cannot, or should not, be armed on board an airliner because if a bullet should penetrate the skin of a pres-surised cabin the aircraft could disintegrate or passengers be sucked out.

This is not so, pressurised B29 bombers were frequently bullet and shrapnel-riddled during raids over Japan yet returned. The greatest danger is that a fuel line or hydraulics might be punctured. Skymarshalls use low-velocity bullets to lessen the risk.

Hijackings in general are beyond the province of this history. They may subject passengers to severe trauma (at the very least they are likely to suffer a boring political diatribe), they may involve assassination; only occasionally do such situations result in the destruction of an aircraft.

In June 1989 a Russian-built Antonov 26 military transporter converted for civil use by Ariana Afghan was hijacked on a flight from Kabul to Zaranj in the south-west of Afghanistan. From agency reports that reached the West from Iran it seems that the pilot, Mirvis Patkia, resisted the hijackers, but somehow lost control of the twin-engined machine. It crashed in south-eastern Iran near the town of Zabol, close to the border with Afghanistan. There were reported to be twenty-six survivors, but it is not known if this accounts for all on board.

Following tighter airport security the number of hijackings has declined in recent years. Now the most serious non-accidental threat to airliners is the prospect of a bomb being placed on board, most likely by terrorists. In the past, however, the destruction of an aircraft would be likely just to murder one passenger – with comparatively little danger of the culprit being caught.

As far back as 28 March 1933 an Imperial Airways Armstrong-Whitworth Argosy biplane airliner en route from Brussels to Croydon was brought down near Roulers, Belgium, following what is accepted as having been an explosion on board. It was a bright afternoon, cold at 1,200m (4,000ft) where *City of Liverpool* cruised at two and a half kilometres (a mile and a half) per minute. The English Channel lay ahead. By sunset Captain Lionel Leleu aimed to be home in Purley, near Croydon, to take his pregnant wife out for the evening. Pilots then had open cockpits, with leather coats, goggles and a scarf to keep out the cold. Back in the passenger cabin people sat in wicker chairs and could even open the windows.

Farm workers looked up at the airliner as it cruised sedately across the sky. One later stated that he saw a puff of smoke appear above the rear of the fuselage and then a streak of flame from near the tail. The Argosy nosed down into a shallow dive. At that moment something tumbled out of the fuselage and plummeted to earth. It was one of the passengers: Albert Voss, a sixty-eight year old German Jew who had become naturalised British and practised as a Manchester dentist. He must have been one of the first flying businessmen, visiting Germany five or six times a year, ostensibly to deal in dental instruments, but possibly he was engaged in more nefarious activities.

On the day of the fatal flight he was accompanied by a younger associate named Dearden, reputed to be involved in smuggling. At Brussels both men took out 35-franc insurance policies worth £500 to their dependants should they die in an air disaster.

As Voss's body smacked into the soil Captain Leleu was fighting to achieve a controlled emergency landing for *City of Liverpool*. Flames could be seen inside the cabin as she came low, heading towards a line of poplars that bordered the Essen road. He was standing up in the cockpit, heaving back on the control column. He almost achieved a touchdown in an open field, but when only 300km (200ft) or so from the ground there were two sharp reports like bullets being fired, and *City of Liverpool* broke in two by the passenger door. The forward section rolled on to its back and then plunged vertically down, the twisted wreckage instantly erupting into fire on impact. Just before it struck the ground a female passenger was thrown from the rear portion, her dress billowing around her like a parachute. She, too, died. Her name was Lotte Voss, no relation of Albert Voss but suspected, though this has never been proved, of being his mistress.

Every piece of the wreckage was examined for traces of inflammable chemical, though none was ever found. The inquest returned an open verdict. Officially the file on this disaster remains open.

A not dissimilar incident befell a Douglas DC-3 of Canadian Pacific Airlines in September 1949, but in this case the perpetrators were brought to justice. The airliner took off from Quebec's L'Ancienne Lorette Airport for the short trip to Baie Comeau to the north-east with a total of twenty-three people on board. Fishermen and a steamer crew watched it as it passed over the forests bordering the Saint Lawrence River and approached Mount Torment, some sixty kilometres (forty miles) from Quebec, where it exploded in mid-air killing all on board.

When crash investigators and the Royal Canadian Mounted Police sifted through the wreckage they concluded that a dynamite charge had been responsible for this mass murder. Meanwhile back in Quebec one Marguerite Pitre attempted to commit suicide. She was a mistress of Albert Guay, a jeweller whose wife had perished in the crash. Just a month before he had been fined for illegally being in the possession of a gun following a disturbance in a restaurant with Pitre. He had only recently separated from his wife after, it would later be revealed, attempting to murder her three times.

Guay had power over Marguerite Pitre, having loaned her money. Telling her that the police suspected her of having been the perpetrator of the crime, he gave her pills with which to kill herself; but when this attempt went wrong she revealed all from her hospital bed. The bomb had been constructed by her brother. All three were sentenced to death.

The murderers of all eighty-one persons on board a Middle East Airlines Boeing 720 have not been brought to book, however. On New Year's Day 1976 it took off from Beirut for Saudi Arabia. At 11,100m (37,000ft) over that country's desert a bomb in the forward cargo hold blew the machine apart, an event that has become tragically familiar in recent times.

Between the inception of commercial air travel and 1985 there were nearly forty confirmed instances of bomb explosions on board aircraft.

Philippines Air Lines was stuck three times; British European Airways (now British Airways) lost a Comet 4B over the Mediterranean in a 1966 attempt to kill Cypriot guerilla leader General Grivas. Perhaps fore-warned, he was not on board, but the sixty-six persons who were died.

Most west to east trans-Atlantic flights are timed to land at Heathrow at breakfast-time. Air India's Boeing 747 *Kanishka* stopped over at Heathrow on her frequent flights from the United States to her homeland. But she never made it to Heathrow on the Sunday morning of 23 June 1985. Flying over 100 minutes late and two and a half hours from London, she was still over the Atlantic off the coast of Eire at 06.00 GMT. She was cruising slightly slower than normal: Mach 0.81 instead of 0.84. She was fitted with five engines: there are mounting points beneath the port wing of all Boeing 747s to enable them to carry a non-working engine there. A defective engine had been fitted to *Kanishka* before she left Montreal for this service to Bombay via London and New Delhi. This and the stream-lined fairings fitted to the cowling accounted for the speed reduction and was partly why the flight was late.

Meanwhile 9,600km (6,000 miles) away it was afternoon in Tokyo where at Narita Airport baggage containers were being offloaded from a Canadian Pacific Airlines Boeing 747 which had arrived as Flight 003 from Vancouver with 390 on board. In one of those containers was a suitcase marked for trans-shipment to Air India Flight 301 to India via Bangkok.

India was a nation in turmoil. Internal strife in the state of Punjab brought about by Sikh demands for a separate nation of Khalistan had come to a head in June 1984 when the Indian Army stormed the Golden Temple at Amritsar, the Sikhs' holiest shrine. Shortly after that bloody massacre the Indian President Indira Gandhi was murdered by one of her Sikh bodyguards. Fighting broke out on the streets of New Delhi as Hindus murdered Sikhs in retribution.

Now, almost a year later, Indira Gandhi's son Rajiv was president. His life, too, was under constant threat. At least one assassination attempt had already been foiled. Two Sikhs, Lal Singh and Ammand Singh were wanted for questioning.

It was 15.19 Local Time (06.19 GMT) when Narita Airport shook to the detonation of a bomb. Two baggage handlers were killed and four seri-ously hurt as a suitcase that would have been loaded into Air India Flight 301, and had arrived on Canadian Pacific Airlines Flight 003, detonated. *Kanishka* was still far out over the Atlantic at that time, and the first unde-tailed reports of the Tokyo explosion were only just being transmitted as Captain Hanse Singh contacted Shannon air traffic control at 07.05 GMT. The Boeing was at 50'N, 15'W travelling at a groundspeed of 519 knots and heading at 098' Magnetic to cross the Bristol Channel and approach Heathrow from the west. There were 307 passengers on this leg of the flight and a total of 22 crew. The co-pilot was Satninder Singh Bhinder, and the Flight Engineer Dara Dumasia, on his last flight before retire-ment.

In Shannon air traffic control, M. Quinn and T. Lane were looking at the slowly moving flash of the radar return on the radar screen as *Kanishka* flew on. It was 07.14 when that dot flared and then vanished. In the same moment the two controllers heard a clicking on the radio receiver as if a transmit button was pressed. *Kanishka* had been blown apart.

The cargo vessel *M.V. Laurentian Forest* confirmed the horror two hours later as it sailed into wreckage and corpses floating on the sea. Eventually 131 bodies were recovered. Using sonar, the British *Gardline Locator* located the wreckage at a depth of 2,010m (6,700ft). Contemporary flight recorders are fitted with radio beacons, the batteries for those on *Kanishka* enabling them to send out a signal for up to thirty days. Thus located, the cockpit voice recorder was brought up by midget submarine on 9 July. The following day the flight recorder was also found on the sea-bed, and handed over to the Indian authorities.

For what little is at present known about the perpetrators of this crime we have to look at Royal Canadian Mounted Police evidence. Here was an investigation far more complex than the Guay and Pitre case. The examination of passenger lists and computer records indicated that an L. Singh had checked in at Vancouver for Canadian Pacific Flight CP003, but had failed to board it. A passenger of the same name was also booked on Air India's Flight AI301 from Narita Airport to Bangkok. Also on 22 June an M. Singh checked in at Vancouver Airport for Canadian Pacific Flight CP060 to Toronto. There was an argument as this person demanded that his luggage be checked through to Air India Flight 182 although this booking could not be verified. This Singh claimed that he had just phoned Air India who had told him that his booking was confirmed. The luggage was interlined for transfer to the Air India Boeing. At 16.18 GMT Canadian Pacific Flight 060 left without M. Singh on board – but with the luggage. Canadian Pacific Flight 003 departed Toronto for Tokyo at 20.37 GMT. Just five minutes later Flight CP060 swept down on to the same runway. Baggage handlers ran out the containers from the hold. The suitcase with the bomb inside was transferred to the waiting Air India 'jumbo'.

We know that the bomb that was to explode at Narita Airport, although clearly the Air India flight from Japan was the real target of the device, was constructed within the frame of a hi-fi tuner that had been manufactured by the Sanyo Corporation in 1979. The Royal Canadian Mounted Police discovered an electrical retail shop in Vancouver that had sold this obsolete model to two Sikhs, distinctive in their turbans, three months before.

Enough 'plastic' explosives to destroy a 'jumbo' jet can easily be hidden within the frame of a hi-fi tuner, tape recorder, briefcase or even a camera case. It is only necessary to rip a tear in the skin of the aircraft, metal that is only a millimetre or so (less than a twentieth of an inch) thick, and the five hundred knot slipstream and the explosive effects of depressurisation will do the rest.

The explosives were not detected by airport security because the X-ray machine at Toronto airport was faulty that day. Security staff there ran a hand-held explosives 'sniffer' over the luggage being transferred from Canadian Pacific Flight 060 to Air India Flight 182. But if the explosive were Czechoslovak-manufactured Semtex it would have been undetectable to such devices.

The *Kanishka* incident is listed in the International Civil Aviation Operator's Accident Index as 'structural failure'. This patently verges on the ludicrous, yet because the Indian authorities have not to date released full information or a copy of their report it could not be labelled as anything else. Had the information been available world-wide then perhaps the tragedy to happen on the night of 21 December 1988 could have been avoided.

The dark veils of dusk came early that night, the winter equinox and the longest darkness; a night for witches and evil plots.

It was almost the end of a year that had seen a terrible catalogue of disasters in Great Britain: a horrific fire at London's Kings Cross Underground station, the explosion of a North Sea oil rig, and just days before a triple collision of trains at London's Clapham Junction, Britain's busiest station and a calling place for my commuter service home to the south-western suburbs.

In a still-united USSR, rescuers were still digging for survivors amidst the rubble of towns, villages and cities razed by the Armenian earthquake in which the estimated death toll was 55,000. Who could predict that before another day, during the mildest winter since records began another disaster would sweep away the post-mortems of the year's catastrophes to be replaced by banner headlines spreading the news of the heinous murder of all on board a Boeing 747?

Perhaps I glimpsed it that night, coming in from America; perhaps it was one of those aircraft, mostly ignored through familiarity, pacing the train as it swept through the inner suburbs, the winking of their navigation lights mirroring the Christmas illuminations that glowed in windows flashing by. Every day the airliners swept over my home, usually on their landing approach to the world's busiest international airport: Heathrow; their flaps down, airbrakes extended, wheels stretching out like talons for the first smoky contact with the runway just a few miles away.

I glanced up at them as I walked home from the station: one, two, three visible together in the clear sky of that evening; Douglas DC-9s and DC-10s, the all-conquering Boeing series; 727s, 737s, 757s and the mighty 747 'jumbos', spotlights illuminating the operator's logos on their giant tail fins: Trans World Airlines, British Airways, Air France, Pan American. The last company had retained some of the nautical terms once associated with their flying boats. It was with Boeing 'ships' that they had established their North Atlantic service just before World War II. The *Yankee Clipper* flew newsreel film of the British Monarch's American tour in the final summer of peace across the ocean for showing in British cinemas just a day after the footage was shot, a remarkable achievement at the time and a precursor of the end of the Blue Riband liners. Now, pictures of the destruction of a Pan American trans-Atlantic aircraft would be flashed around the world within hours.

In deference to their history Pan American's radio call sign was not the expected Papa Alpha but Papa Clipper. Their intercontinental airliners still bore nautical names. A Boeing 747 of their fleet was sitting on the concrete apron at Heathrow that evening. She had been christened *Clipper Maid of the Seas* and for nineteen years had carried this name through the air currents of the skies. She had been refuelled and cleaned, new promotional literature and 'snack bags' had been tucked into seat pockets. The lavatory tanks had been flushed and fresh water piped into the tanks. Meals and duty-free goods were being loaded by the thirteen cabin crew.

Captain Jim MacQuarrie and co-pilot Ray Wagner had programmed the three inertial navigation system computers that could navigate and automatically fly the 'jumbo' across the Atlantic on yet another trip to New York. No human hand can compare with the efficiency of these systems. Perhaps pilots are only really carried on long-range commercial aircraft now to deal with emergencies and to allay the fears of the more nervous passengers!

As the first passengers for Pan American Flight 103 boarded the luggage containers were being slid into the two cavernous holds. Some luggage was being transferred from another Pan American aircraft, a triple-engined Boeing 727, standing alongside on Pier 7-Left. This had taken off from Frankfurt in West Germany at 16.50 to form the first leg of Flight 103. Working beneath the glare of floodlights at some point a baggage handler unwittingly loaded a bomb into the forward hold of *Clipper Maid of the Seas*. A warning had been given. But security was seriously lax and wanting as Flight 103 was being prepared that unseasonably mild night.

Pan American had been placed on top-level security alert by Frankfurt Airport's security chief Horst Hanstein and his Pan American counterpart Martin Hüpner from 7 December following a threatening telephone call to the US Embassy in Helsinki. The caller had warned that Pan American Flight 103 would be bombed before Christmas. Such threats had been made before: every day unbalanced, or simply malicious, people phone up airlines, airports and security services. Hoax callers far outnumber terrorists.

As the 109 passengers of the connecting flight checked in at Frankfurt they were asked questions concerning the reason for their journey and whether they had packed their own luggage; also, whether they were carrying any luggage belonging to another person. Pan American's security contractor, Alert Management Systems Incorporated, opened and inspected some of the luggage that was presented; that belonging to English or American passport holders was, it seemed, ignored, the innocence of such passengers being presumed purely on the basis of their apparent nationality – yet, as terrorists have proved in the past, it is not beyond their resources to obtain false passports, and there are blond-haired, blue-eyed, white-skinned Arab terrorist group sympathisers. Of the seventy items of baggage that would be transferred to *Clipper Maid of the Seas* at Heathrow, only seven or eight items had been hand-searched, though all items had been fed through an X-ray check and an explosives 'sniffer', neither of which are foolproof.

As the Boeing 727 was airborne over the congested skies of western Europe the 194 passengers joining Flight 103 at London were milling around the check-in desk. The staff at Heathrow had not been informed of the threatening call to Helsinki. In Terminal Three non-US passport holders put their luggage through an X-ray machine under the eye of Alert Management Systems Incorporated *before* checking in. Only a few bags are believed to have been hand-searched before they were swept away by conveyor belt to the baggage handling area for packing into the pallets that would be loaded on to the 747. The baggage handlers were involved in a race against the clock: for *Clipper Maid of the Seas* to get away on schedule they had just one hour to sort the baggage from the Frankfurt connection and to load that along with the items checked in at Heathrow into the Boeing 747.

Among the baggage loaded was that of New York businessman Jaswant Singh Basuta who had gone through the security checks into the departure lounge, but missed the last call for the flight while he was in the duty-free shop. His inattentiveness was to save his life, but that doomed Flight 103 was to soar away with his luggage on board. That this was permitted to happen breached security and disregarded lessons that should have been learnt from the *Kanishka* incident: no aircraft should leave with the luggage of an absent passenger.

Heathrow is one of the world's greatest transit camps, a city enclosed within security fencing; a melting pot for the mixings, greetings and partings of our argumentative and peaceless species. The jet airliners that made such liaisons easily possible – that bring and fly away the lonely, the dispossessed, the smugglers and the hunted – were arriving and departing heavily-laden that night. In a time of such heavy traffic it was hardly surprising that *Clipper Maid of the Seas* was twenty-five minutes late as she took off from Runway 28 Left. All runways are numbered according to their compass direction. This was one of the two main parallel runways awkwardly aligned so that the prevailing wind usually blows across them. The behemoth paused momentarily at the threshold for clearance.

And then she was off, rolling, the four mighty Pratt and Whitney turbofans – each harnessing the total power of a World War II four-engined bomber – sucked greedily for air at first, desperate to feed their combustion chambers, and then the power began to rise by the moment as the slipstream forced more and more moist December air into those cavernous intakes where it would be compressed, blended with kerosene, and expelled from the nozzles as a deadly stream of superheated gases that could drive the Boeing forward on yet another of the thousands of flights that she had already made across the tempestuous waters of the Atlantic.

The wings flexed, stiffened, bowed a little as they took the weight; leading edge slats (firmly locked now with the modifications made after the *Hessen* incident at Nairobi) were diverting extra air across the smoothly curved upper surfaces to make the pressure there lower than beneath where the huge drooping flaps – though not lowered to their maximum which would have added too much drag – were helping to trap the air so that obeying the laws of flight and defying those of gravity over three hundred tons of volatile fuel, electrics powerful enough to supply a small town and 259 souls (in airline parlance the passenger complement of a flight are referred to as 'persons', the total on board including the crew as 'souls') soared into the sky.

Who first coined the phrase: 'When I see an elephant fly?' – what would they think to see *Clipper Maid of the Seas* lift her nose towards the stars glinting between the torn shreds of thin cloud and then climb away as if flying towards them. As the winking anti-collision lights of the clipper faded to the north, blending with others also departing, and relying on the air traffic controllers hunched over their glowing radar screens at West Drayton traffic control centre, to keep them safe from the horrors of mid-air collision, friends and relatives of those on board fought their way out from the throng of the terminal to cars, buses, taxis and the Underground. The most dangerous part of the journey was over, their loved ones would be in New York in a few hours time, hurtling through the night. The winter dawn would come first to these islands, a dawn lit by the flames of destruction. Leaf-strewn Great Britain would rise to the horror and carnage of its worst air disaster and greatest mass-murder: the sabotage of Flight 103 over the peaceful Scottish border town of Lockerbie.

By 18.58 the aircraft was already nearly 480km (300 miles) north of London and cruising at over four-fifths the speed of sound: 864kph (540mph). The Solway Firth lay 9,300m (31,000ft) below, its waters and those of the small River Sark that drained into it being the historically disputed border between England and Scotland.

To the east, perhaps visible to those seated on the starboard side who had not closed their blinds, glowed the lights of Carlisle. Seven miles north of England's last major town and just over the Scottish border, its lights no brighter than distant glow-worms in the dark from the 747's altitude, was the village of Gretna; once the destination of eloping lovers coming to get married without parental consent under more liberal Scottish laws and still as a romantic, if over-commercialised, location for such arrangements.

Soon *Clipper Maid of the Seas* would turn to the west, towards the ocean and the United States, a pilgrim of the jet age. Eight and a half million revolutions of the engines should take her there at almost sixteen kilometres (ten miles) per minute. Flying with the ghosts of the aerial pioneers of less than a lifetime before who had fought the might of the Atlantic, and failed: Ray Hinchcliffe, Elsie Mackay, Princess Ludwig Lowenstein-Wertheim, Leslie Hamilton; half-forgotten names in a world of 'jumbos' and supersonic aircraft and whose frail and unreliable machines had plummeted down into those dark and heaving seas to disappear forever.

But Flight 103 was not a stick-and-string machine of aviation history about to battle the jetstreams on a wing and a prayer; to the north-west Prestwick air traffic control was watching over the 747's flight. It was a blip on the radar screen of the duty clearance officer, Tom Fraser, as the Boeing entered Scottish air. Below now lay the soft hills and rolling fells of the border country, sheep farming land today, but once a wild landscape that the Roman empire had been unable to conquer. Hadrian's Wall already lay behind Flight 103, but slipping ten kilometres (six miles) below at over 800kph (500mph) were the archaeological remains of ancient battles between the legions and the Picts. Just to the west was the dual-carriageway A74 trunk road to Glasgow, its course entwined with the electrified west coast route railway line from London to Scotland. Heading north the two paths cross and re-cross each other as they wind up Beattock Pass. First they go through the little market town of Lockerbie, the last station for nearly fifty kilometres (thirty miles) before that barren and wind-scoured land; a town of low-built stone houses huddled together against the wind.

Co-pilot Ray Wagner's voice cut through the silence of that bleak terrain as he radioed Prestwick control: 'Papa Clipper 103 requesting oceanic clearance. Estimating 59 North, 10 West at flight level 310, mach decimal 84.'

It was 19.02 as Tom Fraser, the duty clearance officer, replied 'Papa Clipper 103, you are cleared from 59 North, 10 West to Kennedy.' He glanced at his screen where the steady sweeps of the radar were projected as a box containing the blip of the 747 with beside it, in glowing figures, the information PAA 103, 310 (the altitude, 31,000ft [9,300m]), 059 (direction).

Everything was normal; *Clipper Maid of the Seas* was now cleared to cross the ocean. On board the cabin crew were preparing to serve dinner. Many passengers dozed or slept, ready to face a working day in New York, or perhaps even a day's Christmas shopping. Perhaps at least one person on board had no thoughts of Christmas cheer, only of death: at the time of writing the possibility of this being a suicide bombing has not been discounted. Perhaps whoever smuggled the bomb on board knew that down below in the hold destruction was primed, by time-switch or by altitude-trigger.

In Prestwick control's operations room controller Alan Topp also had the aircraft on his screen now, moving eighty kilometres (fifty miles) south of Prestwick. In a flash the symbols changed: where there had been one box representing the aircraft there were now five. He blinked in disbelief. It had to be a mistake, surely. Yet each sweep of the radar stubbornly revealed five returns – five pieces of aircraft – spreading apart, and beginning to descend now.

It was 19.03. When the bomb exploded – either because the delay on the time-switch had expired or a few metres (feet) of altitude had been gained as the clipper rode the air currents – the airliner was streaking towards the town of Lockerbie. Most of those on board *Clipper Maid of the Seas* died instantly. The bomb first decapitated the airliner, detonating behind and below the cockpit and destroying the nerve centre, the electrical substation attached to the front bulkhead behind the nosewheel bay. This front section of the fuselage with the cockpit crew and those first-class passengers not ejected into the void would fall to earth fastest.

Passengers in the centre cabins were subjected not only to a 800kph (500mph) plus blast of air, but also bombardment by any loose items. In this tornado of destruction the aircraft broke up, the tail shearing off. Passengers and cabin crew who were standing or not strapped in would plummet to earth separately, a hail of unconscious humanity would pepper the hillsides and the town. It took two minutes for them – and for the pieces of airliner – to hit the ground. This had been the fate of *Kanishka* and her passengers, too.

There was no time to escape from the falling death. By the time the townsfolk of Lockerbie heard the roar of the pieces of Boeing screaming down it was upon them. Sherwood Crescent was just a quiet street, although the A74 London–Glasgow road passed just yards from there. Soon it would be time for the popular early-evening soap opera. Some were finishing dinner, settling down for a quiet night in those cosy little homes, private stages for the dramas of families. The wings and centre section of the fuselage struck. In an instant 225,000L (50,000gall) of aviation fuel exploded in a fireball that roared ninety metres (three hundred feet) into the night sky. Sherwood Crescent was obliterated. Where the neat houses had stood was a nine metre (thirty foot) deep crater ringed by burning rubble amidst which glittered fragments of airliner.

A short distance away in Rosebank Crescent was an equally horrific scene: nearly fifty bodies, some still strapped in their seats, landed in the garden of widow Ella Ramsden. She survived, although part of the economy class cabin had crashed into her home while she was inside.

It took many hours for all of the horrors to be found: on the fairways and greens of the golf course to the east of the town lay another sixty corpses; in back gardens, on the A74 and in side streets lay other. One woman found a corpse hanging from a tree on the outskirts of the town; a driver died at the wheel of his car on the dual-carriageway when blazing pieces crashed around him.

Kate Anderson and her husband were in their farmhouse kitchen in the hills south-east of the town when the sky was lit by an eerie glow. They stepped outside. The graveyard was only a few yards away. The peace and solitude of the hillside was only disturbed by the trickle of the Waters of Milk stream as it bubbled downstream. Suddenly, there was a whistling noise in the air: in the blink of an eye something else appeared on the hillside within yards of the gravestones: the cockpit and forward first-class cabin of *Clipper Maid of the Seas* smashed on to the grass. The portion fell on its port side and there she lay like a huge smashed egg. Her name pointed at the moonlit sky from whence she'd come. The starboard cockpit windows were not even broken.

Kate Anderson stepped inside that wreckage. She came upon the body of a stewardess, her flesh still seemed warm. Possibly, she was still alive for just a few moments, but died as Kate touched her. Other corpses inside that hell seemed to be crushed and boneless, just pulped remains of humanity. Spread around the cockpit section outside were other bodies. When the ochre light of another dawn came to that hillside and glinted off the white paint of that section of fuselage photographs of it would come to symbolise not only the Lockerbie disaster but Christmas 1988.

From a distance the whole town of Lockerbie seemed to be on fire. The emergency services could only seal it off and establish a temporary morgue at the town hall. By 21.00 the first news reports had been flashed around the world; by midnight talk of sabotage was filling the airwaves. How could such catastrophe come to a little Scottish town that most could not geographically place mentally? Journalists consulted atlases. I recalled the town as a convenient stopping place when driving between London and Glasgow. In latter years one has even had to drive off the main road to enter the by-passed town. It was difficult to imagine such horror occurring there; streets burning, notes pinned to the door of the town hall as people sought news of friends and relatives. Residents of some of the homes that were destroyed were on holiday so it would take some days to establish the death toll of Lockerbie folk: eleven would be the final figure, many others were made homeless.

Before the chimes of midnight rang out many were travelling through the darkness of that solstice night towards Lockerbie: police reinforcements to make the cordon as effective as possible, servicemen to assist with the recovery of corpses and the detritus of disaster, fire tenders from nearby towns, accident investigators from Farnborough, the National Transportation Safety Board 'Go' team from Washington, Boeing officials, journalists of both quality and 'gutter' press, friends and relatives of crew, passengers and townsfolk, and the looters, the dregs of humanity we have met before in these pages at the wrecks of *Shenandoah* and a Trident – the ghouls and sensation seekers who came to gawp and plunder. In the weeks after the disaster over thirty would appear at Dumfries Magistrate Court on charges related to the theft of possessions and sections of wreckage. Others must have escaped undetected.

They cancelled Christmas in Lockerbie that year. Throughout the holiday period the soft Scottish hills were criss-crossed by Army Chinook and Lynx helicopters searching for wreckage, while other teams combed the land on foot. They found Christmas cards that had been in the Boeing's hold up to fifty-six kilometres (thirty-five miles) away. Streams and rivers were dragged to bring up pieces. The only brief pause was for a Christmas morning service in the town's church.

In the United Kingdom 999 is the universal telephone number for fire, police or ambulance assistance. The cynics amongst us have in recent times commented that these three numbers should also instantly link one to a politician. Within hours of the disaster the British Prime Minister Margaret Thatcher was on the scene and visiting townsfolk survivors in hospital, her presence requiring a large security contingent to protect her from any terrorist murder attempts when all the available manpower would have been better employed in the clearance operations. The author is not the only person who feels that along with the credit and donor cards in his wallet there should be one that reads 'In the event of being involved in a newsworthy disaster I do not want to be filmed in hospital with any politicians'.

Government Cabinet member and Secretary of State for Transport, Paul Channon MP, also came to Lockerbie. Immediately afterwards he flew off to a holiday in Mustique, a move which was politically naive for he was pilloried by the media for deserting the scene. In truth most of those professionals involved with the investigation were probably pleased not to have him getting in the way. Such political appointments are merely short-term and it is ludicrous that the British transport supremo needs to know nothing about the technicalities of his portfolio.

On the Wednesday following the disaster it was officially announced that a bomb was responsible. Traces of plastic explosive were found on pieces of a suitcase and a baggage pallet, almost certainly Semtex manu-factured by the Czechoslovak government at Pardubice, sixty miles from Prague. Although the Czechs would not sell the explosive directly to terrorists, it could be passed on to the breed by countries such as North Vietnam and Libya. The latter country in particular was an avowed enemy of the West and had previously sold Semtex to the Irish Republican Army. In November 1988 one hundred pounds of the explosive was found by police in a south London flat, a find that possibly prevented a Christmas bombing campaign.

The speculation of who was responsible for the outrage was height-ened. The Palestine Liberation Organisation, or one of its splinter groups, or an Iranian group acting in revenge for the 'Vincennes incident' were the most suspected.

Confirmation that a bomb could escape detection by security checks came when journalists proved that it was simple to get employment in the secure areas of Heathrow using forged references,or even to sneak unde-tected on to the flight decks of aircraft to hide boxes of chocolates in lieu of bombs behind panelling.

It is common knowledge to those engaged in clandestine activities that acting in a natural manner as if in a place by right rarely results in being challenged; only months before the Lockerbie bombing the author, while employed as a Press Officer, was photocopying confidential documents and handing them over for newspaper publication in plain view of those who wanted the information kept secret. No one suspected because I was acting so openly!

It is foolish to believe that a change in political flag would assist security. Intercontinental airliners at least occasionally take-off without the owner of a piece of baggage that is in the hold; having to search through pallets to off-load a single suitcase causes great delay and expense. If security was to be made total traffic would grind to a halt. This was to be dramatically demonstrated by Doctor Jim Swire, an American whose daughter perished in the Lockerbie disaster. In June 1990 he flew Heathrow–New York on British Airways carrying a radio/cassette recorder in which was hidden a dummy bomb. Heathrow's security did not detect it, a very embarrassing affair though their later excuse would be that they were aware of the identity of Doctor Swire (a prominent critic of the investigation and security precautions) and that he would hardly be a potential bomber.

However, other tragedies were to occur before Doctor Swire's exposures and the British Minister of Transport would be replaced. In an astonishing blunder in March 1989 Paul Channon informed five journalists over lunch at London's Garrick Club that by 'the most brilliant piece of detective work in history' the bombers had been identified. Yet no one was brought to book or specifically named. It may be that Channon's statement, which he later denied ever having made, compromised the detective operation.

In a re-shuffle of Thatcher's cabinet in July, Channon was dismissed to the back benches of Parliament and replaced by a former high-flier (no pun intended) of the Government who was trying to re-establish his career following a scandal of a few years earlier when he had become the father of his secretary's child. No commentators mourned the departure of Channon, few welcomed Cecil Parkinson, this 'baby battered' replacement; just another expendable politician whose head could be a sacrificial offering in the event of another catastrophe viewed by the public as avoidable.

Less than a year had elapsed from the Lockerbie disaster when a DC-10 of the French operator UTA was blown up in mid-air. On 19 September 1989 the scheduled flight took off from Brazzaville en route to Paris via N'Djamena, the capital of Chad. In 1984 a bomb had been placed on a DC-8 operating this service but it had detonated on the ground. One person was killed. Private security guards had been placed on Chad flights following that event but they had been withdrawn earlier in 1989, according to Union des Transports Aériens on advice from the French Interior Ministry, though the DGSE (French secret service) denied this.

The DC-10 was destroyed north of the Termit mountain range in Niger, West Africa. The wreckage was scattered over forty square miles. All 171 souls on board must have perished instantly.

Only two months later in South America a Boeing 727 of Avianca with 110 on board was blown up near Bogota, Columbia. This time, it was likely to be the victim of drug barons. There were no survivors.

While the hunt for the perpetrators of these three bombings continued one aircraft saboteur was brought to justice. Twenty-seven year old Kim

Hyon-Hue was so serenely beautiful that she was dubbed 'the virgin terrorist'. Could this vision of loveliness really be the face of a woman who had planted a radio containing a bomb in the luggage hold of a Boeing 707 forming Korean Airlines Flight 858 from Baghdad to Seoul on 29 November 1987? The Boeing exploded over the sea off the Malayan coast killing all 115 on board. Kim was arrested in Bahrain after an abortive suicide attempt. Her partner in the exploit, Kim Sung-Il, swallowed a cyanide capsule, thus escaping the justice of the South Korean courtroom where friends and relatives of the dead shouted abuse as sentence on Kim was passed by Judge Chung Sang-Hak.

But were these the real criminals? Kim Hyon-Hui at least would seem to be a tragic dupe; the real instigator of the bombing was believed to be the North Korean government who wished to disrupt the Olympic Games due to be held in Seoul the following summer.

And of the perpetrators of the Lockerbie mass murder? The incident has become immersed in a quagmire of secrecy, half-truths, hyperbole and usually ill-informed conjecture. Initial suspicions centred upon Iran with probable assistance from Syria in retribution for the shoot-down of Iran Air 655. The 1990 Iraqi invasion of Kuwait saw new political alliances formed however: Syria and Iran becoming half-allies of the 'Western' nations who formed a pact to eject the forces of Iraq's despot President Saddam Hussein; forces that they had armed.

Suspicions shifted (truer to say that they were shifted) towards an old thorn in the side: Libya. United States Air Force F-111 bombers based in Great Britain had tried to kill that country's leader, Colonel Gaddafi, by bombing his palace in 1986. Now, the American Central Intelligence Agency named Abdel Basset Ali Mohamed and Ali Amin Khalifa Fhimah as the bombers of both Pan Am Flight 103 and the UTA DC-10.

Rather than pointless conjecture on the true instigators and saboteurs of these incidents, this book is concerned with safety and it is the implications that must be addressed.

International pressure saw the Czechs agree to introduce a detectable odour to Semtex but it is certain that a great deal of the explosive remains stockpiled around the world. The Palestine Liberation Organisation, for example, has in recent years been known to use detonators left behind by the British in 1948. Also, we should not look upon terrorists as isolated groups of malcontents. The story of Korean Airlines Flight 858 is just one example of how terrorism is sponsored by sovereign states. This raises the frightening prospect of other incidents to rival that at Lockerbie.

At the time of flight 103 catastrophe the Russian Army, just as the British had done a century before them, were withdrawing from Afghanistan. As the Antonov and Ilyushin transports flew out of government-controlled Kabul they ejected flares to decoy any infra-red heat-seeking missiles fired by rebel forces surrounding the city. For many years now shoulder-launched missiles such as the Russian SAM 7 have been in existence. Armed with one of these a terrorist could quite easily fire upon an airliner from a field or roof near to an airport, causing complete destruction.

On 17 August 1988, just before the Lockerbie disaster, the Lockheed C-130 Hercules carrying the ruler of Pakistan, President Mohammad Zia, and thirty-six others blew up near Bahawalpur shortly after take-off. All on board perished. A bomb may have been secreted on board, but there is a strong possibility that it was shot down by a surface-to-air missile.

The following press agency report rated just one paragraph in a few British newspapers in July 1989:

Rebels in Angola used a missile to shoot down a plane on an internal flight killing forty-two passengers and injuring six.

Imagine the furore if the incident had occurred in the West. Why bother to risk smuggling a bomb on board an airliner when it is possible to simply shoot it down from the ground.

Will airliners soon have to be fitted with Electronic Counter Measures?

11
On Rotary Wings

One of the early helicopters was built by Irish inventor, Louis Brennan, and demonstrated in 1922. But it crashed at Farnborough in 1925. The Spaniard Cierva built a series of auto-giro rotor-assisted aircraft in the inter-war years and in Germany, Hanna Reitsch flew the Focke-Achgelis Fa61 *inside* the Deutschlandhalle in Berlin in 1938. But it was left to Igor Sikorsky, the emigré Russian who had built the famous flying boats in the 1930s, to demonstrate, in 1939, the world's first practical helicopter, the VS-300.

Before the great conflict was over both Germany and the United States had helicopter production lines. The clatter of rotary wings would soon be heard above battlefields; from Korea to Vietnam to Afghanistan the 'whirlybird' filled the skies. They soon found more peaceable uses, too, from plucking foolhardy weekend sailors from stormy seas to bringing medical aid to the victims of natural disasters.

In the early years of rotary wing operations some foresaw the helicopter supplanting conventional aircraft, though this will never happen. The helicopter is more complex and expensive to operate, and its rotors do not merely circle but also flap. During the forward stroke a blade provides only lift, not thrust, and this imbalance subjects it to enormous stresses. A slow-motion film reveals rotors bending in seemingly horrific ways. This makes them prone to our old enemy: fatigue failure.

Piloting a helicopter is rather akin to patting one's head while circling a palm around one's stomach, every movement of the collective stick needs a counter-balance by use of the cyclic stick. Whereas fixed-wing aircraft with side-by-side controls are universally captained from the left-hand seat, a helicopter is captained from the right on the basis that before auto-pilots for such machines were introduced (they are still rare owing to the great complexity involved) the chief pilot, assuming he was dexter, could not take his right hand off the collective control, so sitting on that side enabled him to operate the radio and other switches on the centre console more easily. The more junior pilot on a dual-control machine pays the penalty of either having to reach over with his left hand or swap his grip on the collective.

Ironically, it is the manoeuvre that is most fascinating – hovering – that is the easiest to achieve with a helicopter. It is when forward motion is required that the problems begin. In the hover all that is necessary is that the tail rotor is countering the torque of the main rotor; if the tail rotor fails, instead of the blades circling the fuselage the fuselage will circle the blades – with predictable, and unfortunately oft-demonstrated, results. The principle is slightly different on those machines such as the Boeing Vertol Chinook which have twin main rotors both mounted in a horizontal plane, contra-rotation provides their main balance and they are universally twin-engined; one engine can power both rotors. This is a convenient point to dispose of one often-believed myth of helicopter flight: if the engine (or engines, most large helicopters are twin-engined even if driving only one main rotor) stops it will plummet to earth like a stone: in fact unpowered the blades will auto-rotate for a controllable landing (though like a glider there is no 'go around' for a second attempt!) Indeed, rotary-wing pilots must prove their competence at such a landing at least once a year to keep their licence.

Like the hovercraft, the helicopter has not been the all-conquering success its original proponents hoped for. The air-cushion vehicle has the problem of being difficult to steer, the helicopter suffers from the very facet that has made it so useful – vertical take-off and landing needs proportionately greater power than with an aircraft and uses more fuel in the process: think of childhood learnings, how a weight can be lifted by means of an inclined plane using less power than to lift the same load vertically, the principle is the same and explains why we have not yet seen long-range vertical take-off airliners. Off the record, pilots of the British Harrier 'jump-jet' will tell of how the fuel gauge goes down like an elevator needle when the fighter is in the 'hover-mode', the type makes conventional take-offs and landings in normal circumstances and can lift a much greater weapons load in the process.

Military and mercy duties aside, the future for the helicopter seemed to lie in inter-urban transport using heliports near city centres. Such schemes have tended to founder on resistance from pressure groups concerning noise and danger. The fixed-wing aircraft has also fought back with STOL (short take off and landing) designs such as the Dash 7 which can operate from strips that would have been deemed as too small for anything but helicopters twenty years ago.

An early commercial success for helicopters was in the linking of airports. Chicago Helicopter Airways, for example, established a service linking Midway and O'Hare Airports. However, this shuttle service struck disaster on 27 December 1960 when a Sikorsky S-58C carrying two pilots and thirteen passengers crashed on a cemetery at Forest Park, Illinois. No one survived.

The helicopter had arrived at Midway Airport at 22.15. It took just fifteen minutes for it to be 'turned round' for departure. The crash occurred twenty-seven kilometres (seventeen miles) from the airport at 22.38, at the mid-point of the journey, when a section of one main rotor blade broke away. With landing lights blazing the S-58 came down with the unbalanced remaining blades producing a sound like the cracking of a whip. Before impact the tail cone complete with the rear rotor separated.

The accident investigation body of the time, the Civil Aeronautics Board, deduced fatigue failure of the main rotor blade that had sheared.

Los Angeles, too, quickly established helicopter shuttles to link its airports. By 1968 Los Angeles Airways was operating with the highly successful Sikorsky S-61 design. On 22 May one of these was operating Flight 441, one of some thirty made daily linking Anaheim Heliport with Los Angeles International Airport, a distance of forty kilometres (twenty-five miles). With three crew and twenty passengers the Sikorsky lifted off from Anaheim into afternoon sunlight to fly under Visual Flight Rules to Los Angeles International. At 17.50 near the Pomona freeway intersection it passed another helicopter whose crew later reported Flight 441 to be at 600m (2,000ft) and apparently flying quite normally. But just thirty seconds later the pilot of that helicopter and Los Angeles Airways Flight Control heard a last panic-stricken message: 'LA, we're crashing! Help us!'

The end of Flight 841 and all on board it was witnessed from the ground: observers reported that the helicopter suddenly descended to 180–240m (600–800ft) with a seemingly erratic action of the main rotor blades. A witness with a helicopter maintenance background reported that there was then a violent yaw to the left of nearly ninety degrees as one rotor blade seemed to be out of track and turning high. The remaining blades began to chop into the fuselage fore and aft, and sections were shed before the Sikorsky pitched down into a near-vertical dive. As it struck the ground the fuel ignited in a mushrooming explosion. The precise cause was never established, though the wreckage did reveal that the main rotor blade damper unit was faulty.

Less than three months later Los Angeles Airways suffered another disaster with their S-61 fleet. Helicopter N3007 had already completed three round trips to various Los Angeles destinations from the International Airport on 14 August before taking off as Flight 417 to Anaheim at 10.26. Just ten minutes later and at 450m (1,500ft) over Compton a main rotor blade was seen to separate from the central hub. As the machine spun to destruction the tail cone sheared off. The three crew and eighteen passengers perished. The cause this time was a metallurgical fault during manufacture of a main rotor blade spindle. A fatigue crack had developed in an area of sub-standard hardness that had not been properly shot-preened.

On the opposite coast of America a helicopter service had been established between the airports and the roof of the Pan American building in downtown New York. At 17.35 on 16 May 1977 an S-61L of New York Airways was perched on that roof with its rotors turning. Four passengers had boarded and others were just doing so, greeted by a smiling stewardess. Suddenly the helicopter rolled on to its starboard side, the undercarriage leg having sheared off through fatigue. Those already on board received only minor injuries, but four people on the roof who had been approaching to board were killed by the disintegrating rotors as they struck the roof. One main rotor blade lanced down to the streets. A pedestrian standing at the corner of Madison Avenue and 43rd Street was killed and another injured by it.

In a remarkable coincidence the very next day a similar fate befell an S-61 of British Airways at Scotland's Aberdeen Airport, but in this case it was an electrical fault that caused the starboard main undercarriage leg to retract. None of the fifteen on board were injured as the machine rolled over.

The helicopter has become a workhorse of the off-shore oil industry. Flights to service the rigs are often made under some of the most difficult conditions for aircraft operation. Landings have to be accomplished on a trembling platform jutting out from the rig, high above an often storm-stirred sea.

On 1 February 1958 an S-58 of Humble Oil and Refinery Company took off from an off-shore rig near Grand Isle, Louisiana, with two pilots and nine workmen on board. Immediately after lift off the pilot had hovered to complete his centre of gravity check (to make sure that the loading of the machine was balanced). During this process the helicopter started to spin to the right. This rapidly became uncontrollable and was accompanied by a loud metallic clatter from the rear. The tail rotor was mechanically overloaded. As it failed the fuselage tried to rotate around the rotors. In seconds the machine toppled into the Gulf of Mexico. One pilot and three of the passengers drowned before rescuers from the rig could haul them into boats. The survivors were chemically burnt by gasoline bubbling to the surface from the wreck.

Sikorsky promised to look into this tail rotor failure, but exactly four months later before there could be any outcome from these investigations another S-58 of the same oil company plunged into the Gulf with the loss of all six on board. The cause in this latter instance was never discovered. The problems of these early S-58s were soon solved with later variants that were turbine powered, a form of propulsion that delivers the power more smoothly with less attendant risk of mechanical strain or vibration fatigue.

The S-58/Wessex design was to have a long and noble record in the rig support role. As late as 20 April 1976 a Wessex 60 was in service with Great Britain's Bristow fleet serving that country's North Sea rigs. In an amazing moment of forgetfulness the pilot took off from Gas Rig 48 without first removing the fabric engine intake cover! The result was predictable as the engine gulped for air, but only drew in the cover. Fortunately all fourteen who had been on board were pulled safely from the sea.

Bristow was less fortunate the following day however when another S-58 with ten on board went out of control as it was about to alight on the helipad of Charlie Platform in the Forties Oilfield. The machine plunged 42m (140ft) to the deck of a crane barge moored alongside the rig. One passenger was killed and five injured. Tail rotor fatigue was diagnosed, but the cause was not.

Norway, too, owns rigs inthe tempestuous waters of the North Sea, and it was en route to one of these that an S-61 of Helikopter Service plunged into the waters off Varhaug on 23 November 1977 killing all twelve on board. The wreckage was dredged up from a depth of 300m (1,000ft) and the fatigue failure of one blade damper given as the cause of disaster. Helikopter Service faced catastrophe again on 26 June the following year when another S-61 flying from Bergen to the Staifjord Alfa platform went down with sixteen passengers and two crew, approximately sixty kilometres (forty miles) off Bergen. No Mayday was transmitted, although the machine had been in radio contact with its base just minutes before. There were no survivors. A beacon guided searchers to the wreckage lying some 230m (770ft) down on the seabed, and main rotor blade spindle failure was established as the probable cause of the disaster.

Returning to the S-61s of New York Airways, their Flight 972 of 18 April 1979 lifted off from Newark International Airport for a flight to New York shortly after 18.00 with a total of eighteen on board. It was over one kilometre (one mile) east of the airport and had climbed to just over 300m (1,000ft) when one of the five tail rotor blades sheared off. The resultant vibration caused the entire tail rotor gearbox and rotor assembly to separate from the helicopter when it was 45m (150ft) above the airport where the pilot was attempting an emergency landing. The machine went into rapid nose-down right hand turns and impacted with such force that three passengers were killed, ten others and three crew members seriously injured.

Metallurgical examination revealed a fatigue failure across ninety per cent of the failed tail rotor blade's leading edge. The National Transportation Safety Board in their report also pointed out that seat failures contributed to passengers' injuries when the decelerative forces exceeded the relatively low design strength of the Federal Aviation Administration approved seats. This safety aspect is also relevant to fixed-wing aircraft: in recent times this matter was investigated in the wake of the Boeing 737 incident near Britain's East Midlands Airport in 1989 (see Chapter 4). Seat supports that crumple like a car's bumper to absorb impact have been suggested, but most share common supports across two, three or even four seats, not all of which may be occupied, so at what g-force should the supports begin to compress? Universal single seats would involve a cost and weight penalty that no airline is likely to absorb unilaterally. It is also normal practice for seats to be mounted in multiples on rails so that they can be quickly reorganised for different services, so if single seats became mandatory the timing of turn-arounds would be slowed.

The Aérospatiale/Westland SA 330 Puma is a type in wide service with the British and French armed forces, but the machine with its two Rolls Royce/Turbomeca 1,300 horsepower engines was also made available for sale to commercial operators. Petroleum Helicopters were the owners of the machine that was attempting to land on an oil rig in the Gulf of Mexico on 8 December 1977. A crosswind gusting at up to thirty knots was blowing across the helipad. The Puma drifted left as the pilot tried to bring her down. Full right cyclic would not bring her back and now, belatedly, the pilot commenced a go-around for another attempt. As he did so the main rotor blades struck a steel cable stretching down from a crane boom near the edge of the helipad. The Puma smashed down on to the pad then bounced off to plunge into the sea. The fuselage split open and sank immediately. Only one pilot and one passenger of the total of nineteen on board were saved.

An S-61N of British Airways was flying over the North Sea in clear weather at 450m (1,500ft) returning to Aberdeen with fifteen oil rig workers on 11 March 1983 when it was suddenly rocked by an explosion in the main gearbox. The number one engine ran down and the oil pressure fell from its normal 50 psi to just 30 while a loud high-frequency vibration shrieked through the aircraft.

The captain decided to set the helicopter down in a favourable sea 123km (77 miles) north-east of Aberdeen. This was safely accomplished and there she rode the swell with her flotation gear out and a sea anchor deployed. Everyone felt seasick as they waited for help to come. In case a sudden evacuation was needed the captain ordered the co-pilot to launch and inflate the life raft from the rear door. This was apparently successful and the co-pilot returned to the cockpit, but passengers soon reported that the raft had punctured. The co-pilot now deployed the forward life raft, but he did this wrongly for it inverted during inflation and could not be righted from the cockpit door. Then it too punctured. Fortunately a Sea King rescue helicopter arrived, lowered a life raft successfully and also winched up the seasick men. Gearbox failure was the cause of the power loss, but further practice in emergency procedures would also have been in order.

The twenty-three passengers on board another British Airways S-61 later that year were not oil rig workers but fare paying passengers flying the scheduled service from Penzance Heliport to the Scilly Islands southwest of England. The helicopter was flying under Visual Flight Rules at just 75m (250ft) despite the low cloud as it approached the island's capital of St Mary's. In a moment's inattentiveness by the pilot, the machine suddenly plunged into the sea. The heavy machine, travelling at over three kilometres (two miles) per minute, burst apart. St Mary's lifeboat picked up six survivors, but nineteen passengers and the stewardess died.

The Air Accidents Investigation Branch concluded that the weather conditions were not suitable for Visual Flight Rules operation and also noted the lack of height warning equipment. While fixed wing aircraft are fitted with such equipment to prevent them landing 'wheels up', it was not seen as necessary on helicopters. In conditions of no visible horizon even the best pilot can only orientate himself for approximately forty-five seconds. After that time they may believe that they are climbing when in fact descending, turning port when actually turning starboard. It is essential both to watch and believe the artificial horizon; all too often pilots have believed this instrument to be faulty when in fact their senses are being deceived.

The Chinook is a wind that blows over America's Rocky Mountains and is considered to be dangerous to aircraft that venture into it. It is also, perhaps unfortunately, the name given to the large machine in Boeing Vertol's range. The Chinook is of the twin-horizontal rotor configuration. It is the heavy-lift helicopter of the British and American armed forces, but has also been widely sold as a commercial machine.

British International Helicopters Limited had purchased the type for their North Sea oil rig supply contracts. In the late autumn dawn of 6 November 1986 engineers were working on one of these machines in a hangar at Sumburgh Airport. While being pre-flight checked an oil leak was discovered in the left engine's gearbox. A breather pipe was replaced and after running engines the crew were satisfied that all was well. At 08.50 the machine lifted off bound for the Brent oilfield. Ninety minutes later it departed from Brent Platform 'C' with forty-four workers returning home on leave. It climbed to 750m (2,500ft) and flew towards Sumburgh on track M of the helicopter air routes. At 11.08 it was sixty-four kilometres (forty miles) from the Shetland Islands and receiving the signals of the VHF omni-range (VOR) beacon. Twenty minutes later permission to land was granted. The pilot subsequently recalled how the perilous rocks of Sumburgh Head were in sight when he noticed an increase in the engines' noise level. They were only minutes from landing. He flew on for a few seconds – it is not bad judgement on his part that he did not immediately cut power and auto-rotate down to the sea. Even as the two pilots scanned the instrument panel for indications of what the problem might be, there was a loud bang. The rotor blades touched and broke up, and from 150m (500ft) the Chinook plunged into the sea.

Only two survivors – the captain and one passenger – were rescued from those waters. In such cold seas survival time is just minutes. By early afternoon the Air Accidents Investigation Branch had chartered the diving support vessel *Deepwater 1* which sailed from Peterhead in Scotland that evening.

On 7 November part of the forward fuselage was located 100m (333ft) down on the seabed and at midday the cockpit voice recorder was brought up. By darkness on the following Monday 75 per cent of the fuselage and 95 per cent of the transmission had been raised. A catastrophic fatigue failure of the spiral bevel gear in the forward rotor gearbox was diagnosed by the Farnborough investigation team.

A previous problem with the Chinook design was that operators had had to check bolts on the gear assembly every three hundred operating hours, an expensive and time-consuming process. To solve this problem, Boeing introduced a modification that was endorsed by the American Federal Aviation Administration and accepted by the British Civil Aviation Authority subject to there being regular inspections.

'The manufacturer and airworthiness authorities considered the modification to be a relatively straightforward improvement to the previous design standard,' the accident report would later state, 'consequently, they failed to appreciate that there was a real possibility that it might perform in a fundamentally different way to forward and aft transmission joints of earlier modified states, or indeed to a modified aft transmission under test. With the benefit of hindsight this might have been avoided if more realistic and rigorous testing had been required'.

The benefit of hindsight is no compensation to the friends and relatives of victims. The AAIB inspectors urged that the Civil Aviation Authority should investigate new ways of detecting problems within helicopter engines before they could become tragic. Upon reading the conclusions Boeing declared that the original gear modification had not been correctly carried out. The company said that the senior engineer of British International Helicopters had felt two months before the disaster that there was something wrong with the modified transmission and that it should be removed with the 'check bolts every three hundred hours' version reinstated until further investigation of the new version was carried out. This was not done, however.

In the light of Boeing's challenge a review board looked at the findings again before publication of the report. This board concluded that the Chinook had been maintained in accordance with the correct procedures and that the modified ring gear had been fitted correctly. By now over two years had elapsed since the disaster and Boeing were ordered to pay the costs of the review. But the company had not accepted defeat yet. They tried to persuade the British Secretary of State for Transport (Paul Channon) that there had been a miscarriage of justice. Channon dismissed the claim in April 1989, but at the time of writing the affair is not yet closed.

What is certain is that the incident saw the withdrawal of the Chinook type from North Sea operations following a refusal of workers to fly in them. Instead the venerable S-61 type took over the service with detrimental effects on operators' finances because it carries a lighter payload per trip. In military service the Chinook had suffered what some felt to be an inordinately high accident rate. Those with fears of the safety of the design seemed to have these founded in July 1989. On Monday 24 July five servicemen were injured when a Chinook of the RAF's 27 Squadron crashed during take off. The following day another two servicemen were hurt when a machine of 78 Squadron came down at Mount Pleasant in the Falkland Islands. All training exercises involving the type were suspended. Service chiefs ordered that the machines should only be used for essential duties. In less than ten years' service thirteen servicemen had been killed and six machines had been lost in accidents.

It is interesting to speculate the future of the rotary wing machine. The types examined in this chapter have been in the most basic of layman's description 'egg-shaped fuselage beneath a fan' or 'cylindrical fuselage beneath two fans' types, the universal perception of the helicopter yet thirty years ago the British aircraft industry had indicated one possible way forward with the revolutionary Fairey Rotodyne. This took off as a rotary-wing machine and then cruised as a fixed-wing aircraft. Each stubby wing of this convertiplane had a Napier Eland turboprop engine. On take off most of the power of these engines was used in driving pressure jets at the tip of each of four twenty-three foot long rotors. No counter-torque tail rotor was needed with this method of propulsion. Once airborne the wings would give 85% of the lift with the rotors providing the remainder as they auto-rotated and thrust was provided by conventional propellers. Although the author never witnessed this machine he has heard it said that the incredible noise it produced was one of the major factors that saw it fail as a commercial proposition (Concorde's commercial prospects would be affected by the same alleged problem less than twenty years later).

While multi-blade fans have replaced tail rotors on some machines (the Aérospatiale Gazelle and Dauphin being common examples) and machines with compressed air jets replacing tail rotors have been flown the future would seem to lie with the convertiplane but in a different configuration from Rotodyne. Manufacturers have experimented with aircraft on which the wings can be rotated through ninety degrees so that propellers (rotating in opposite directions for obvious reasons!) can lift the machine vertically, conventional fixed-wing forward flight being achieved by gently rotating the wings back to horizontal. The problem has been: what happens if one engine fails? Boeing-Vertol now have type-approval for such a design but with the engines linked by a common shaft through the wings and fuselage (the engines of conventional helicopters such as the Chinook are also linked to give single-engine safety –a term that many see as relative with that design!)

Convertiplanes would overcome the helicopter's main disadvantage: their very slow forward speed. Most cruise at only some 120 miles per hour. It is hard to believe that the *thwack-thwack* of types such as the S-61 will not be a sound soon extinct.

12
Landing Accidents

For more than ten hours the pilot has been confined to his cockpit. He has crossed several time zones. He is probably wearing two watches, one adjusted for local time, the other set on his home's time. It is dark outside. Undiffused by the dust drifting in the lower levels of air the stars gleam with a brightness not normally seen by the naked eye.

Let us assume that it has been a quiet trip, that there has been no trouble from the passengers or problems with the aircraft's systems, that the pilot has not been troubled by family worries. He has begun to doze during the flight, perhaps even slipped in and out of micro-sleep. His heart rate has perhaps dropped to sixty beats per minute. It is time to begin the let-down to landing. Yet his biological clock is telling him that it is time to sleep. He yawns and mentally shakes himself; it is time to concentrate.

The pilot has decided to handle the landing himself. His eyes are to remain fixed on the sky, the co-pilot will watch the instruments, adjust the throttles, listen for the radio beacons (assuming that this is not an Instrument Landing System approach) and lower the flaps.

As the aircraft enters cloud, rain spatters the windscreen, the wipers slap hypnotically, the pilot shakes his head to drive away the tiredness. Is this air traffic controller helpful? Pilots consider that those of some countries will accept no responsibility in the event of problems, afraid of being cited as culpable if disaster strikes. Perhaps the controller is over-worked and tired. Perhaps he has family problems of his own that are affecting his concentration.

Has the altimeter been re-set to the barometric pressure prevailing at the airport? Is the 'bug' on it set at the right altitude to ensure that they climb out to a safe height in the event of an overshoot? What's the correct heading if we abort this approach? Watch out for that crosswind. Didn't they have a big prang here last year? A hundred and fifty metres (five hundred feet) – why are we still in cloud? Didn't he say cloud base a hundred and eighty metres (six hundred feet)! There it is, there's the runway – is this the right airport? – remember the guy who landed at Northolt thinking he'd made a perfect touch-down at Heathrow? This isn't the taxiway is it, like the chap who put the BAC One-Eleven down on Gatwick's taxiway at Gatwick in 1988 and nearly rammed a 737 head-on – drifting right now, a little left rudder's in order, whoops, too much, back the other way a bit – we did put the wheels down, didn't we? There we go

– perfect – a greaser.

But sometimes it isn't a greaser; sometimes it's disaster.

Forty-seven year old Captain Gale Kehmeier did not have a perfect record of handling jet aircraft when he took command of a United Air Lines triple-engined Boeing 727 at Denver on 11 November 1965. Of his 17,743 hours flight time only 334 had been logged on the type. In 1960 he had failed his oral examination for graduation from the piston Douglas DC-6/7 series to the new jet DC-8s. His jet conversion training was suspended on 6 February 1961 and he returned to flying DC-6s, on which he was rated average/above-average.

He tried to get his jet 'ticket' again in May 1962 and after two simulator checks was given Boeing 720 clearance. On 5 February 1965 a Federal Aviation Administration inspector rode behind Kehmeier on a Boeing 727 flight. He recounted at the disaster enquiry that the captain flew in a manner a little below average and was lax in airspeed and altitude maintenance.

The Fairchild Model 5424 flight recorder told the story of this disaster. The flight was a scheduled service that had commenced at New York's La Guardia and was due to terminate at San Francisco. Kehmeier hauled her into the sky over Denver at 16.54. Less than an hour later he was approaching Salt Lake City Municipal Airport. Air traffic control requested his indicated altitude. 'Ten thousand feet at 250 knots, runway in sight,' Kehmeier responded. Landing permission was given.

The 'No Smoking – Fasten Seat Belts' sign was turned on, the flaps were pumped down, the wheels swung down from their wells. The white, blue and silver Boeing was descending at 600m (2,000ft) per minute. This was an Instrument Landing System approach. The First Officer, Philip Spincer, who had logged just eighty-four hours on the B727 type, was watching the glide slope indicator on the instrument panel – the instrument was calling for a 180m (600ft) per minute descent. Spincer's left hand stretched out for the throttles to add power to arrest this too rapid descent. Kehmeier prevented him from doing so. 'Not yet, son.'

Less than twenty seconds later Keheier pushed the levers forward. He felt that the power was not increasing as it should. They were at just 300m (1,000ft), and thirty seconds from impact. Kehmeier pushed the throttle levers against their stops for full 'go around' power. But it was too late, the Boeing was sinking remorselessly towards the runway threshold and there was no time for the Pratt and Whitneys to spool up. That they did so however was confirmed by Second Officer and Flight Engineer Ronald Christensen who heard them respond normally.

The impact came 100m (335ft) short of Runway 34 Left with a bone-jarring force of 4.7g. The main undercarriage oleos could not withstand such an impact and sheared off as the Boeing smashed over the runway threshold lights. The rear of the fuselage threw up a shower of sparks as it seared along the runway. Travelling on her belly and nosewheel, the Boeing slid for nearly 900m (3,000ft) and veered right on to grass before lurching to a halt 45m (150ft) east of the runway. The port engine had already fallen off by then. Worse, as the starboard undercarriage broke off it had ruptured the fuel and number three generator lines.

Fire broke out even during the bone-shattering slide. It first entered the cabin by the starboard seat 18E and raced up the cabin panelling. Yet more fuel was being pumped in to feed these flames by the still operating boost pumps.

There was panic as passengers fled from the fire. Choking smoke filled the cabin. A stewardess was struggling with the main door – crumpling of the fuselage had jammed it in its frame. Two fire tenders reached the burning airliner in three and a half minutes (a long response time compared to the events at Manchester Airport, England, twenty years later) and began laying foam over the fuselage, but because the flames had first ignited inside the cabin the fire fighting was ineffective until the cabin roof had been burnt through. There was also a stoppage in fire fighting when the water supply ran dry. Salt Lake City tenders arrived in ten minutes to add their efforts to the rescue. Most who survived were out of the wreck by then.

Trapped in the cramped passageway leading to the central staircase were a stewardess and two male passengers. The flames were advancing towards them. The stewardess put an arm through a crack and waved frantically for help. Unable to pull the three clear, firemen passed a hose to her. For nearly thirty nightmare minutes the stewardess and passengers fought off the flames, finally escaping when a hole was burnt through the cabin wall and they were able to scramble out.

Forty-one passengers died on the spot, another two subsequently in hospital. All six crew were among the forty-eight survivors. One of the stewardesses recommended that cabin staff should be seated nearer the emergency exits, as she had had to fight through panicking passengers in order to reach the door. United Air Lines reacted to this idea, and now this arrangement is almost universal.

The official report recommended that the fuel pipes and generator leads should be separated, the former going through the centre area of the floor beam. Emergency lights should also be turned on for all take-offs and landings. Twenty years later in the wake of the Manchester Boeing 737 fire we would find investigators recommending floor-mounted lights to guide passengers to the exits.

Kehmeier was guilty of one of pilots' most common errors: he was trusting to his own eyesight and senses. In the wake of the Salt Lake City disaster twelve pilots made Boeing 727 simulator landings with the altimeter blanked out. Eleven of the twelve 'crashed'; long, thin runways lured them to disaster by making them sense that they were higher than was the case. The successful pilot was one who had formerly operated from an aircraft carrier. Clearly, the solution would be a standardised runway width. Such world-wide agreement and reconstruction is beyond the realms of possibility, so the onus remains on pilots to believe in their instruments or the red-over-white runway lights where equipped.

If Kehmeier was the villain of the piece at Salt Lake City, Captain Al Haynes of the same airline was the hero of the Sioux City crash twenty-four years later. With an unblemished thirty-three year flying record Haynes was just two years from retirement as he lifted Flight 232 into the air, again from Denver but this time flying eastbound for Chicago. As the Douglas DC-10 soared high above America's Midwest the passengers were served a lunch of chicken fingers in breadcrumbs, biscuits and a peach. The flight had been airborne for almost an hour and was over Alta, Iowa, at 8,700m (29,000ft) when the aircraft's number two, the tail, engine exploded, ripping off the tail cone and tearing jagged holes in the tailplane and engine cowling. The detonation was so violent that it hurled standing passengers and cabin crew to the floor. The DC-10 pitched down into a dive.

Alfred Haynes gently eased back on the column to pull her out of the dive. Cabin crew calmed the passengers. They radioed Minneapolis air traffic control. So far the crew knew that there had been a major failure of the tail engine, but the problem did not yet seem serious; the flight could safely be landed on the wing engines. Only slowly did the true implications of that engine detonation become clear: the wide-bodied giant began to bank steeply and Haynes had trouble bringing her back to the horizontal. The hydraulic controls to the rudder, tailplane and ailerons were becoming less effective by the moment. When the engine had exploded the 1.8m (6ft) blades of the turbo-fan engine rotating at four hundred revolutions per second had peppered the control surfaces with shrapnel; also, the three hydraulic circuits, all of which had to pass through the tail section, had been punctured. The precious hydraulic fluid was streaming away. The electrical circuits had also been disrupted. Few instruments remained working on the cockpit panel. At 15.17 Haynes reported an almost total loss of hydraulic power and requested directions for an emergency landing. Just three minutes later he declared a total emergency.

Control directed the flight back towards Sioux City, the nearest airport with a runway long enough to handle a potentially unbraked DC-10, but over thirty minutes' flying time distant. Haynes was faced with a perilous situation, his only control by varying the power of the two remaining engines. Could he bring such a crippled DC-10 in for a safe landing? Haynes radioed his operations base in San Francisco to see if anyone there could offer any assistance. 'If you have any suggestions, holler!' he told them. But the operations base was incredulous that he had suffered such a catastrophic engine failure. An off-duty pilot who had been travel-ling on the flight was kneeling before the DC-10's throttles and manipu-lating them. 'How many times do you have to tell them?' the assisting pilot cried. Slowly, so slowly, on what little aileron control was left and by using the engines, they managed to turn the giant. The cabin crew demonstrated the emergency landing position – crouch forward with your head between your knees – to passengers. It was calm in the cabin now, some praying, some writing out wills on odd scraps of paper.

The DC-10 was at 3,000m (10,000ft) now, there was absolutely no hydraulic pressure left and they were lost. Electrical failure had wiped out all the navigation systems. 'We need something to land on, a highway, a field, or something,' Haynes radioed. Sioux City tower drew the crew's attention to Interstate 20, forty-eight kilometres (thirty miles) east of the city. Haynes decided to try to make it to the airport where emergency tenders could be waiting. He spiralled down towards it in three clockwise circles, port throttle advanced a little more than the starboard. 'Whatever you do keep us away from the city,' he called.

Sioux City control tower tried to guide Haynes on to Runway 31, but with so little control the pilot did not feel able to turn the plane. He asked to land on the disused Runway 22 that was then blocked by waiting emergency vehicles. The trucks and tenders rolled away. The last moments of the DC-10 were filmed from the ground, later to be prime-time news footage. The approach looked good, the landing gear was gravity-dropped, power increased slightly to counter its drag. The aircraft came in towards the airport fast but level, just under 320kph (200mph) without flaps. She was just short of the runway threshold when the star-board wing dipped. It was probably just a gust of wind, but without aileron control at such low level there could be no recovery. The wing tip struck the ground, the nose was pulled down and she began to slew around through almost 180°. When the heavy tail section smashed down she somersaulted. Could anyone survive this?

She was on fire now, too. The fuselage split into three main sections, the cockpit bouncing away to come to rest some way distant of the inverted main cabin. Some passengers were thrown out, others came to hanging from their seatbelts in the upside-down cabin. Flames were crackling around them; the screams of the trapped and the noise of the emergency vehicles cut through the air.

Some passengers walked away from the wreckage of that DC-10; others were rescued by the emergency crews. Haynes survived. His comment was; 'I lost that baby.' Yet it was a superb example of airmanship testified by the 186 survivors. The death toll was 111.

'Yet Another DC-10 Disaster' headlines screamed, many reports ignoring the fact that it was not the airframe that had failed but the engine, and that it had failed in a catastrophic way not experienced before. The last of the type had only just rolled off the production line and there are over 350 in service around the world at the time of writing. Was there a design fault? Could this be the start of a catalogue of related disasters? Indeed, is it wise to mount an engine above the tailplane and below the rudder? The type's replacement on the production line, the MD-11, has the same configuration.

Few responsible authorities thought that the Sioux City incident was anything but an isolated fault, until just over one week later. Then on

27 July 1989 another DC-10 crashed after the pilot reported engine problems.

Korean Airlines Flight KE803 was carrying workers from Seoul to Libya
when it came down nearly five kilometres (three miles) short of Tripoli
Airport, ploughing through two houses and killing a family of four as
they slept. At least eighty people on board the airliner were killed and
110 injured. The disaster occurred in fog. A Russian airliner heading for
Tripoli had already diverted to Malta, but the Korean pilot, Captain Kim
Ho-Jung, insisted that he had to attempt a landing. The Libyan news
agency, Jana, reported that contact with the flight was lost fifteen minutes
before the crash.

The eventual report on the Sioux City incident was to conclude that
the failure and separation of the rotor assembly in stage 1 of the number
two (rear) engine led to the loss of all three hydraulic systems that
powered the flight controls.

United Airlines' engine overhaul facility had failed to detect a fatigue
crack originating from a previously undetected metallurgical defect as
manufactured by General Electric. And the Libyan incident: a full explanation has not been logged in the ICAO Accident Summary; just another
airliner that flew into the ground.

Let's return briefly to an earlier breed of Douglas, the graceful DC-8.
One of these machines came to grief at Toronto International Airport on
5 July 1970 following a disagreement between the captain and co-pilot.
First Officer Philip Spincer might have saved United Air Lines' Boeing
727 at Salt Lake City in 1965 if he had been allowed to or had insisted on
advancing the throttles, but in Canada that summer day it was the First
Officer's deploying of the spoilers to 60° as they approached Runway 32
that caused disaster.

Unprepared for this, the pilot fought to stretch the glide of the rapidly
descending jet, but it struck the runway with terrible force. The number
four, starboard outer, engine was shed on impact. The aircraft was
streaming fuel from ruptured pipes and yawing to the asymmetrical
power but the pilot hauled her into the air again in an attempt to make
another circuit. She was critically damaged, however. At 900m (3,000ft)
there was a series of explosions, and the number three engine and a large
portion of the starboard wing separated. She plunged almost vertically to
destruction. Nine crew and one hundred passengers were killed instantly.

Airliners nowadays carry sufficient fuel to be able to divert to another
airport should the original destination be veiled in storms or fog.
However, even today there is no diversion facility should Moscow be
closed in – it's a case of get in or crash. Similarly El Al (Israeli Airlines)
would have difficulties being accepted at some airfields should they need
to seek an alternative set-down point.

The Russian-built four-engined turboprop Ilyushin Il-18 Moskva of
Ceskoslovenske Aerolinie left Zurich in the dusk of a July evening in 1961
to fly sixty-four passengers to Rabat, Morocco. Thirty minutes after

midnight it made contact with Rabat tower. On the ground visibility was a mere thirty metres (hundred feet). The flight was advised to divert to Casablanca. The Ilyushin flew on in the darkness to arrive there shortly after 01.00. Conditions at Casablanca were little better than at Rabat. The Ilyushin did make one approach, but overshot and climbed away again to 450m (1,500ft). The cloudbase was 150m (500ft) and worsening. Now the captain requested permission to land at the US Air Force base at Nouasseur. Casablanca air traffic control asked him to circle while it sought permission. At 01.24 the flight was asked its fuel situation. The captain estimated ninety minutes flying time.

Immediately after radioing the fuel estimates the captain must have seen what he believed was a 'window' in the weather that would enable him to fly in to Casablanca. However, disaster struck. Just before 01.30 the Ilyushin smashed into a hillside at 135m (450ft). It was in line with the runway but still nearly thirteen kilometres (eight miles) short of it. When rescuers got there thirty minutes later they found only one passenger still alive who had been thrown clear, though others could be heard calling for help from the flames of the burning wreckage. Soon there were no more cries, just the crackle of flames. The passenger who had been flung clear soon succumbed to his injuries, making a total death toll of seventy-two.

We know exactly what the pilot of another Russian-built aircraft was thinking before his airliner crashed on the final approach to Rijeka Airport, Yugoslavia, for he lived to tell the tale. The Tupolev Tu-134A of Aviogenex was forming charter flight JJ130 carrying seventy-five British tourists from Gatwick on 23 May 1971. It was an unpleasant trip for all on board; early summer storms were swirling over much of Europe, pummelling the jet. Doubtless the passengers were relieved to hear the announcement that they would soon be landing. As the let-down began the Tupolev was buffeted by the wild air; airsickness bags were used.

This was an Instrument Landing System approach, the concentration of the crew fixed on the glide slope indicator, the co-pilot called off the distance to run. Less than a minute and just over three kilometres (two miles) from the runway an updraught caught her. The Tupolev was thrown upwards and off the ILS beam.

Under such circumstances the pilot should have abandoned the approach and overshot for another attempt, but instead he applied down elevator and reduced engine power to try to get her back on the approach beam. Perhaps it was over-correction on the pilot's part, perhaps a downdraught now caught her, but eighteen seconds before impact the throttles were opened up again and the pilot tried to haul her into a climb-out. He was probably totally disorientated by now. As the Tupolev came over the runway threshold at an excessive 260 knots he believed that he was lower than he really was. His final 'flare', the pull on the control column that lifts the nose and punches the mainwheels on to terra firma, was too high. Stalled, or almost so, she smashed down with such force that the main spar was shattered. The starboard wing broke off. The airliner toppled on to her side and burst into flames as she screeched along the ground. All but one passenger and four of the seven crew were killed, all through just a moment's hasty decision.

The very day after the British Overseas Airways Corporation Boeing 707 was ripped apart by clear air turbulence near Mount Fuji in 1966 (see p. 102), air disaster came to that nation again. This time it was the Boeing 707's contemporary and competitor, a Douglas DC-8, that ended up as shattered and burning wreckage.

On 4 March 1966 the Canadian Pacific Airlines Flight 402 scheduled service to Vancouver left Hong Kong at 16.14, routed via Taipei, Kagoshima and Oshima. It started its descent from 7,500m (25,000ft) towards the Tokyo call at 19.12, levelling off at 4,200m (14,000ft) in the Kisarazu holding pattern. Below, boiling storm clouds veiled the Japanese capital. For over thirty minutes the DC-8 flew in the rectangular holding pattern in the hope that the rain would disappear. At 19.42 the captain radioed air traffic control to say that if there was no improvement within fifteen minutes he would divert to Taipei.

At 19.50 Tokyo advised that there had been some improvement. Visibility was 720m (2,400ft). The pilot began to descend through the flight levels within the holding pattern, but as he came down to 900m (3,000ft) the airliner began to rock in the rough air and rain lashed against the windscreen. He aborted this attempt and pointed the Douglas's nose towards Taipei. He had hardly settled on this new course when a message from Tokyo air traffic control made him change his mind again: their visibility had cleared to 750m (2,500ft). Once again the snub nose of the airliner was pointed towards Tokyo.

This was a Ground Controlled Approach, the ground operator calling off the height and headings, guiding the DC-8 down the invisible beam to Runway 33R. Eight kilometres (five miles) from touchdown the pilot was advised of a light tail wind, five knots at 150°.

Runway 33 stretched out across Tokyo Bay. The DC-8 was one and a half kilometres (one mile) from it when the GCA operator advised: 'You are twenty feet below the glidepath, level off momentarily.' But the approach continued to be too low. In the last moments the pilot asked for the lighting intensity to be reduced. Dazzled, tired, or trusting to his own humanly fallible senses, the pilot brought the four-engined giant down far too steeply. A main undercarriage oleo struck number 14 approach light some 840m (2,800ft) short of the touchdown point; it then hit each light up to number 3 and at 20.15 smashed against the sea wall. The aircraft was thrown back on to the runway in blazing pieces. There were eight survivors, albeit seriously injured, from the total complement of seventy-two.

Before looking at more recent incidents in the closing pages of this history it is appropriate to return for the last time to those early post-war years when aviation was perhaps over the 'golden days' of 1930s but still seen as exciting, an age before aerial traffic jams and intercontinental travel became mundane; back to the days of the British Avro Tudor.

The story of how the loss without trace of *Star Tiger* and *Star Ariel* saw the Tudor design removed from scheduled passenger operation was described in Chapter 8 but they would remain on charter operations until the early 1960s. Only a year after the loss of *Star Ariel*, on 10 March 1950, a Tudor V of Fairflight left Llandow Airport, west of Cardiff in South Wales, with five crew and seventy-eight passengers to fly to Dublin, Eire. The return journey was on 12 March and all seemed normal as it approached Llandow's Runway 28. However, just before touchdown the four-engined airliner fell away to starboard and crashed, killing all on board.

The Ministry of Civil Aviation Court of Investigation under Sir William McNair K.C. concluded that the aircraft had been incorrectly loaded so that the centre of gravity was pitched too far aft, indeed more than one ton of luggage or ballast loaded forward would have been needed to balance the airliner.

The Managing Director of Fairflight was the legendary Air Vice-Marshall Bennett, wartime leader of the RAF Pathfinder squadrons of Bomber Command. He vehemently disagreed with the conclusions of the accident investigation. He had himself examined the wreckage and noticed that the pilot's seat was not locked onto its rails, indeed its supports were not bent whereas those of the co-pilot's were. Bennett felt that the pilot must have lost control when his seat moved as he pulled at the control column. The Court of Investigation dismissed Bennett's views however.

In these days of multi-million pound compensation for the victims of air disasters (at the time of writing claims for the victims of the Turkish Airlines DC-10 incident near Paris in 1973 were only just being settled following legal wrangling in American courts) it is instructive to record the criminal costs imposed against Fairflight: a £50 fine for incorrect loading and £150 costs!

When choosing a holiday, people rarely consider whether or not the airport they will be flying to is safe, trusting in the airlines, air traffic controllers and airport administrations. Airliners have brought tourists and their foreign exchange to countries and islands throughout the world, including St Thomas in the Virgin Islands. Pilots of jetliners were more than unhappy about the mere 1,500m (5,000ft) length of the runway at Harry S. Truman Airport, Charlotte Amalie: to brake a heavily-loaded Boeing 727 in one and a half kilometres (one mile) allowed for no leeway with regard to the touchdown point. Yet still the jets swept down on to that short and narrow strip, for to get agreement between the pilots' unions from operators around the world to boycott it was not easy. Without such backing no pilot would risk his career by refusing to fly there. It seemed that Harry S. Truman Airport was a location waiting for disaster to happen. 27 April 1976 was the fateful day.

A Boeing 727 of American Airlines took off from Rhode Island with eighty passengers for the scheduled service which descended over St Thomas in mid-afternoon. The triple-jet's flaps were drooping down at 30°, a configuration appropriate for a landing there into a twenty knot headwind. Yet on that afternoon 40° of flap should have been selected in a gusting wind striking the Boeing from 120° at 12 to 14 knots. This error in the forecast winds seems to have been made by the airport operators. The pilot did know this treacherous approach well, yet that minor difference in flap selection was enough to add ninety metres (three hundred feet) to the landing distance. Even more relevant, however, was that it made the machine more subject to the danger of windshear.

The Boeing was flying ten knots faster than the reference (ideal) speed as it came over the runway threshold. The wheels were almost on the ground when windshear of a mere five knots struck her. It was just a breath of wind, but was enough to keep her airborne, wafting along three metres (ten feet) above the runway, every moment eroding any minimal safety margin.

With just 600m (2,000ft) of runway still stretching ahead of him the pilot decided to overshoot, but just like Kehmeier over twenty years before with another B727 he believed that the Pratt and Whitney JT8D-1A engines were not spooling up as they should. Now he cut the power, thumped her down and stood on the brakes. But it was too late. With the nosewheel still pawing at the air, smoke from burning rubber streaming from the mainwheels and travelling at well over one and a half kilometres (a mile) per minute, the silver machine struck the Instrument Landing System antenna at the end of the runway. This tore off a wing. The aircraft crashed through the perimeter fence, searing across a road and came to rest in flames on a petrol station. The flight deck crew survived, but thirty-seven of the eighty-eight occupants perished in the fire and thirty-nine others, including one person on the ground, were injured.

The runway at Harry S. Truman Airport was lengthened in the wake of this accident. However, there are still other runways which are too short, or airports which are ill-equipped to rescue survivors from disaster. The length of Gatwick Airport's only runway is a cause for concern. In 1988 a Boeing 747 slashed through the upper branches of trees just after take-off from there, fortunately without causing major damage, but it does demonstrate that if a heavily-laden machine should encounter problems at take-off velocity there is no option of safely braking to a halt – the aircraft is committed to flight or disaster.

The peril of windshear, however, is being overcome. Just as computers can fly aircraft far more accurately than humans, they can also detect windshear, adjusting the controls and throttles to compensate for the effects as the aircraft lands, leaving the pilot free to concentrate on his set-down point and heading. Pan American, before their demise, placed an order with Sundstrand to equip 158 Boeing 727s, 747s and Airbus A300s with windshear warning computers. While there is as yet no legal requirement to enforce the fitting of such systems, they will almost certainly soon become universal.

New England and the north-east states of America were deep in the grip of winter. Although the temperature was still just above freezing point as night fell at Boston-Logan International Airport on 23 January 1982, there was little melting of the hard-packed snow that glazed Runway 15R. Rain was falling from heavy cloud at 240m (800ft) as the Douglas DC-10 of World Airways Flight 30H from Oakland, California descended.

The useable runway length of 15R was 2,757m (9,191ft). However, with fresh rainwater lying on ice that had been compacted by the weight of the numerous wide-bodied aircraft that had used it, this was perilously short. Just as the safe stopping distance of the Boeing 727 at Harry S. Truman Airport had been eroded by finally touching down too far along its length, this DC-10 had already overflown nearly nine hundred metres (three thousand feet) before the pilot got her down. He had accepted an excessive approach speed derived from the autothrottle speed control system. The real problem was the ice: eighteen hundred metres (six thousand feet) was just too short to pull up the DC-10 loaded with 212 people. At 19.36 the pilot swerved to avoid the approach light pier at the departure end of the runway. Now ahead of him lay the waters of Boston harbour. The DC-10 crunched through the ice at the water's edge and pitched into the black sea, the nose section of the aircraft breaking off as it did so. Passengers from sunny California found themselves fighting through freezing water to escape; two were lost and presumed drowned.

While not ranking as a major air disaster in terms of death toll, this incident clearly highlighted the problems of landing on runways effectively shortened by ice. The National Transportation Safety Board heard evidence from other pilots who had landed at Boston-Logan International that day. Several pilots reported braking conditions as 'poor'; one reported 'poor to nil'. The airport management was criticised for not measuring the friction coefficient of the runways, and the air traffic controllers for not relaying warnings of poor grip to approaching traffic; two hours before the crash a ground vehicle had reported the braking conditions as fair to poor.

Just over a week later, on 1 February 1982, the pilot of a Grumman 1159 executive aircraft did consider the probability of difficult braking conditions as he approached Anderson Airport's snow-covered runway. He planned to land as close as possible to the end of the runway which had just been snow-ploughed. He was not told that the plough had deposited the snow that it had planed across the runway threshold. As he came down out of the murk he was unable to distinguish the runway lights because they were obscured by snow. His mainwheels struck the hump of snow, the left gear failed and the light aircraft skidded along on the ice. The two lucky pilots and two passengers stepped out of the wreckage shaken but unhurt; though somewhat bemused.

At what is now almost the close of this history it is appropriate to take a look into the crystal ball of the future. Computerisation/automation – these are the key words on which future air travel will be built. TCAS, windshear protection and all the other safety precautions developed in seventy years of commercial flight have made flying the very safest mode of travel so why, one may ask, do airliners so very often seem to become funeral pyres strewn in broken pieces across the earth?

Over eighty percent of aircraft accidents involve some degree of human failure. Based at Farnborough, England, is the Royal Air Force's Institute of Aviation Medicine whose research includes the Confidential Human Incidents Reporting Programme (CHIRP) to which any member of aircrew can confidentially give information. The aim is to understand the psychology of the flight deck; why pilots often simply do not believe warning systems, to understand what kind of personality makes the safest pilot.

It must also be realised that each advance in technology brings with it new problems. A new generation of airliners is coming into service which are fly-by-wire: the controls are not linked directly to the flying surfaces but to a computer. The pilot should not be able to put the aircraft into a dangerous attitude, the computer will not allow it. It was a fly-by-wire system that allowed an A320 Airbus of Air France to perform a nose-up, very slow fly-past of an airshow at Habsheim, France, on 26 June 1988. It could not stall, the computer would not let it, but the computer could not see the trees looming ahead. Too late, the pilot pushed the throttles forward. The wide-bodied jet plunged into the woodland. Moments later, horrified watchers saw a plume of fire appear. Incredibly, of 136 people on board only three were killed. A false sense of security, akin to the motorist whose car has anti-lock brakes so he follows one inch behind the vehicle in front? Other pilots have commented that they would rather not fly an aircraft 'which decides whether or not I'm an idiot before doing what I tell it'

While there can be little humour in the subject of air disasters one incident of pure comedy (if expensive for insurance companies) will finish this history on a lighter note. Some readers may remember the Bristol 170 as the aircraft that flew motorists with their vehicles across the English Channel from soon after World War II until the late 1960s. This was a twin-engined design with the cockpit mounted above clam-shell nose doors. Designed as a military transport it was to be a success in civil service, too.

Qantas Airways hired one of these machines from the Bristol Corporation in 1947 and on 22 October were demonstrating landings on the 1 in 12 slope of Wau airfield, a jungle strip in New Guinea. With five crew on board the freighter rolled to a halt, the flaps were retracted, the propellers windmilled to a stop. The pilot flipped off the electrical switches and started gathering himself to leave the aircraft.

That was when he glanced out of the side window and realised that the machine was rolling gently backwards! With no engine power to check this the crew could only hold tight and brace themselves as the Superfreighter rolled for nearly half a mile before slewing into a ditch, crumpling the starboard wing and tearing off the undercarriage. The machine was beyond repair, a 'write-off', but none of the crew were hurt.

The International Civil Aviation Operators Accident Index records the 'probable cause of accident' as: 'Parking brake cable failed'.

The Air Accidents Investigation Branch

History of the Accidents Investigation Branch – Air (AAIB) Since November 1987

The Accidents Investigation Branch was formed in 1919 as a result of public concern about the numbers of aircraft accidents at that time. The existence of the Branch was formalised with the Air Navigation Act of 1920, which required the Minister responsible for civil aviation to make regulations providing for the investigation of accidents arising during the course of air navigation within the United Kingdom. The Act also called for provisions to be made for the investigation of accidents to British registered aircraft elsewhere in the world. Two years later the Air Navigation (Investigation of Accidents) Regulations 1922 called for an Accidents Investigation Branch to be established as part of the Air Ministry.

In its early days the Accidents Investigation Branch was a part-military organisation concerned mainly with military aircraft accidents. Civil air transport was at this time very much in its infancy. After World War II, when civil aviation underwent a period of rapid expansion, the Branch was transferred to the Ministry of Transport and Civil Aviation. However, the Accidents Investigation Branch continued to assist the Royal Air Force with its aircraft accident investigations and does so to this day.

The Branch is now in the Department of Transport, having been transferred in 1983 from the Department of Trade. However, as an Inspectorate, it is quite independent of any policy making division or regulatory authority and the Chief Inspector of Accidents reports direct to the Secretary of State. The Branch is based as a lodger unit at the Royal Aircraft Establishment, Farnborough.

Accident Investigation Procedure

The remit of the Accidents Investigation Branch and the rules under which it operates are detailed in the Civil Aviation (Investigation of Accidents) Regulations 1983. The Branch's task is to investigate all accidents to civil aircraft, in the United Kingdom, in order to determine the circumstances and cause(s) with a view to the prevention of similar accidents in the future, not to attribute blame.

There are, on average, about 250 reportable civil air accidents in the United Kingdom per year; in 1986 there were 220 (including 9 involving public transport aircraft). Of these, 49 involved Inspectors deployed in the field and 6 are the subject of full 'Inspector's Investigations' culminating with a formal AIB Report published by HMSO. In addition to the formal reports, AIB publishes a short account of all notifiable accidents in the AIB Bulletin which is published monthly. To carry out its task the Branch employs a staff of 41, of whom 29 are investigators. The Inspectors of Accidents are drawn from two disciplines – pilots and engineers.

Branch Investigations

The initial response to the report of an accident is determined by the Chief Inspector of Accidents, the Deputy Chief, or, in their absence, by the Duty Co-ordinator for the day. Co-ordinators are nominated for each twenty-four hour period from among the Principal Inspectors.

The commander of an aircraft and the aircraft operator are legally obliged to report any accident. Reports are also received from the Police, Air Traffic Control, Airport Authorities and members of the public. These reports are received by the AIB Duty Co-ordinator who will decide whether to despatch a team to the accident site.

In order to respond quickly to any accident whether it be at home or abroad a duty roster is maintained which consists of three Inspectors (Operations) and three Inspectors (Engineering) and a Flight Recorder Specialist.

In the case of minor accidents involving light aircraft, and when there are no casualties, the Co-ordinator may decide that they may be dealt with adequately by requiring the pilot to complete an Accident Report Form; or alternatively, if the accident involves a glider, hang-glider, a microlight aircraft or a balloon, he may decide to delegate the investigation to the relevant association.

In the case of more serious accidents, or any accident where the cause is obscure, where fatalities are involved or which involve aircraft engaged in public transport, the Co-ordinator will initiate a Field Investigation by a team consisting of at least two Inspectors – one Operations and one Engineering. The size of the team depends on the type of accident. If the accident involves fatalities, a pathologist from the RAF Institute of Pathology and Tropical Medicine will form part of the team.

On the evidence elicited by the Field Investigation, the Chief Inspector decides whether the accident will be the subject of a limited investigation, involving the production of a Bulletin, or whether a full Inspector's Investigation shall be carried out, normally culminating in the publication of the Inspector's report.

Before the report can be finalised, however, the Inspector is obliged, under the Regulations, to consult the directly interested parties such as the aircraft commander, the operator, and anyone whose reputation may be adversely affected, and to take into consideration any representations they may wish to make. The final version of the report is then submitted to the Secretary of State, who normally agrees to its publication (by HM Stationery Office). However, before it can be published, the interested parties have twenty-one days in which to ask for a Review Board to review those findings and conclusions which may adversely affect them. Requests for a Review Board are comparatively rare, there having been only three cases since 1969, the year in which they were instituted under revised regulations.

It should be said that despite the care and time expended in order to produce as fair a report as possible, any recommendations regarding the safety of aircraft are passed to the relevant authority or organisation, usually the Civil Aviation Authority, as soon as possible, and in advance of publication of the report. In addition to the investigation of accidents, the Chief Inspector also has the power to investigate incidents involving the safety of aircraft, including 'air misses'.

Public Inquiries

In the case of a major aircraft accident, the Secretary of State may decide to order a Public Inquiry. The Inquiry is held by a commissioner appointed by the Lord Chancellor; the Branch undertakes the technical investigation and produces its evidence to the Treasury Solicitor, who in turn presents it to the Inquiry. Thereafter, the members of the Branch concerned are available to the Inquiry as specialist witnesses.

The Commissioner makes his report, including any safety recommendations, to the Secretary of State, who normally agrees to its publication.

The most recent Public Inquiry was that into the British Airways Trident accident near Staines in 1972.

Branch Participation in Foreign Investigations

As well as having the responsibility for investigating accidents in the United Kingdom, the Branch may also participate in overseas investigations when a British registered or British manufactured aircraft is involved. The arrangements covering accredited representatives in foreign investigations are laid down in ICAO Annex 13 to the Convention on International Civil Aviation. In addition, the Branch receives many requests for assistance from foreign countries, either to loan expert advisers or to read out Flight Recorders or Cockpit Voice Recorders.

Assistance in RAF Investigations

The Branch has a long-standing commitment to the Royal Air Force to lend the specialist services of Inspectors (Engineering) to assist Boards of Inquiry into accidents involving RAF aircraft.

Liaison

The Branch maintains a close liaison with the Civil Aviation Authority in all matters regarding flight safety, airworthiness of aircraft, operating procedures, air traffic control, etc. Also with overseas safety authorities, aircraft manufacturers, both British and foreign, and airline operators.

Associated Activities

Branch Inspectors lecture on the various aspects of accident investigation to a large variety of organisations including the Police, the Cranfield College of Aeronautics, and international safety organisations.

The Branch also has its own training programme, under which Inspectors are kept current on a wide variety of aircraft types, ranging from large passenger transport aircraft to small private aircraft.

Chief Inspector of Accidents
January 1985

Appendix 2

Chronological Index of Accidents Included in Book

Date	Place	Type	Operator	Description
1785	English Channel	Balloon	Pilatre de Rozier	Hydrogen-filled envelope exploded. Death of first authenticated pilot.
12 Nov 1870	Paris, France	Balloon *Daguerre*		Shot down escaping from siege of city. First victim of anti-aircraft fire.
June 1897	Germany	Experimental airship	Dr. Wölfert	Hydrogen-filled envelope ignited by sparks from engine.
17 Jan 1906	Lake Konstanz, Germany	Airship LZ2	Count F. Zeppelin	Crashed into trees following engine failure.
1907	Stuttgart, Germany	Airship LZ4	Count F. Zeppelin	Dashed to ground by wind while moored. Hydrogen exploded.
17 Sep 1908	USA	Wright *Flyer*	Orville Wright	Demonstration flight for US Army. Structural failure of aircraft. Army officer killed, first passenger to die in aeroplane accident.
8 Oct 1914	Düsseldorf, Germany	Airship Z9	German Navy	Bombed by British aircraft
31 May 1915	London, England	Airship	German Navy	Five killed by bombs. First airship raid on the city.
7 June 1915	Belgium	Airship L37	German Navy	Shot down by British aircraft.
2 Sept 1916	Cuffley, England	Airship	German Navy	Shot down by British aircraft.
1916	Little Wigborough, England	Airship L33	German Navy	Shot down by artillery.
1921	Yorkshire, England	Airship R34	Royal Navy	Structure crumpled after flying into hillside. No injuries. Returned safely to East Fortune base before collapse became complete. First airship to cross North Atlantic.
23 Aug 1921	Near Hull, England	Airship R38	Royal Navy/US Navy	Structure failure and fire.
April 1922	Near Paris, France	Farman Goliath & DH18	Grands Express Aeriens & Daimler Airways	First mid-air collision involving commercial airliners.

Date	Place	Type	Operator	Description
21 Dec 1923	Off Sicily	Airship *Dixmude*	French Navy	Exploded after being struck by lightning.
1924	Croydon Airport, England	DH34	Imperial Airways	Crashed on landing. First accident involving airliner fitted with tachometer.
3 Sep 1925	Ohio, USA	Airship *Shenandoah*	US Navy	Structural failure in storm.
5 Oct 1930	Allonne Ridge, France	Airship R101	British Air Ministry	Struck ground en route to India following probable failure of forward envelope. Fire broke out when engines or calcium flares carried in control cabin ignited hydrogen.
28 Mar 1933	Roulers, Belgium	Armstrong Whitworth Argosy	Imperial Airways	Suspected sabotage by bomb placed on board.
4 Apr 1933	Off New Jersey, USA	Airship *Akron*	US Navy	Structural failure in storm.
11 Feb 1935	Pacific Ocean	Airship *Macon*	US Navy	Elevator had not been properly repaired following earlier failure and was torn off in storm. Crashed in sea.
5 May 1935	Rocky Mts, USA	Douglas DC-2	Trans World Airways	Flew into dead-end ravine in storm. This accident the catalyst of the establishment of safety bodies in USA.
6 May 1937	Lakehurst, USA	Airship *Hindenburg*	DELAG	Exploded while mooring shortly after electrical storm. Possible sabotage.
23 Aug 1944	Freckleton, England	Consolidated B-24	USAAF	Crashed on village school during storm. Worst wartime disaster involving civilian casualties.
15 Dec 1944	English Channel	Noorduyn Norseman	USAAF	Believed lost without trace, but possibly destroyed by bombs being jettisoned by RAF bombers. Glenn Miller was a passenger on this aircraft.
13/14 Feb 1945	Dresden, Germany	Avro Lancasters	RAF, USAAF	Night bombing raid followed by daylight raids. An estimated 55,000 or more people were killed, mostly in firestorm, the largest number of people killed in a single air-raid, including nuclear strikes on Japan.
5 Dec 1945	Off Florida coast, USA	5 Grumman Avengers & Martin Mariner	US Navy	Became lost during navigation exercise. Ditched in ocean, but wreckage never found. Mariner amphibian exploded in mid-air while on search mission for missing Avenger flight.

Date	Place	Type	Operator	Description
19 Dec 1946	Northolt, England	Douglas DC-3	Scottish Airways	Crashed on house shortly after take-off in freezing conditions. Aircraft probably lacked lift through iced flying surfaces.
21 Aug 1947	Woodford Airfield, England	Avro Tudor II	Avro Aircraft Corp.	Crashed on take-off owing to control cables of ailerons having been reversed. Designer Roy Chadwick killed in this accident.
22 Oct 1947	Wau Airfield, New Guinea	Bristol 170	Qantas on hire from Bristol Aircraft Corp.	Brake cable failed following landing. Aircraft rolled backwards into ditch.
6 Jan 1948	Near Northolt, England	Vickers Viking	BEA	Crashed on approach in freezing weather. Altimeter possibly not correctly adjusted.
27 Jan 1948	In sea off Bermuda	Avro Tudor IV	BSAA	Lost without trace. Cause unknown.
20 Oct 1948	Near Prestwick Airport, Scotland	Lockheed Constellation	KLM	Struck power lines during overshoot approach to runway. Crashed on hillside.
17 Jan 1949	In sea off Bermuda	Avro Tudor IV	BSAA	Lost without trace. Cause unknown. *See also* entry above.
30 Jan 1949	Near New York, USA	Cessna 195 & Lockheed Constellation	Private owner & Pan American	Mid-air collision.
9 Sept 1949	Mount Torment, Canada	Douglas DC-3	Canadian Pacific Airlines	Sabotaged by bomb placed on board.
1 Nov 1949	Washington DC-	P-38 fighter & Douglas DC-4B	US Dept of Defense & Eastern Airlines	Mid-air collision. P-38 was being tested by Bolivian pilot for possible purchase by that country's airforce. Both aircraft plunged into River Potomac.
10 Mar 1950	Llandow Airport, Wales	Avro Tudor V	Fairflight	Charter flight from Dublin. Crashed on landing owing to incorrect centre of gravity.
3 Nov 1950	Mont Blanc, French-Swiss Alps	Lockheed Constellation	Air India	Crashed into mountain near summit on approach to Geneva Airport. *See also* 24 Jan 1966.
6 Sept 1952	Farnborough, England	D.H.110	De Havilland	Wing buckled during supersonic fly-past at airshow. Wreckage struck public enclosure.

Date	Place	Type	Operator	Description
26 Oct 1952	Ciampino Airport, Rome, Italy	Comet 1	BOAC	Pilot aborted take off, but could not stop within runway limit. No major injuries.
20 Dec 1952	Larson Air Force Base, USA	C-124 Globemaster	USAF	Control locks not removed. Crashed immediately after take off.
3 Mar 1953	Karachi Airport, Pakistan	Comet 1	De Havilland	Failed to become airborne during delivery flight to Canadian Pacific Airways.
2 May 1953	India	Comet 1	BOAC	Disintegrated climbing into tropical storm. Possible structural failure.
25 June 1953	Dakar Airport, Senegal	Comet 1	UAT	Overshot runway on landing. Pilot inexperienced with jet operations a contributory factor. No serious injuries.
10 Jan 1954	In sea off island of Elba, Italy	Comet 1	BOAC	Structural failure – hitherto unidentified metal fatigue.
7 Apr 1954	In sea off Naples, Italy	Comet 1	South African Airways on charter from BOAC	Structural failure (see above).
16 Apr 1954	Bromma Airport, Stockholm, Sweden	Vickers Viscount	Air France	Cargo hold door sheared off in flight and struck engines. Safe emergency landing accomplished.
July 1956	Over Michigan, USA	Vickers Viscount	Trans Canada Air Lines	Gearbox failure in engine. Propeller sheared off puncturing fuselage and killing one passenger.
30 June 1956	Over the Grand Canyon, USA	Douglas DC-7 & Lockheed Super Constellation	United Air Lines & Trans World Airlines	Mid-air collision after both pilots elected to change from Instrument to Visual Flight Rules. No survivors.
9 Sept 1956	Bartlesville, Oklahoma USA	DC-3 & Cessna 170	Continental & private owner	Mid-air collision
1 Feb 1958	Gulf of Mexico near Grand Isle, Louisiana, USA	Sikorsky S-58	Humble Oil and Refinery Co.	Tail rotor overloaded and failed.

Date	Place	Type	Operator	Description
6 Feb 1958	Munich Airport, W. Germany	Airspeed Elizabethan	BEA	Failed to get airborne from slush-covered runway, a degree of icing also present on flying surfaces of airliner. Charter service carrying Manchester United Football Club team from Belgrade to Manchester; many players killed along with sports commentators.
1 June 1958	Gulf of Mexico	Sikorsky S-58	Humble Oil and Refinery Co.	Plunged into sea en route from offshore rig.
4 Apr 1960	Hickory, N. Carolina, USA	Fairchild F-27 & Cessna 310	Piedmont & private owner	Mid-air collision.
19 May 1960	Near Orly Airport, France	Sud-Aviation Caravelle & Stampe	Air Algerie & private owner	Mid-air collision. Light aircraft crossed ahead of jetliner on landing approach. Stampe could claim right-of-way, but Caravelle obviously unable to avoid collision. Stampe destroyed; airliner landed at Orly airport damaged.
16 Dec 1960	New York, USA	Douglas DC-8 & Lockheed Constellation	United Air Lines & Trans World Airlines	Mid-air collision. Jet airliner overshot its allocated airspace.
27 Dec 1960	Forest Park, Illinois, USA	Sikorsky S-58C	Chicago Helicopter Airways	Fatigue failure of main rotor.
15 Feb 1961	Brussels Airport, Belgium	Boeing 707	Sabena	Overshot on first landing approach, circled then dived to destruction. All on board died instantly. Cause unknown.
May 1961	Near Sydney, Australia	Douglas DC-4		Pilot probably died of heart attack during landing approach and toppled across throttle controls when trying to leave his seat. Co-pilot unable to pull pilot off controls. Aircraft crashed on mudflat off coast.
12 July 1961	Casablanca Airport, Morocco	Ilyushin Il-18	Ceskoslovenske Aerolinie	Crashed on final approach in poor weather.
21 Dec 1961	Esenboga Airport, Turkey	DH Comet 4B	BEA	Artificial horizon on pilot's instrument panel had loose cowl. Pilot deceived into making excessively steep climb. Stalled and crashed.

Date	Place	Type	Operator	Description
8 Dec 1963	Over Elkton, Maryland, USA	Boeing 707	Pan Am	Probably lighting strike. Crashed in flames killing 80.
29 Feb 1964	Glungezer Mountain, Austria	Bristol Britannia	British Eagle Airways	Premature descent to Innsbruk Airport while flying under Visual Flight Rules in poor weather.
9 July 1964	Knoxville, Tennesse, USA	Vickers Viscount	United Air Lines	Mid-air fire in passenger cabin from unknown causes.
8 Feb 1965	Over Atlantic Ocean off New York, USA	Douglas DC-7 & Boeing 707	Eastern Air Lines & Pan Am	Near-collision. DC-7 overstressed by avoiding action; plunged into sea; landed safe.
11 Nov 1965	Salt Lake City, USA	Boeing 727	United Air Lines	Pilot made final approach too steep. Undercarriage sheared by impact followed by fire.
4 Dec 1965	Carmel, New York, USA	Lockheed Constellation & Boeing 707	Eastern Air Lines & Trans World Airlines	Mid-air collision.
24 Jan 1966	Mont Blanc, French-Swiss Alps	Boeing 707	Air India	Smashed into mountain near peak at almost same spot as another Air India aircraft (see also 3 Nov 1950). Debris from this accident found following an avalanche in August 1989. Bodies still missing.
3 Mar 1966	On slopes of Mount Fuji, Japan	Boeing 707	BOAC	Ripped apart by clear air turbulence at approx 3,000m (10,000 ft).
4 Mar 1966	In sea near Tokyo, Japan	Boeing 727	All Nippon Airways	Plunged into sea on final approach. Cause unknown.
4 Mar 1966	Tokyo Int Airport, Japan	Douglas DC-8	Canadian Pacific Airlines	Pilot descended below GCA directions. Aircraft destroyed by heavy landing.
22 Apr 1966	Oklahoma, USA	Lockheed Electra	American Flyers	Pilot had falsified his medical record to conceal heart condition. Suffered coronary during landing approach.
3 June 1966	Felthorpe, England	Trident I	British Aircraft Corp.	Entered deep stall during airworthiness certification trials. See also 18 June 1972.
22 May 1968	Los Angeles, USA	Sikorksy S-61	Los Angeles Airways	Main rotor blade damper faulty, but positive cause not established.

Date	Place	Type	Operator	Description
14 Aug 1968	Los Angeles, USA	Sikorsky S-61	Los Angeles Airways	Fatigue crack in main rotor blade spindle.
5 July 1970	Toronto International Airport, Canada	Douglas DC-8	Canadian Pacific	Co-pilot deployed spoilers in error before landing.
23 May 1971	Rijeka Airport, Yugoslavia	Tupolev TU-134A	Aviogenex	Tried to land after slipping off ILS glideslope. Pilot disorientated. Crashed in poor weather.
6 June 1971	Over Duarte, California, USA	F-4 Phantom & Douglas DC-9	USMC & Air West	Mid-air collision. Fighter pilot did not see airliner while performing acrobatics. Phantom observer the only survivor.
30 July 1971	Over Shizukuishi, Japan	F-86 Sabre & Boeing 727	JASDF & All Nippon	Mid-air collison similar to above. No survivors.
11 June 1972	Detriot Met. Airport, USA	Douglas DC-10	American Airlines	Cargo door sheared off owing to design fault. Safe emergency landing. *See also* 3 Mar 1973.
18 June 1972	Nr. Heathrow Airport, England	Trident I	BEA	Entered deep stall when leading edge slats prematurely retracted during confusion on flight deck owing to captain suffering coronary.
29 Dec 1972	Everglades, Florida, USA	Lockheed L-1011	Eastern Airlines	*First wide-bodied jet disaster.* Descended unknown to crew when autopilot accidentally disconnected as they tried to change faulty warning light.
3 Mar 1973	Near Paris, France	Douglas DC-10	THY (Turkish Airlines)	Design fault in cargo hold door not corrected properly after 11 June 1972 accident at Detroit.
3 June 1973	Goussainville, France	Tupolev Tu-144	Aeroflot	Broke up in climbing turn while on display flypast at Paris airshow. Probably collision avoidance emergency.
31 July 1973	Boston-Logan Airport, USA	Douglas DC-9	Delta Airlines	Crashed on landing. No positive conclusion of cause; possible instrument failure.
1 Sept 1974	Farnborough, England	Sikorsky Blackhawk		Pilot entered second roll when too low to recover during press preview of airshow.
19 Nov 1974	Nairobi Airport, Kenya	Boeing 747	Lufthansa	Took off with leading edge slats retracted. Stalled immediately after lift-off. *First major B747 disaster.*

Date	Place	Type	Operator	Description
4 Apr 1975	Near Saigon, South Vietnam	Lockheed C5-A Galaxy	USAAF	Structural failure of rear loading ramp. Military aircraft flying orphans out of country. 190 killed.
24 June 1975	Near Kennedy Int. Airport, USA	Boeing 727	Eastern Airlines	Probably lightning strike. Crashed on highway.
1 Jan 1976	Kastrup Airport, Copenhagen, Denmark	Douglas DC-10	SAS	Bird strike caused flame out of port engine. Safe return and landing.
1 Jan 1976	Saudi Arabia	Boeing 720	Middle East Airlines	Bomb in forward cargo hold. Total destruction when it exploded over desert.
20 Apr 1976	Gas Rig 48, North Sea	Sikorsky S-58 Wessex	Bristow	Pilot took off with engine intake cover still in place which was ingested causing failure.
21 Apr 1976	Charlie Platform, North Sea	Sikorsky S-58	Bristow	Possible tail rotor fatigue.
27 Apr 1976	Harry S. Truman Airport, Virgin Is	Boeing 727	American Airlines	Windshear caused pilot to land deep on known short runway. No room to stop.
10 Sep 1976	Over Zagreb, Yugoslavia	Trident 3 & Douglas DC-9	British Airways & Inex-Adria	*Worst mid-air collision to date.* Air traffic controller error. No survivors.
5 Jan 1977	Near Bromma Airport, Stockholm, Sweden	Vickers Viscount	Linjeflyg	Ice allowed to accumulate on tail surfaces. Aircraft pitched into vertical dive.
27 Mar 1977	Los Rodeas Airport, Tenerife	2 Boeing 747s	KLM & Pan Am	*Worst air disaster to date.* Collision on runway when KLM aircraft made unauthorised take-off roll with Pan Am machine still taxiing down runway. 583 killed.
4 Apr 1977	New Hope, Georgia, USA	Douglas DC-9	Southern Airways	Crashed on highway after both engines flamed-out in storm.
16 May 1977	Pan Am Building, New York, USA	Sikorsky S-61	New York Airways	Undercarriage leg sheared off. Helicopter toppled over with engines running.

Date	Place	Type	Operator	Description
17 May 1977	Aberdeen Airport, Scotland	Sikorsky S-61	British Airways	Electrical fault caused undercarriage oleo to retract while engines were running.
23 Nov 1977	North Sea off Varhaug	Sikorsky S-61	Helikopter Service	Fatigue failure of blade damper.
8 Dec 1977	Gulf of Mexico	SA Puma	Petroleum Helicopters	Rotor blade hit cable on oil rig. Crashed in sea.
20 Apr 1978	Kem, Russia	Boeing 707	Korean Airlines	Forced down by Russian fighters.
26 June 1978	North Sea off Bergen	Sikorsky S-61	Helikopter Service	Main rotor blade spindle failure.
18 Apr 1979	Newark Int. Airport, USA	Sikorsky S-61	New York Airways	Tail rotor blade fatigue failure.
25 May 1979	Cardiff Airport, Wales	Vickers Viscount	British Airways	Fatigue failure of undercarriage bolt jammed oleo leg. Emergency landing without injury.
25 May 1979	Chicago O'Hare Airport, USA	Douglas DC-10	American Airlines	Fatigue failure of engine pylon caused by incorrect servicing procedures. Port engine fell off during take-off roll. Aircraft crashed on mobile home park seconds after lift-off. No survivors.
28 Nov 1979	Mount Erebus, Antarctica	Douglas DC-10	Air New Zealand	INS programming fault by airline's navigation division. Pilot flew into volcano while flying visually in whiteout conditions. Sightseeing flight.
19 Apr 1980	Riyadh Airport, Saudi Arabia	Lockheed L-1011 Tri Starboard	Saudia	Aircraft made emergency landing following fire in cargo hold. All 301 on died when fire and fumes spread to cabin before evacuation could be carried out.
1981	Taiwan	Boeing 737	Far Eastern Air Transport	Corrosion. All on board killed.
13 Jan 1982	Washington DC-	Boeing 737	Air Florida	Crashed on to highway bridge and then into River Potomac after taking off with ice on wings.
23 Jan 1982	Boson-Logan Int. Airport, USA	Douglas DC-10	World Airways	Could not stop before end of ice-covered runway. Plunged into Boston harbour. Two killed.
1 Feb 1982	Anderson Airport USA	Grumman 1159	Private owner	Light aircraft. Landed close to runway threshold owing to ice and lost undercarriage oleo in ploughed snow piled there. No injuries.

Date	Place	Type	Operator	Description
24 June 1982	Off coast of Indonesia	Boeing 747	British Airways	Flew into volcanic ash from eruption of Mount Galunggung. All four engines failed. Longest unpowered flight in a machine not designed for the purpose. Engines restarted and safe landing made at Jakarta.
13 Jul 1982	Off coast of Indonesia	Boeing 747	Singapore Airlines	Flew into ash as above. Three engines failed. Safe landing at Jakarta.
13 Sept 1982	Malaga Airport, Spain	Douglas DC-10	Spantax	Careered through runway perimeter after captain aborted take-off roll owing to vibration. Investigation later revealed thrown tread on tyre. Fire after crash. 50 dead, 344 survivors.
11 Mar 1983	North Sea, north east of Aberdeen	Sikorsky S-61	British Airways	Set down on sea following gearbox failure. No injuries.
16 July 1983	Off Scilly Is	Sikorsky S-61	British Airways	Flew into sea flying under visual flight rules in cloud.
1 Sept 1983	Off Moneron Is	Boeing 747	Korean Airlines	Shot down by Russian fighter plane. No survivors.
23 June 1985	Narita Airport, Japan			Bomb in cargo container exploded while being transferred from Canadian Pacific to Air India aircraft killing airport workers. *See also entry below.*
23 June 1985	Over Atlantic off cost of Eire	Boeing 747	Air India	Bomb planted on board by Sikh extremists. No survivors. *Worst death toll to date in sabotage incident.*
2 Aug 1985	Near Fort Worth Airport, Dallas, USA	Lockheed L-1011 Tri Star	Delta Airlines	Crashed near runway in storm.
12 Aug 1985	Mount Osutaka, Japan	Boeing 747	Japan Airlines	Fuselage ruptured following failure of previous repair on fuselage rear pressure bulkhead. *Worst accident to date involving one aircraft.* 520 killed.
22 Aug 1985	Manchester Airport, England	Boeing 737	British Airtours	Combustion can in port engine exploded. Aircraft stopped on runway, but was burnt out.
6 Nov 1986	Off Shetland Is	Boeing Vertol Chinook	British International Helicopters	Believed forward rotor gearbox failure. Conclusion still in dispute at time of writing.
29 Nov 1987	Off Malayan coast	Boeing 707	Korean Airlines	Bomb placed on board by North Korean agents. 115 killed.

Date	Place	Type	Operator	Description
29 Apr 1988	Off Hawaii	Boeing 737	Aloha Airlines	Corrosion failure. Section of forward cabin ripped away. Stewardess sucked to her death. Emergency landing made.
30 May 1988	Coventry, England	Gloster Meteor VII		Preserved jet fighter crashed at airshow when pilot failed to retract air brakes during acrobatics.
26 June 1988	Habsheim, France	Airbus A320	Air France	Crashed into trees following low-level flypast at air show
3 Jul 1988	Over Strait of Hormuz	Airbus A300	Iran Air	Shot down in mistake for hostile F-14 fighter by US warship.
17 Aug 1988	Bahawalpur, Pakistan	Lockheed C-130 Hercules	Pakistani Air Force	Shot down or destroyed by bomb while carrying President Zia. All on board killed.
28 Aug 1988	Ramstein, W. Germany	3 Aero-Macchi MB-339As	Italian Air Force	Mid-air collision of Frecce Tricolor at airshow. *Worst air display disaster to date.*
28 Aug 1988	Kleine-Brogel, Belgium	Valmet Redigo	Finnish Air Force	Crashed at air show.
15 Dec 1988	Off Anchorage, Alaska	Boeing 747	KLM	Flew into volcanic ash cloud.
21 Dec 1988	Lockerbie, Scotland	Boeing 747	Pan Am	Sabotage. Bomb on board. Total destruction. Wreckage fell on town.
8 Jan 1989	Near East Midlands Airport, England	Boeing 737	British Midland Airways	Crew isolated a good engine believing it to be failing. Faulty engine became total failure as landing attempted. Aircraft crashed on M1 motorway.
20 Jan 1989	Chicago O'Hare Airport, USA	Boeing 727	Piedmont Airlines	Lost engine on take off. Made circuit and landed on one engine.
8 Feb 1989	Santa Maria, Azores	Boeing 707	Independent Air	Collided with high ground.
13 Feb 1989	Over Pacific Ocean	Boeing 747	United Airlines	Cargo door and section of fuselage ripped out at 6,600m (22,000 ft). Nine passengers sucked out.
June 1989	Paris, France	MiG 29	Russian Air Force	Engine flamed-out while aircraft in near-stalled attitude at airshow. Either bird ingested or debris in intake fell back into turbine blades. Pilot survived very low-level ejection.
18 June 1989	Zabel, Iran	Antonov 26	Ariana Afghan	Crashed while pilot was trying to over-power hijackers.

Date	Location	Aircraft	Operator	Cause
18 July 1989	Sioux City Airport, USA	Douglas DC-10	United Airlines	Centre engine exploded in flight. Crashed attempting to land without hydraulic power.
24 July 1989	Middle Wallop, England	Boeing Vertol Chinook	RAF	Emergency landing. Cause not known at time of writing.
25 July 1989	Mount Pleasant, Falkland Islands	Boeing Vertol Chinook	RAF	Emergency landing. Cause not known at time of writing.
26 July 1989	W. Germany	Tornado IDS & Micro-light	Luftwaffe & private owner	Mid-air collison.
27 July 1989	Tripoli, Libya	Douglas DC-10	Korean Airlines	Crashed in poor weather approaching Tripoli Airport.
19 Sep 1989	Over Niger, Africa	DC-10	UTA	Sabotage – bomb on board.
27 Nov 1989	Bogota, Columbia	Boeing 727	Avianca	Sabotage – bomb on board.

Bibliography

Barker, Ralph. *Great Mysteries of the Air* (Chatto & Windus, 1966)

Clarke, Basil. *The History of Airships* (Herbert Jenkins, 1961)

Hersh, Seymour. *The Target is Destroyed – What Really Happened to Flight 007* (Faber & Faber, 1986)

Johnson, R.W. *Shootdown – the Verdict on KAL 007* (Chatto & Windus, 1986)

Kusche, Lawrence David. *The Bermuda Triangle Mystery – Solved* (New English Library, 1975)

Launay, André. *Historic Air Disasters* (Ian Allan, 1962)

Masefield, Sir Peter G. *To Ride the Storm* (William Kimber, 1982)

Moorhouse, Earl. *Wake Up, It's a Crash* (David & Charles, 1980)

Moran, Peter and Brown, Russell. 'Freckleton Disaster', *FlyPast Magazine* (January 1988)

Moynahan, Brian. *Airport International* (Pan Books/Macmillan London Ltd, 1978)

Nesbit, Roy Conyers. *Failed to Return* (Patrick Stephens Ltd, 1988)

Tootell, Betty. *All Four Engines Have Failed* (André Deutsch, 1985)

Vette, Gordon with McDonald, John. *Impact Erebus* (Hodder & Stoughton, 1988)

Weston, R. and Hurst, R. *Zagreb One Four – Cleared to Collide?* (Granada, 1982)

Flight International

Index